Nature Embodied

Nature Embodied

GESTURE IN ANCIENT ROME

Anthony Corbeill

PRINCETON UNIVERSITY PRESS

PRINCETON AND OXFORD

Library of Congress Cataloging-in-Publication Data

Corbeill, Anthony, 1960–
Nature embodied: gesture in ancient Rome / Anthony Corbeill.
p. cm.
Includes bibliographical references and indexes.
ISBN 0-691-07494-1 (acid-free paper)
1. Rome—Social life and customs. 2. Gesture—Rome. 3. Latin literature—History
and criticism. 4. Gesture in literature. I. Title.
DG78.C592 2004
302.2′22—dc21   2003045782

British Cataloging-in-Publication Data is available

This book has been composed in Goudy

Printed on acid-free paper.∞

www.pupress.princeton.edu

Printed in the United States of America

1 3 5 7 9 10 8 6 4 2

For Three Graces

CONTENTS

ILLUSTRATIONS

FIGURES

TABLE

ABBREVIATIONS

CLE   F. Bücheler, *Carmina Latina epigraphica* (Leipzig: vol. 1, 1930²; vol. 2, 1897; vol. 3, ed. E. Lommatsch 1926).

CIL   *Corpus Inscriptionum Latinarum* (Berlin 1862–).

FIRA   S. Riccobono et al., eds., *Fontes Iuris Romani Antejustiniani* (Florence 1941–1943) 3 vols.

KS   R. Kühner and C. Stegmann, *Ausführliche Grammatik der lateinischen Sprache*, 2d ed. (Leipzig 1912 and 1914) 2 vols.

Lewis and Short   C. Lewis and C. Short, *A Latin Dictionary, founded on Andrews' edition of Freund's Latin dictionary* (Oxford 1966).

LHS   M. Leumann, J. B. Hofmann, and A. Szantyr, *Lateinische Grammatik*, vol. 2: *Syntax und Stilistik* (Munich 1972) rev. ed. Handbuch der Altertumswissenschaft 2: 2.2.

LIMC   H. C. Ackermann and J.-R. Gisler et al., eds., *Lexicon iconographicum mythologiae classicae* (Zurich 1981–) 8 vols.

LSJ   H. G. Liddell and R. Scott, *A Greek-English Lexicon*, 9th ed. Rev. by H. S. Jones and R. McKenzie, with supplement (Oxford 1968).

LTUR   E. M. Steinby, ed., *Lexicon topographicum urbis Romae* (Rome 1993–2000) 6 vols.

OED   J. A. H. Murray et al., eds., *The Oxford English Dictionary* (Oxford 1961) 3d ed.

OLD   P.G.W. Glare, ed., *Oxford Latin Dictionary* (Oxford 1982).

ORF   E. Malcovati, *Oratorum Romanorum fragmenta liberae rei publicae* (Turin 1976) 4th ed.

PGM   K. Preisendanz, ed., *Papyri graecae magicae* (Stuttgart 1973), A. Henrichs, 2d ed.

PHI disk   Packard Humanities Institute CD of Latin authors, version 5.3.

RE   A. F. von Pauly and G. Wissowa, eds., *Realencyclopädie der classischen Altertumswissenschaft* (Stuttgart 1894–).

SVF   H. von Arnim, *Stoicorum veterum fragmenta* (Leipzig 1964) 4 vols.

TLL   *Thesaurus linguae Latinae* (Leipzig 1900–).

Walde-Hofmann   A. Walde and J. B. Hofmann, *Lateinisches etymologisches Wörterbuch* (Heidelberg 1938, 1954) 2 vols., 3d ed.

ACKNOWLEDGMENTS

THIS BOOK began many years ago as an ambitious idea, and I am certain it would have remained an idea if not for the American Academy in Rome, which provided nine months of thinking, questioning, and travelling in 1994–1995 through a Rome Prize funded by the National Endowment for the Humanities. I thank the Academy for providing food, housing, and confidence, as well as for the hospitality received on subsequent visits; I hope it is not invidious to single out for particular thanks Malcolm Bell III, Mellon Professor during my stay, and Chris Huemer, head librarian. My home institution, the University of Kansas, has generously supported subsequent stages of writing and revision, funding summer salary from the General Research Fund and a semester of sabbatical leave. The Hall Center for the Humanities at KU provided office space and a fellowship for an additional semester.

Versions of each of these chapters have been delivered orally at various venues since 1995. I am grateful to my hosts on each occasion as well as to members of the audience whose comments have caused me to reevaluate many of my original ideas; I thank in particular John Bodel, Douglas Cairns, Michael J. Clarke, Christopher Craig, Michael de Brauw, Peter Holliday, Eleanor Leach, Barry Powell, and Garth Tissol. A final draft of the entire manuscript was completed during a two-week visit to the University of Texas at Austin as a Big-XII Fellow, where Andrew Riggsby and Stephen White offered both a gracious welcome and healthy skepticism.

Different parts of the book have benefited from comments of the following scholars: Alan Boegehold, John R. Clarke, David Fredrick, Erich Gruen, Brian Krostenko, Robert Morstein-Marx, Arthur Riss, Tara Silvestri Welch, and two anonymous readers from the press. Nicholas Horsfall has been warmly encouraging and sharply critical since the inception of this project, and has improved the manuscript throughout. For enduring conversations about gesture, I thank Aaron Binderup and Mac Bell; David Abram inspired my work from early on. In the final stages of preparing the manuscript Robert Cohon, Nancy de Grummond, Peter Holliday, and Paul Rehak provided advice concerning illustrations, while Bob and Chris Elsdale graciously allowed me to reproduce Bob's inspiring artwork on the jacket.

An earlier version of chapter 2 has appeared in *Memoirs of the American Academy in Rome* 42 (1997) and an earlier version of chapter 4 in D. Fredrick, ed., *The Roman Gaze* (Baltimore 2002). All translations of Latin and Greek are my own.

A final thanks to the human and more-than-human must be given for my previous twelve years in Lawrence, among unparalleled colleagues and students in the Classics Department at KU; and for those in the dedication.

Nature Embodied

Introduction

GESTURE AS A CULTURAL SYSTEM

WHEN GREGORY BATESON was conducting fieldwork in New Guinea, his friends among the native Iatmul could not understand why he had to work so hard to learn their language: "But our language is easy to understand" they told him, "we just talk."[1] I wonder how Romans would react to an American studying their gestures from a distance of two millennia. A predictable response would be that their body language is easy to understand; they just move. It is in this common lack of self-reflection that both the complications and rewards of studying ancient gesture lie. Since gesture normally does seem the natural thing to do with the body from day to day, the texts and visual representations from antiquity tend to be uninterested in depicting the particulars of how Romans moved their bodies as they interact with their environment and each other. At the same time, however, this very lack of interest makes the subject ideal for a cultural critique. When our sources mention a gesture being performed, and its intention being understood by a viewer, we gain access to a shared area of knowledge, one based not on the expression of individual will but on cultural circumstances.[2] As an early modern historian has remarked in introducing a group of essays intended to apply the study of gesture to the humanities, to "interpret and account for a gesture is to unlock the whole social and cultural system of which it is a part."[3] To give an example that has recently engendered much discussion and that I shall not discuss in this book: when a Roman man scratches his head with his middle finger, and his audience is able to understand that he wishes through this gesture to advertise his sexual availability to another man, the common area of belief underlying the practice affords the scholar a glimpse into a world of homoerotic activity for which Roman texts of the period otherwise give only shadowy outlines.[4] In researching and writing about Roman gesture I have kept in mind Bourdieu's concise formulation concerning the role of the body in the social and political life of the individual: "It is because agents never know completely what they are doing that what they do has more sense than they know."[5] The

---

[1] Bateson 1991.216.

[2] Schmidt 1953.235, speaking of folk gestures generally.

[3] Thomas 1992.11.

[4] For the gesture, see Corbeill 1996.164–65; on its value as evidence for a male homosexual subculture, see esp. Richlin 1993, Taylor 1997, Williams 1999.218–24, and Frier 1999.

[5] Bourdieu 1990.69.

modern scholar, therefore, confronts a rare opportunity in which distance from the subject studied can be construed as an advantage. Gestures provide access to a system of thought and prejudice otherwise not accessible to us—and one often only dimly perceived by contemporaries.

It has become a cliche to say that the body "speaks." I wish to consider the implications of this cliche of the speaking body by demonstrating how much of the gestural language displayed on the streets and in the houses of Rome can in fact be shown to belong to a self-consistent language, and to one no less complicated and subject to exploitation than the spoken language of Latin. In antiquity, Roman authors debated the extent to which Latin grammar and syntax ought to be regularized or whether it should be allowed to develop in anomalous and potentially difficult directions—the so-called analogy-versus-anomaly controversy.[6] The analogists wished to rationalize grammar to eliminate unusual formations from the language—the deponent form *adsentior*, for example, should yield to the formally regular *adsentio*; Julius Caesar proposed that Latin adopt a present participle for the verb "to be" (*ens*) in order to fill an inconvenient gap in Latin morphology. Cicero, by contrast, was a strong opponent to the analogists, insisting that speaking a rule-bound Latin constituted speaking against Roman tradition.[7] This topic of debate, centered on the distinction between "natural" and "unnatural" changes to the language, has implications beyond the grammatical, involved as it is in the politics of excluding provincials and the undereducated from the ranks of the late Republican elite.[8] In similar ways, elite authors of rhetorical and philosophical texts are found debating the relationship between the body and nature and underlining the importance of maintaining particular bodily etiquettes.[9] Not only does Roman society depend upon moral codes being as stable as Latin morphology, but it also demands that those codes emerge in visible, easily detectable signs. By using notions of the body simultaneously to create and reinforce social distinctions, the elite in Rome could check the power of marginalized groups such as women and ambitious politicians from outside Rome.

The clearest example of this need to control the public body on display can be found in the third section of the eleventh book of Quintilian's *Institutio oratoria*.[10] Modern scientific research into the role of the body in spoken lan-

---

[6] For this ancient linguistic controversy, see Rawson 1985.117–31, esp. 120–23.

[7] Cic. *orat.* 155.

[8] Sinclair 1994.92–96.

[9] For concise surveys of Roman writings that discuss gesture, see Schmitt 1989, Fögen 2001.

[10] For a range of recent approaches to this section of Quintilian, see Fantham 1982 (source study), Maier-Eichhorn 1989 (commentary), Graf 1992 (orators and actors), Wülfing 1994 (pedagogy), Aldrete 1999.3–43 (Roman oratorical practice), and Gunderson 2000.59–86 (construction of Roman masculinity).

guage has uncovered increasing evidence for the claim that "the gesture and the spoken utterance are different sides of a single underlying mental process."[11] Such claims Quintilian would have found self-evident. His discussion of oratorical delivery, which covers approximately fifty pages in modern editions, includes numerous minute details of how to hold the head and fingers. To quote one example of the complexities that faced the aspiring orator as he strove to master the hand position appropriate to his words: "Grasp the tip [of the index finger] lightly on both sides and gently curve the remaining two fingers—the little finger less so [than the ring finger]. This gesture is appropriate for argument. If you wish to seem to argue more keenly, grasp instead the middle joint of the index and have the last two fingers contracted more tightly to correspond with the tighter position [of the thumb and middle finger]."[12] Quintilian's remarks do not only show the types of details the student of oratory was expected to internalize; in order for these gestures to possess any kind of persuasive power, we must also presuppose an audience trained at some level to interpret these gestures correctly. This tacit understanding between speaker and audience ultimately works to distinguish between bodies that accurately convey a speaker's mind by moving in accordance with nature and those that can be marked as unnatural and therefore in some way deviant.[13] It is not surprising, then, that the gestures taught in "foreign schools" are on one occasion singled out for derision (11.3.103); the non-Roman, as often in Latin texts, is marked as morally suspicious. Quintilian is perfectly clear on the body's role in persuasion: emotional appeals to an audience fail to convince when they are not "set aflame" by the skillful use of vocal inflection, facial expression, and "the carriage of nearly the entire body."[14] And yet, in a paradox not lost on the author, formal training is necessary to act naturally.[15] This need for training has further repercussions beyond the exclusion of non-Roman elements. Easily understood pantomime gestures—such as pretending to reach for a cup or threatening to strike a blow (11.3.117; see also 90, 104)—are discarded by Quintilian's handbook in favor of the less direct, and less easily mastered, system he describes. Commonly understood gestures are constructed as beneath the orator's dignity. The gesture that is widely recognized (vulgaris) becomes distinct from the more desirable form that derives from art (ex arte; 11.3.102).

[11] McNeill 1992.1.

[12] Quint. inst. 11.3.95: summo articulo [indicis digiti] utrimque leviter apprehenso, duobus modice curvatis, minus tamen minimo, [gestus] aptus ad disputandum est. acrius tamen argumentari videntur, qui medium articulum potius tenent, tanto contractioribus ultimis digitis, quanto priores descenderunt.

[13] Gesture reflecting mind: e.g., Quint. inst. 11.3.65; among Quintilian's many remarks on the "naturalness" of the body: Quint. inst. 11.3.88.

[14] Quint. inst. 11.3.2: adfectus omnes languescant necesse est, nisi voce vultu totius prope habitu corporis inardescunt.

[15] See, for example, Quint. inst. 11.3.10–13.

The particular configuration of knowledge-as-power that we see at work in Quintilian resembles a recent assessment of the role twentieth-century education plays in replicating class distinctions:

> The judgments that teachers make with regard to students . . . take into account not only knowledge and know-how, but also the intangible nuances of *manners* and *style*, which are imperceptible and yet never unperceived manifestations of the individual's relationship to such knowledge and know-how and the "half-uttered or unuttered or unutterable" expression of a system of values which are always deciphered in terms of another system of values which themselves are just as unuttered and as unutterable.[16]

These remarks are applicable to the specific context of the control of the body. "Unuttered and unutterable" rules legislate the elite orator's body movement and, as a result, the physical demeanor of the right-thinking citizen. Pliny the Younger offers a rare glimpse of an ancient awareness of how such elite mannerisms undergo silent replication: "It has been established since antiquity that we should learn from our elders *not only with our ears but also with our eyes* the things that we must ourselves do and, in turn, pass on to our descendants."[17] Pliny describes the *tirocinium fori*, the period of education during which sons of the elite received instruction in the fine points of speechmaking and statesmanship by observing the successful friends of their fathers. This training is then repeated for each subsequent generation, insuring replication within the elite ranks.

Modern scholarly research on Roman gestures has been dominated by two works.[18] Sittl's *Die Gebärden der Griechen und Römer*, published in 1890, offers a magisterial survey of gesture in both Greece and Rome that has not been replaced. Yet this groundbreaking and comprehensive study must primarily concern itself with providing taxonomies, and the tendency to conflate Greek and Roman practice offered few opportunities for Sittl to provide extensive culture-specific analysis. The second landmark in the study of Roman gestures is Brilliant's *Gesture and Rank in Roman Art*. Although primarily restricted to how status is represented in sculptural and numismatic sources, the work contains much of value to a study of bodily expression in Roman society in general. Especially helpful is Brilliant's notion of a Roman "appendage aesthetic." In contrast with the Greek artist, who tends to glorify the individual parts and particular musculature of the body, Roman art "is characterized by the manipulation of significant parts of the image without reference to the physi-

---

[16] Bourdieu and Saint-Martin 1974.338–39 (original emphases).

[17] Plin. *epist.* 8.14.4: *erat . . . antiquitus institutum ut a maioribus natu non auribus modo verum etiam oculis disceremus quae facienda mox ipsi ac per vices quasdam tradenda minoribus haberemus* (italics added in translation).

[18] De Jorio 1832 also deserves mention for its delightful tone and remarkable prescience.

cal qualities of the body to which they are attached."[19] Those parts consist primarily of the arms, legs, and head, the appendages Quintilian describes most fully in his analysis of the importance of rhetorical gesture. Since the 1980s the tremendous growth throughout the humanities of scholarly interest in the body has accordingly given rise to a number of detailed studies on gesture and the body in ancient Rome. I hope that this book will complement these already published specific studies of the body with a general consideration of why and in what ways gesture in ancient Rome was able to assume so much importance.

It should by now be clear that I do not intend in the following to provide a taxonomy of the types of gestures used in Rome and to describe the range of their uses. In particular I will not be adopting the distinctions among gestures that one finds in modern studies of nonverbal behavior. A common category employed in these works comprises those gestures normally referred to as "emblems" or "quotable gestures," gestures that "may be quoted and provided with verbal glosses so that they can be listed apart from the contexts of their use."[20] These gestures are distinct from so-called batons or beats, that is, movements of the hand that act in tandem with speech by punctuating and emphasizing the spoken word.[21] Recent studies have shown that the great majority of quotable gestures, as used in modern situations, are "concerned with the regulation of interpersonal relationships, with displays of one's own current mental or physical condition, or with an evaluative response to another."[22] They are, in other words, concerned first and foremost with conveying and interpreting internal states through unspoken means. Many Roman gestures of this type would be quite familiar to the modern viewer: Romans pointed with the index finger to draw attention to a person or object,[23] scratched the head and bit the fingernails in anxiety,[24] and put a finger to the lips to request silence.[25] And yet Sittl's compendium of many of these "quotable gestures" in his sixth chapter (tellingly entitled "Symbolische Gebärden") reveals that the ancient authors who preserve even such apparently straightforward gestures do not consider their uses restricted to interpersonal communication. Rather, the gestures frequently derive their validity from a perceived relationship between their individual expression and workings in the world that exist outside the gesture's ad hoc usage. The most familiar example of the coexistence of a human and transhuman element in gesturing is the ex-

[19] Brilliant 1963.10; I discuss the value of this observation particularly in chapter 4.
[20] Kendon 1984.94–104 analyzes these types of gestures in detail (quotation is from 94).
[21] McNeill 1992.15–16, who offers a survey of other types at 12–18.
[22] Kendon 1984.95; compare Bateson 1972.412–13.
[23] Kendon 1984.90 remarks on the apparent universality of this gesture (on which compare Lucr. 5.1030–32).
[24] Hor. Sat. 1.10.70–71; Pers. 1.106.
[25] TLL 5.1: 1124.38–45 (J. Rubenbauer).

tended middle finger. Originally representing the erect phallus, the gesture conveys simultaneously a sexual threat to the person toward whom it is directed and an apotropaic means of warding off unwanted elements of the more-than-human.[26]

This possibility, that *even common gestures are perceived to have connections with a world beyond interpersonal communication*, is the first of three basic assumptions that underlie my project. A corollary of this belief is the possibility that gestures originally represented not arbitrary signifiers but had a stage that was somehow mimetic, even if the precise connotations of that imitation are now lost.[27] Many students of gesture, for example, attribute the Western head shake of disagreement to the movement of a feeding infant's head from its mother's breast when done nursing.[28] As a second assumption, I presuppose *a continuity of gesture across the time and space of the ancient Roman world unless there exists clear evidence to the contrary.*[29] Third, I assume that *there exists a principle of gestural economy.* If a gesture can be demonstrated as having one meaning in one context, then that same gesture will tend to retain a single primary meaning in different contexts within its single, coherent culture. An instance of the workings of gestural economy in the modern United States is in the meaning of the sign consisting of the index and middle finger forming the letter "V." This sign, interpreted in English-speaking countries beginning with the First World War as the "V-for-victory" salute, now commonly connotes "peace" (apparently originally in the sense "victory for peace"), regardless of the context in which the gesture is made. These latter two assumptions—of gestural continuity and gestural economy—are particularly crucial for a study of gesture in antiquity, since the limitations of our sources for bodily movement will often force me to employ evidence not only from different media but from different centuries. I would like now to demonstrate briefly how these three assumptions can be applied to a specific case. In the next three paragraphs I shall apply each to an analysis of thumb gestures in Roman antiquity.[30]

I begin with the first assumption, that gestures originate from some mimetic principle that connects the body with the world outside the body (a detailed demonstration of this assumption occupies chapter 1). Ancient authors remark on the etymology of *pollex*, the Latin word for "thumb," an etymology that distinguishes it from the remaining fingers and appears to be unique

---

[26] For Roman examples of the extended middle finger, see Mart. 2.28.1–2; Suet. *Cal.* 56; Priap. 56.1–2; Groß (1968) 7.930; for the relationship between sexual insult and apotropaism, see Röhrich 1967.21–24. Compare, too, the connotations of sticking out the tongue in derision: Pers. 1.60 with Sittl 1890.90–91 and Schmidt 1953.239–40.

[27] Kendon 1984.103.

[28] Darwin 1998.272–77 was the first to suggest this parallel.

[29] For the principle, see Röhrich 1967.14.

[30] Chapter 2 offers a more detailed treatment of these issues.

among the Indo-European languages: "the thumb (*pollex*) received its name from the fact that it has power (*pollet*)."[31] This etymological connection between the thumb and power is supported by the ways in which the Romans refer to thumbs in diverse areas of their culture: in contrast with the other fingers, it alone is used in synecdoche for activities involving the entire hand, such as spinning and writing;[32] the thumb plays a prominent role in preparing medicines and effecting cures, with the result that it is occasionally designated in combination with the ring finger as one of the "medicinal fingers."[33] The living connection between words and things reveals in this case the thumb's access to a power that lies outside the human physique.

This etymology may also inform the origins of the sign that is referred to in ancient texts as the "hostile thumb" (*infestus pollex*), which provides a clear example of my second assumption, that of gestural economy. On the basis of philological evidence it can be argued with virtual certainty that this gesture resembled the modern "thumbs up" (a gesture that itself did not have positive connotations until the twentieth century). The Roman manifestation of this particular thumb gesture demonstrates the principle of economy in two ways. First, its position accords with a notion of economy of structure, since the thumb in this gesture resembles the erect phallus in ways similar to the erect middle finger.[34] In this light, it is fitting that this sign can be identified with that given in the gladiatorial arena to request the death of an unsuccessful combatant, the firmly attested "turned thumb" (*verso pollice*).[35] The hostility of the openly erect thumb brings death to those vanquished in combat. A second type of economy displayed in the case of the *infestus pollex* is that of diametrically opposed gestures conveying opposite meanings; one can compare the Roman head nod forward in assent with its precise opposite, the nod of the head backward in denial. By this principle, it follows that the sign for sparing would represent an opposing thumb position, in this case that of the thumb pressed firmly on the closed fist. And in fact there is independent evidence that such a gesture had positive connotations. The pressing of the thumb on the closed fist corresponds to a Roman gesture of well-wishing that Pliny the Elder attests as being used frequently in Roman society.[36] The principle of economy, therefore, allows us to connect the commonly attested "hostile thumb" with the gestures for death and mercy in gladiatorial contests.

[31] Ateius Capito fg. 12 Strzelecki (= Macr. *Sat.* 7.13.14); see too Lact. *opif.* 10.24, Isid. *orig.* 11.1.70.

[32] For example, Ov. *met.* 4.34–36 (spinning), Ov. *epist.* 17.266 (writing).

[33] Marcell. *med.* 28.72; see, too, 2.9, 25.13, 32.5, and Plin. *nat.* 23.110, 28.43; Niedermann 1914.329–30.

[34] Sittl 1890.102–3, 123.

[35] *Anth. Lat.* 415 (413 Shackleton Bailey).27–28: *sperat et in saeva victus gladiator arena, / sit licet infesto pollice turba minax*; for (*con*)*verso pollice*, see Juv. 3.36–37, Prud. *c. Symm.* 2.1097–99.

[36] Plin. *nat.* 28.25.

My third assumption concerns the stability of the meaning of Roman gestures through time and among the various peoples that inhabited Roman territory. In the case of texts, the thumb's "power" is a theme shared by a diverse range of authors, from Republican etymologists to medical writers of the early Empire to a poet composing riddles in the fifth century CE. This type of stability also applies to artistic representations. Two pieces of material evidence from different parts of the empire offer evidence for the thumb gesture requesting that a fighter be spared. These two representations, one a stone relief sculpture (apparently from Rome), the second an appliqué medallion in terracotta from the Rhône valley, show the thumb pressed firmly on the closed fist.[37] In both the textual and material evidence, therefore, the gesture survives both across the span of centuries and within the culturally coherent space of Rome.

Reconstructing the rudiments of a grammar of Roman gesture produces an epistemology of physical movement that can allow us to understand why the Romans invested so much in manipulating their own bodies and in reading those of others. On several occasions I will be pointing out differences between Greek and Roman gesture. What I focus on in analyzing these differences are not those bodily movements that the two cultures do not share, but those in which a gesture shared with the Greeks becomes integrated into the culture and naturalized as uniquely Roman.[38] For this process of naturalization another analogy from the study of spoken language will help illustrate my practice. It is a common phenomenon for a word new to a language to acquire a different meaning on the basis of how the word "sounds" in its new linguistic context. For example, the English adjective "husky" originally denoted anything that "had the qualities of a husk," in accordance with normal rules for producing adjectives from nouns by adding the suffix -y. Eventually, however, the sound of the word, produced deep in the throat, caused a new meaning to evolve, so that voices that are hoarse or deep are now described as "husky."[39] Gestures are similarly subject to unpredictable changes in signification. Usage, as often, determines meaning. A particularly clear case that I will discuss in chapter 2 involves the gestures of mourning women. Acts of self-degradation that are shared by grieving women in numerous cultures—tearing the hair, scratching the cheeks, beating the breasts—acquire new meaning in a Roman context. Rather than offering the women as targets for the pollution of death, these actions in fact celebrate the uniquely feminine power of giving and nurturing life.

---

[37] For illustrations and discussion, see chapter 2.

[38] In addition to Brilliant's notion of an "appendage aesthetic," other studies that treat how the Romans viewed the body differently from the Greeks include Torelli 1992 (historical reliefs), Lateiner 1996 (nonverbal behaviors in epic). For a general analysis of how Romans naturalize the educational aspects of their Greek inheritance, see Corbeill 2001.

[39] Jesperson 1922.405–11.

I have chosen for the subjects of the book's five chapters bodily behaviors that cover as wide a spectrum of ancient Roman culture as possible. In order of presentation, I explore how physical deportment assisted in clarifying and reinforcing religious ritual, medical practice, gender roles, and political ideologies. I summarize my individual arguments in the following paragraphs.

Chapter 1 surveys the gestures of priests and doctors to develop a working epistemological model for gesture. My sources include noncanonical texts from medical writers, the natural scientist Pliny, and papyri describing magical ritual. Effective prayer to the Roman required physical as well as mental activity. The body technique of doctors and priests, in mimicking a prayer or incantation's goal, depends upon an understanding of how symbolic positioning and movement by the body can affect external reality. In the second century BCE Cato the Elder demonstrates how mending a twig can mend a fractured leg, and gynecologists advise a man to alternately bind and loosen his wife's clothing when she has trouble in childbirth. What all these practices share, I argue, is a desire to harmonize the movements of the human body with the external, more-than-human world. It is here that my title "embodied nature" takes on its full meaning. Physical gesture is characterized as being, above all, coextensive with the nature of which it is a part.

In chapter 2 I turn from this broad consideration of the world of nature to a close analysis of one small component: the Roman thumb (*pollex*). By evaluating various aspects of this digit, from its etymological meaning to its everyday manifestations, I demonstrate how the Romans located in this single body part a notable source of power. I close the chapter by using this discussion to reconstruct the outward appearance of the "turned thumb" that spectators deployed at the gladiatorial games to bid that a fighter be killed or spared.

Chapter 3, following up on the idea of death in the arena, examines the social function of Roman gestures of lamentation. After surveying how expressions of grief divide along gender lines—men reconcile the loss of the deceased as a former member of the community, whereas women ensure that the dead person successfully enter an afterworld—I focus particular attention on the function of self-mutilation and degradation on the part of women. I suggest that the violent physical expressions of women do not transform these mourners into offerings for the potentially hostile dead, a scapegoat theory that has been offered from Roman antiquity (Varro) up through the twentieth century (especially by Durkheim and his followers). Instead I show how this violent mourning should be understood as part of "woman's work." Female mourning practice has its own end in effecting the successful separation of the corpse from the surviving society; it replicates the birth process, thereby ushering the deceased into its new phase of existence. Numerous acts, many peculiar to Italic ritual, support this belief: the prescription that the deceased be removed from the house feet-first is a conscious inversion of the fetus emerging from the womb; the preparation of the corpse on bare ground is prefigured by the same positioning of the newborn; women unbind hair and clothing during both lamentation and childbirth; and the nine-day period between burial and funeral feast finds its analog in the nine-month pregnancy. I conclude by examining the textual and visual evidence that suggests how beating the breasts represents a metaphorical "breast feeding" of the corpse to ensure immortality in the afterlife. Contrary to the way the male-dominated literary elite represents their actions, women in grief celebrate the rejuvenating and life-giving powers of the female body.

Chapter 4 shows how the interpretation of gesture can be exploited at a particular historical moment. Using primarily the speeches and philosophical works of the politician Cicero, I analyze the relationship between bodily movement and political programs in late Republican Rome. Physical bearing provided visible indications of whether a politician identified with popular or elite politics. A contemporary Ciceronian moral treatise asserts that certain types of gesture violate natural law (fin. 5.47). Integrating Bourdieu's model of the habitus with Roman notions of how nature is embodied in the "natural" human being, I show how elite figures publicly adapt Cicero's philosophical claim to Roman politics: "popular" politicians, with their identifiable gestures and walk, rebel against the truth of nature. The elision of nature and culture serves the purpose of social exclusion. I close this chapter by conjecturing the ways in which Julius Caesar used gesture as a means for political advancement. An awareness of contemporary cultural attitudes enabled Caesar to exploit elite Roman strictures regarding physical movement. I argue that Caesar intentionally adopted the demeanor of "popular" politicians as an act of defiance toward the elite, who had worked to define this demeanor as deviant. The intentional disjuncture between Caesar's political agenda and the expectations anticipated by his gestures advanced his image as a proponent of social and political change.

In chapter 5 I offer a diachronic analysis of the ways in which Roman writers express a growing dismay about the inability to read the human body. After demonstrating how Republican texts depend on facial expressions being stable and unambiguous signifiers of internal thoughts and character, I turn to a specific text, the first six books of Tacitus's Annals, which were composed in the new political climate of the autocratic Empire. By examining one particular aspect of how Tacitus portrays the relationship between the emperor Tiberius and the senate—the misreading of facial expressions—I analyze the ways in which Tacitus isolates the reign of Tiberius (14–37 CE) as the starting point for the separation of the Roman emperor from the rest of the Roman elite. Facial expression, commonly used in oratory produced during the Republic to indicate character and intention, evolves under Tiberius into a shifting signifier, a reflection of the political uncertainty that arose from the solidification of imperial power. For Tacitus, the accession of Tiberius and the introduction of a new political order have prompted the rise of a new cosmic order, a new perception of the increasingly inscrutable relationship between truth and the body.

Although each of these chapters can be read as an independent case study, in combination they are intended to offer a coherent narrative of the ways in which the Romans came to develop and manipulate relationships between their bodies and the world of which their bodies form a part. That narrative, as conceived here, is one of decline; I offer up a model of innocent and eager Romans, continually striving to harmonize their bodies with the world until political reality intrudes to manipulate an idyllic state of balance. My narrative of this decline doubtless owes much of its pessimism to the ancient authors who are my sources and, in fact, the decline is in many ways only apparent. The harmony with the world that I posit as working in medical practice, religious ritual, and mourning likely continued from archaic times until the fall of pagan Rome and, conversely, these models inevitably were exploited from the very moments of their origin. My adoption of a master narrative of development and decline may open me to charges of being unable to interpret the past outside of my own frame of reference. And yet I consciously embrace this hackneyed trope that sees morality as declining from an imaginary, pristine, and natural state. I cannot help but share with these sources a feeling that something vital in the relationship between bodies and their external environment has been, and continues to be, lost.

Chapter 1

PARTICIPATORY GESTURES
IN ROMAN RELIGIOUS RITUAL
AND MEDICINE

An astronomer looking through a 200-inch telescope
exclaimed that it was going to rain. His assistant asked,
"How can you tell?"
"Because my corns hurt."
—McLuhan and Fiore 1967.68

WE LAUGH AT this anecdote because of its painful truth, especially for those of us who have tricky joints. In this chapter I will consider what aspects of this truth are relevant to an understanding of gesture in Roman culture. Our joints and limbs reacting to the weather constitutes one of the few remaining manifestations of modern, civilized bodies "participating" with nature, and participating in a way that strikes us as mystical and even beyond science. No matter how powerful the telescope, it could never seem to surpass the inherent intuition—the gut feelings—of our aching bodies. As a result of this lingering concession to climate, we tend to suspend judgment when, for example, Pliny the Elder remarks that the autumnal equinox and winter solstice are signaled not just by storms, but by many changes we feel in our bodies.[1] And yet Pliny's statement rests on more than random observation; on the contrary, it assumes the existence of a potentially recoverable network of knowledge. One particularly vivid example will suffice to introduce the ways in which Romans and nature piously interacted. During the annual festival of the Lemuria in the month of May, the Roman homeowner practiced a ritual to drive out unwanted spirits. Rising at midnight, he walked barefoot through his home making the "fig" gesture (hand in the shape of a fist, with thumb inserted upward between index and middle finger) and spitting from his mouth nine black beans. As one scholar has justly remarked: "At first sight it is difficult to imagine Livy or Horace or Agrippa solemnly getting out of bed and going through this ritual. And yet they probably did—at least in a modified form."[2] In Rome,

---

[1] Plin. *nat.* 2.108: *autumnali aequinoctio brumaque, cum tempestatibus confici sidus intellegimus, nec imbribus tantum tempestatibusque sed multis et corporum et ruris experimentis.*

[2] Ogilvie 1969.85, as quoted by Scullard 1981.118–19, who provides details about the Lemuria.

the relationship envisaged between human actors and their natural setting involved a reciprocal engagement: I will be discussing not only how people like Pliny, Cicero, and Cato react corporeally to their surroundings, but also how, like the expectorating homeowner, they work their bodies to manipulate those same surroundings.

Nature may actively determine certain types of physical movement—much as it causes me to limp when a Kansas tornado is approaching—but in Rome these physical movements could in turn be read as a reflection or manifestation of nature written on the body. I have chosen this chapter to open a book about gesture and nature because the practitioners of participatory gestures—from public priests to doctors to everyday users of folk spells and remedies—show clearly how gestures fit into the ways Romans classified knowledge, inasmuch as each of these actors shares ways of mediating between the human and the more-than-human.[3] (I borrow the term "more-than-human" from recent works in anthropology and ecological theory since it neatly avoids the associations of terms such as "supernatural" or "phenomenological world" or the deceptively simple category of the "natural.")[4] In my subsequent chapters I will present Latin texts that detail phenomena resulting from this mediation, such as the way human beings move in the act of mourning the dead to the aristocratic associations of the stately stride to facial expressions that intend to deceive the viewer. In each of these analyses, I maintain that gesture was thought to constitute a legitimate means of determining an individual's character and beliefs; and it is this premise that I will begin to argue in this chapter.

I choose to focus on ritual gestures, a particular area in which Romans constructed their gestures as "natural" in the most literal sense of the word: as conforming with *natura*. A study of ritual gesture benefits from a distinction between two basic types of physical movement. First, there are those gestures that are perceived to be effective as a result of experience, but whose precise relevance to the external world is not immediately clear to the practitioner (*Wirken*).[5] A particularly striking example at Rome is the use of human spittle. Pliny informs us that it is universal medical practice (*in omni medicina mos*) that if one spits three times while praying for a cure, the efficacy of the cure is increased.[6] Yet the only explanation he can offer for this remarkable ability is experience (*vita*). To the second category of gesture belong those movements that are believed to fit into some recognized system and that therefore find their origins in the examination and systematic study of the physical world (*Werken*); this category would incorporate the first class of gestures once

---

[3] On this point, see North 1990a.49.

[4] See most fully the elegant exposition in Abram 1996.

[5] The *Werken* / *Wirken* distinction is discussed by Fischer 1960.342–46.

[6] Plin. *nat.* 28.36: *terna despuere precatione in omni medicina mos est, atque ita effectus adiuvare*; Nicolson 1897 surveys the belief and provides a possible explanation.

they were shown to fit into a detectable pattern, a developmental process that Pliny alludes to frequently in his encyclopedic work on natural history.[7] It is upon this latter category that I shall concentrate in this chapter, as I attempt to locate a consistent underlying structure for some of the gestural movements employed in Roman medicine and ritual.

Cicero indicates a place from which to begin when he highlights a common ground occupied by two opposing philosophical positions of his day. In Book Three of his On the Nature of the Gods the interlocutor Cotta steps up to refute the claims of the Stoic speaker Balbus that had filled the previous book. During the earlier discussion, Cotta had already followed the convictions of his own philosophical school, that of the New Academy, in professing that "it does not so easily occur to me why something is true as why it is false."[8] In light of such emphatic skepticism, it is remarkable that Cotta should be able to locate any points of agreement with the preceding Stoic speaker. And yet, while denying Balbus's claim that the universe (mundus) is god, Cotta nevertheless acknowledges the intricate stability of the natural world. The Latin sentence mirrors the structure he describes:

> illa mihi placebat oratio de convenientia consensuque naturae, quam quasi cognatione continuata conspirare dicebas. . . . illa vero cohaeret et permanet naturae viribus, non deorum. (Cic. nat. deor. 3.28; italics added)

> I was pleased with your remarks on the congruence and consensus within nature which you said coexists in a kind of constant consanguinity. . . . But nature coheres and endures because of the strength of nature, not of the gods.

The skeptical Cotta is unwilling to reject the fundamental principle of nature's coherence. He emphasizes his point with playful repetition of the prefix con-, a prefix denoting unity in place and time. As my subsequent discussion will make clear, this perception of unity within nature reaches outside the boundaries of philosophical discourse and into the world of the everyday, where basic principles of healing and appealing to the gods can also be shown to be predicated on a notion of stable order in nature. This assumption, that the natural world contains a web of harmonious and discordant relationships, came to provide the basic principle around which the elder Pliny organized his investigations into the workings of the universe and all its components.[9] The ancients who used their bodies in Roman medical practice and other

---

[7] For example, Plin. nat. 2.97, 101; Beagon 1992.55–91 evaluates Pliny's complex attitude toward the role of human reason in studying nature.

[8] Cic. nat. deor. 1.57: mihi enim non tam facile in mentem venire solet quare verum sit aliquid quam quare falsum; see, too, 1.60, 2.2.

[9] See, e.g., his explicit statements at nat. 20.1, 37.59. Stemplinger 1919 demonstrates how the principle informs the entire Historia Naturalis. Pliny's disdain for magicians (magi) is attributable to their ignorance of this principle; see Beagon 1992.100–13.

ritual activities share an analogous goal: the desire to learn and thereby participate in the workings of nature.[10]

PHYSICALITY OF WORDS

An analysis of Latin words provides direct access to Roman conceptions of
the body and its movement. My survey of the particular gestures of priests and
doctors complements research regarding the "power of the word" in medical,
scientific, and magical texts.[11] Numerous examples survive of a subset of sympathetic magic that has been aptly termed "verbal homeopathy": cures are
effected or charms succeed as the result of a perceived etymological link between the desired goal and the verbal means that a person employs to obtain
that goal. As a result, if the uvula is sore, one compiler of medical cures prescribes using a dried grape (*uva*). This will ease the pain. Do you need temporary charm? Pliny records the popular belief that eating a rabbit (*lepus*) will
provide you with *lepos*—urbane elegance—but the effects last only for nine
days.[12] Pliny's reflections on this folk-cure are worth recording. After acknowledging that the verbal correspondence represents a "silly joke" (*frivolo quidem
ioco*), consideration of the popularity of the practice makes him serious: "and
yet there must exist some underlying reason for such a widespread belief"
(*tamen aliqua debeat subesse causa in tanta persuasione*). This proviso exposes
an important assumption. Validation through experience supersedes any apparent irrationality of practice. Nature should be trusted even when not fully
understood.

Principles of similarity could also extend beyond the verbal to include physical likeness. Since the tubers of orchids resemble human testicles, orchid
roots are deemed effective for curing sexual ailments among men.[13] In this
particular case, moreover, the word for the orchid bulb is identical with a
common word for testicle (the Greek ὄρχζς), with the result that physical
similarity and name both contribute to the perception that the two objects
are related. It would be impossible to say which, the naming of the tuber or

---

[10] I am not interested in the possible *origins* of this, theory of sympathy (for this, see M. Smith
1983.255, who traces it back to Bolos of Mendes in the second century BCE), but how it fits into
a set of practices already existing in Italy.

[11] See, e.g., McCartney 1927, Köves-Zulauf 1972, and Corbeill 1996.68–74; for the significance of the written word, see Beard 1991.

[12] Marcell. *med.* 14.26: *de uva passa eliges granum, quod unum intrinsecus nucleum habeat, eumque
in phoenicio alligabis et faucibus, id est in regione uvae, inseres et tenebis et dices: "Uva uvam emendat";
mox ipsum phoenicium supra verticem eius tenebis et idem dices cumque ter ipsum feceris et carminaveris,
collo dolentis subligabis*; see, too, 8.128 (*oculi scabri > scarabeus*), 36.46 (*torpor pedium > torpedino
sub pedibus*); Plin. *nat.* 28. 260: *somnos fieri lepore sumpto in cibis Cato arbitrabatur, vulgus et gratiam
corpori in VIIII dies* (i.e., Latin *gratia* = Greek *lepos*; as often, Pliny does not make explicit the
verbal relationships between Latin and Greek); many other examples in McCartney 1927.

[13] Plin. *nat.* 26.95–96 (Isid. *orig.* 17.9.43); Stannard 1982.14–15.

its use as a curative agent, came first in this case and I would argue that, to
the practitioner of the cure, it would not ultimately matter.[14] For this case
resembles a more complex example of a sympathetic relationship that is attested outside the Greek and Roman worlds as well, whereby a disease receives
its name from its similarity to an object in nature and *then* that object is used
to cure the ailment. A recorded cure for venereal disease provides a particularly clear example: the affliction of *carcinoma* (the Greek loan-word for the
disease) derives its name from a presumed resemblance between its visible
manifestation and the crab (the Latin *cancer*).[15] In what might seem a confusion of causal relations, a common remedy for these sores is to grind up a crab
and apply its remains as a poultice to its namesake, the disease. What is op-
erating in these cases, however, is not simply a person observing how nature
creates similarities and then human beings exploiting these relationships—
the so-called "theory of signatures" common in Pliny and elsewhere.[16] Rather,
the case of *carcinomata*, and perhaps of *orchides* as well, shows humans directly
intervening with nature to create verbal relationships and then to exploit
them once created. The interaction resembles Bateson's formulation of the
role of the individual "self" in systems theory, by which the human agent "is
only a small part of a much larger trial-and-error system which does the thinking, acting, and decoding."[17] I shall return at the end of this chapter to the
notion of the body and nature working in tandem within this sort of dynamic,
self-regulating system.

   As a result of a receptiveness among the Romans to seeing nature as an
open system, these cures, in which like affects like, likely arise from more than
superstition. After all, instructors in literature have long had recourse to the
seemingly mystical powers of consonance and assonance, so that an *uva* curing
an *uvula* has fine poetic resonance. And yet, far from originating in some
metaphysical dream world, the practice of verbal homeopathy represents the
pragmatic extension of a conviction that the origins of language are deeply
rooted in nature. The common notion seems to have been most famously
applied to Latin by Nigidius Figulus, a grammarian and mystic of the first
century BCE—the apparent incongruity of these vocations reveals further the
relationship perceived in Rome between language and the more-than-human
world.[18] Aulus Gellius relates the underlying tenet of Nigidius's *Grammatical
Commentaries* as follows: "nouns and verbs arose not by chance assignment,

---

[14] See further the discussion of analogy in Lloyd 1966.172–209, esp. 176–80.

[15] Plin. *nat.* 32.134; Evans-Pritchard 1937.485–87 cites similar examples among the Azande;
further Rosenberger 1998.94, with bibliography.

[16] Conte 1994.92–94 (on Pliny).

[17] Bateson 1972.331.

[18] For attempts to reconcile this incongruity, see Ahl 1988 and, at greater length and with
more imagination, Ahl 1985.

but by a kind of force and reason in nature."[19] This statement does more than posit an onomatopoetic origin of language, a theory now popularly know as the "bow wow" hypothesis, although this is a possible component of Nigidius's general claim. More precisely, Nigidius posits a divine nature that has actively stimulated the production of language. In this aspect Romans could almost be said to be protoecological. A recent analysis of surviving preliterate or partially literate cultures concludes that "spoken language seems to give voice to, and thus to enhance and accentuate, the sensorial affinity between humans and the environing earth."[20] In other words, the ubiquitous "power of the word" grows out of the rootedness of language in the world itself. Words are verbal gestures in which physical action, and not the voice, has primacy. If language in the Roman world is an extension within nature, it should follow that human bodies, to the extent that natural language can affect them, also interact with the coherent patterning of the natural world.

This claim may be justified by continuing to look at words, in particular the Latin words for gestures and gesturing. Even though words constitute the majority of what Roman antiquity has left us in regard to the details of physical movement, this limitation is mitigated by the inherent physicality of the Latin vocabulary. The Latin noun *gestus* ("gesture") derives from the verb *gerere* ("to carry") and refers literally to how the body "carries" itself. As I shall discuss in detail in chapter 4, this carriage can be read by observers as an indication of internal disposition. For now, I would simply wish to observe how this hypothesis helps explain an often misunderstood idiomatic usage of the verb *gerere*. When *gerere* takes as its direct object either a lone adjective or a noun denoting an occupation, the verb acquires the idea that is expressed in English by the phrase "to play the role of." This syntactic trait is shared with other verbs that denote the notion of self-presentation more explicitly than the simple *gerere* would seem to (*praebere, praestare, simulare*).[21] Apuleius, for example, describes a man who "plays the soldier" (*militem gerebat*) by girding himself with a sword-belt (*met.* 11.8); in these cases, carriage creates character. A similar phenomenon, attested as early as Plautus, occurs with the verb *facere* ("to do"); hence the phrase "you do the bold man" means "you behave boldly" (*ferocem facis*; Plaut. *Most.* 890).

The noun *gestus* shares with its verbal form a broad semantic range, indicating not simply different combinations of the fingers and arms, but also the

---

[19] Gell. 10.4.1: *nomina verbaque non positu fortuito, sed quadam vi et ratione naturae facta esse.* Gellius continues: *rem sane in philosophiae disceptationibus celebrem* ("a subject quite common in philosophical discussions"). Collart 1954.258–68 surveys ancient debates over the natural origins of language.

[20] Abram 1996.71; of the linguists he cites, see especially Jesperson 1922.396–411 ("Sound Symbolism"); Jakobson and Waugh 1987.181–234 ("The Spell of Speech Sounds").

[21] See Löfstedt (1942) 1.244–48, who compares the parallel use of *facere*; on *gerere* in particular, see TLL 6: 1940.74–1941.25 (I. Kapp and G. Meyer).

way an individual holds the head or moves the eyes or eats food.[22] The earliest
attested use of the word *gestus* occurs in the mid-second century BCE in a play
by the comic poet Terence. Here gestures act as instruments of deception.
Phormio, the play's title character, needs to deceive a pair of old men who are
about to come on stage, so he chooses to adopt new gestures for the situation.
He informs the audience, "Now I have to take up a new gesture and facial
expression."[23] Phormio presents a bodily attitude designed to influence others'
perception of him. This projection of internal desire via body language is
further reflected in *gestire*, the verb derived from the noun form *gestus*. Having
the root sense of "to make gestures toward," the verb more commonly describes
the feelings of exhilaration or happiness that are conveyed by unusually active
movement of the body.[24] From this conception the verb takes on a complementary infinitive and so acquires the meaning "to desire strongly." This development provides another clear instance of physical movement making
manifest internal emotions and desires.

This brief survey of *gerere* and its cognates indicates that the Latin language
could conceive of desire as literally embodied and, by implication, as readable
in the body. Other aspects of Latin vocabulary indicate this constant presence
of the body in communication. Nigidius Figulus in particular stresses the inseparability of motion and meaning. He sees the verb *adnuo* ("to nod toward"
in assent) as physically expressing internal desire: movement of the head or
eyes toward the petitioner underscores consent. In a related move, a rhetorical
treatise from the Republic permits the orator to stretch forward the neck for
emphasis in the direction of his listeners. This ungainly posture seems at odds
with the emphasis on physical decorum that these treatises normally stress.
Hence, the author is careful to justify his approval on the grounds that this
particular gesture "is granted by nature."[25] The opposing action of nodding
away, the common form of denial in Roman antiquity, operates on similar
principles. The head moves back, away from the petitioner.[26] Some anthropologists claim that the head thrown back or shaken in denial, a type of gesture
almost universally practiced among human beings, including among those
born deaf and blind, derives from the movement that an infant makes in
rejecting the breast after feeding.[27] Nigidius would surely have endorsed such

---

[22] Movement of head: Claud. 5.345; of eyes: Serv. Aen. 7.251; dining: Ov. *ars* 3.755. Although
TLL s.v. *gestus* says the word occurs *maxime manuum* (6: 1969.50 [I. Kapp and G. Meyer]), the
lexicon cites a number of examples that extend beyond simple hand gestures. See, for example,
the straightforward testimony offered by Schol. Ter. *Phorm.* 890: *gestus motus corporis.*

[23] Ter. *Phorm.* 890: *nunc gestus mihi voltusque est capiundus novos.*

[24] Paul. Fest. p. 96; compare Don. Ter. *Eun.* 555.

[25] Rhet. Her. 3.26: *nam est hoc a natura datum.*

[26] Nigid. apud Gell. 10.4.4 (cited fully in n. 28).

[27] Darwin 1998.272–77.

an explanation. Thus far, then, Nigidius's claims about the interaction of the body and the will seem reasonable.

Nigidius continues: not just the pantomime gestures of the head nod, but even more basic elements of the Latin language illustrate bodily participation in the human will. In forming the second-person pronouns *tu* and *vos*, Nigidius remarks that the protruding lips and expelled breath of the speaker make a kind of "natural gesture" toward the intended audience—toward the "you" and "you all." In contrast, the first-person forms *ego* and *nos* cause the speaker to direct the lips and breath inward, toward the speaker or speakers, in a physical act of self-reference.[28] As much as Nigidius's contention may seem extreme, our ancient source for his claim, Aulus Gellius, finds his example "particularly elegant" (*lepidum et festivum*), and we may compare the view of Darwin, who hypothesized an analogous relationship between the body and the origins of language when he posited that "speech was in origin nothing but mouth pantomime, in which the vocal organs unconsciously attempted to mimic gestures by the hands."[29] Modern linguists have assumed a similar correspondence between physiology and semantics in their investigation of "phonetic symbolism" in spoken language, whereby certain vowel and consonant sounds convey specific connotations. In the case of vowels, for example, long *a* tends to be used to describe large or flat objects (English "table"), short *i* to describe small ones (English "little").[30] A similar correspondence is found between vowel sounds and relative "brightness," with the increasing frequency of vocalic resonance marking words with "brighter" connotations. A compelling explanation for this latter phenomenon can be found in the body's physiology: "the acute vowels articulated toward the exterior of our bodies are judged to be 'light,' whereas those articulated toward our interior are imagined to be 'dark,' because 'the further you penetrate into the body, the darker it is there.' "[31] Such claims of "phonetic symbolism" assume that these phenomena reflect an evolutionary development in which all languages derive elements of their vocabulary from basic principles of human physiology. In the case of Latin in particular, other etymological phenomena rush to support the notion that verbal expression derives from internal physical states. The Romans pop-

---

[28] Nigid. apud Gell. 10.4.4: *nam sicuti cum adnuimus et abnuimus, motus quidam ille vel capitis vel oculorum a natura rei quam significat non abhorret, ita in his vocibus quasi gestus quidam oris et spiritus naturalis est* ("Just as, when we nod in assent or denial, the movement of our head and eyes harmonizes with the nature of what the movement indicates, so too in these words [sc. the first- and second-person pronouns] there is a kind of natural gesture of the mouth and breath"). Nigidius seems to derive this example from Chrysippus; see SVF 2.895 (= Galen 5.216 Kühn) and the discussion in Ricottilli 2000.69–80.

[29] Cited by Pei 1965.24.

[30] R. Brown 1958.111–39.

[31] Peterfalvi 1970.63, quoted with disapproval in Jakobson and Waugh 1987.189; but see more recently the sympathetic survey of phonetic symbolism in Pinker 1994.166–67.

ularly derived *vultus* ("facial expression") from the verb *volo* ("to want"), since our outward expression voicelessly "expresses" our inner will. Even more tellingly, the verb *facio* ("to do") produces the noun *facies*, the ancestor of our English "face." Originally, and perhaps until as late as the time of Horace (first century BCE), *facies* is used to describe not simply the face but the entire human physique, presumably because physical appearance is best described in the context of human action, of "doing."[32] We are what we do, especially in the process of doing it. Our body is a facial expression.

HANDS

Even more than the lips, head, and face, the hands provide the readiest opportunities for participation in the world. Accordingly, Latin etymology and semantics repeatedly mark the importance of *manus* in Roman culture: "It is called a hand (*manus*) because it is a gift (*munus*) for the entire body."[33] Extant usage shows that the word *manus* can, in fact, act in synecdoche for the entire arm, most frequently to describe the human embrace or the power of that embrace—men die in the "hands" of their enemies, the hands allow lovers to hug.[34] Parallel to these associations of the hand with comfort and security, when the noun *manus* is compounded to form the verb *mandare*, the commonest verb meaning to "entrust" or "put in the care of," there exists simultaneously both the word's literal meaning ("to give to [one's] hand[s]") as well as the figurative notion of placing someone or something in the embrace of a guardian.[35] In contrast, the common idiom describing surrender, *manus dare/dedere* (literally, "to give the hands"), expresses the opposite notion: in yielding the hands, the vanquished opponent gives over a potent symbol of personal power. In material representations as well, the hand acted as a visual metonymy for the concept of trust and solidarity. Pliny comments that "in other parts of the body there is a kind of religious presence; in the right hand, for example, . . . [which] is offered in trust (*in fide*)."[36] This notion

[32] *Vultus:* Maltby 1991 s.v. cites Prisc. *gramm.* 2.261.16 with 2.528.3, 3.445.3; Cassiod. *anim.* 11 l.78H, *in psalm.* 30.23 l.475A; Isid. *orig.* 11.1.34. For *facies*, see Gell. 13.30, who cites uses from early Roman writers to support this contention, which is repeated by Servius (*Aen.* 6.104, 8.298; v. Serv. auct. *Aen.* 8.194 and Don. Ter. *Eun.* 296); further TLL 6: 1.44.56–70 (O. Hey).

[33] Isid. *orig.* 11.1.66: *manus dicta quod sit totius corporis munus* (*diff.* 2.62 adds *et quod ab ipsis mandimus*). For indications that the hand had greater significance in Roman than Greek culture, see Sittl 1890.130, 133, 134.

[34] Cic. *inv.* 1.108; Ov. *met.* 3.390; TLL 8: 343.3–18 (V. Bulhart).

[35] TLL 8: 262.47–48 (V. Bulhart), where the primary definition of *mando* is given as *respicitur fides vel cura, cui aliquem (aliquid) committimus.*

[36] Plin. *nat.* 11.250: *inest et aliis partibus quaedam religio, sicut in dextera: . . . in fide porrigitur;* further Horsfall 2000.254–55.

of *fides* seems to be represented by the prominent gesture of the right hand in the historical scene on the Esquiline tomb paintings of the third century BCE.[37]

The symbolism of the hand as a guardian of property and preserver of trust informs its importance in Roman law. *Manus* pervades legal terminology. Forms of the word, or compounds derived from it, are used to describe the power the male head of the household has over his wife (*in manu esse*), children (*emancipatio*), slaves (*manumissio*), and inanimate property. Outside the family, when a Roman citizen leads an outstanding debtor to court, the process is described as "the laying on of the hand" (*manus iniectio*).[38] In the physical act of taking possession of animate property, the hand is literally manifest. Gaius, a second-century legal writer, notes that persons and animals must be physically present to make legally valid their transfer as property. Yet this alone is not sufficient; the future owner must also literally hold onto them: "that is why the process is called *mancipatio*, because the object is taken in the hand (*manu . . . capitur*)."[39] A similar procedure takes place in the action of adoption, regardless of whether the adoptee is a child or an adult, and in summoning a witness to testify in court by pulling on his ear.[40] Even in a situation threatening the safety of Rome, verbal orders given by tribunes of the people to release a prisoner were inadequate if the magistrate could not make physical contact with the person in custody.[41] Finally, various pacts were solemnly closed by the formulaic "joining of the right hands" (*dextrarum iunctio*); it is especially well known as a symbol of marriage on countless sarcophagi in the early empire. An indication of the solemnity of this gesture is that it apparently did not exist in the now-familiar manifestation of the "handshake" as a regular means of salutation or leave-taking.[42] It is no exaggeration to say that the hand visually enacts, and ultimately symbolizes, the legal relations that govern commerce, property, and the Roman family.[43]

Visual representations of the hand, depicted in isolation with fingers extended and usually with palm facing the viewer, also date back to early Rome.

---

[37] Boyancé 1964 discusses the significance of the right hand in the cult of the goddess Fides; for the Esquiline paintings, see illustration and bibliography in Holliday 1997.135–36.

[38] Sittl 1890.129–47; Lécrivain 3.1586; Wenger 1953.887–89.

[39] Gaius *inst.* 1.121: *unde etiam mancipatio dicitur, quia manu res capitur* (see too 1.119, 2.24); Sittl 1890.129–30.

[40] Adoption: Sittl 1890.130, with n. 5 for illustration on coins; calling a witness: Hor. *sat.* 1.9.76–77 and Sittl 1890.146.

[41] Cic. *Vatin.* 21; Coarelli (1992) 2.56.

[42] Boyancé 1964.107 is the first to note this. A variation of this gesture is, however, frequently used on Greek and Roman grave reliefs to indicate farewell; see Reekmans 1958.27–30. For the handshake used to seal important agreements among the Greeks, see Neumann 1965.49–58.

[43] Achard 1994.39–40 on hand gestures in law: "Ces gestes sont si forts qu'on leur accorde une authentique valeur juridistique . . . ou qu'on serait mal jugé si on leur résistait"; Täubler 1913.340–41 offers a reconstruction of the origins of the hand's importance in law.

1. Bronze quadrans (*aes grave*) depicting human hand, Rome, 3d c.
BCE (photo American Numismatic Society, acc. no. 1954.263.94).

An *aes grave* of the early third century BCE bears such an illustration, which "would seem to refer to those concepts of possession and power which are explicit in the Roman *manus*" (see fig. 1).[44] This conception of power perhaps extended to Rome's external military conquests as well. Textual sources record that the earliest legionary standards were topped by bundles of hay that were probably meant to resemble a human hand.[45] It is certain in any event that the open right hand becomes the commonest nonanimal symbol for the fighting troops to rally around.[46] The meaning of the symbol is uncertain. One suggestion is that it carries over the idea of "trust" (*fides*) from the legal sphere.[47] More probably the hand, like the animals also found atop the standards, conveys a general symbol of power, perhaps of a deity. The power of a god's hands is certainly attested in the medical tradition. Scribonius Largus,

[44] Brilliant 1963.38; examples in Crawford 1974, nos. 14/4 (plate D, which specimen he dates to 280–276 BCE), 25/7.

[45] Ov. *fast.* 3.115; Plut. *Vit. Rom.* 8.6; Serv. *Aen.* 11.870; Isid. *orig.* 9.3.50, 18.3.5; Reinach 1313, who argues against the claims of the sources that the symbol simply represented the importance of hay.

[46] Domaszewski 1885 provides eight examples (plus one on a praetorian standard).

[47] Domaszewski 1885.53.

who compiled a collection of medical prescriptions in the mid-first century CE, cites with approval a tradition later noted by Galen that called drugs "the hands of the gods"—"for remedies tested by experience have the same effect as divine touch."[48] Whatever the symbolic value of this metaphor, by the Hellenistic period the right hand, either alone or in combination with the left, had become a powerful apotropaic symbol, found frequently on tombs as a warning to potential thieves or as a protection from hostile powers, as in the bronze hands that were found on the ships from Nemi.[49]

Given the hand's significance in law, business, family matters, the military, and as a protection against evil, it comes as little surprise that in the act of prayer the hand was to be kept pure.[50] In official religious activity, it has been noted that the Romans placed greater stress than the Greeks on physical purity of the body.[51] The careful attention to cleanliness can be attributed in part to the fact that direct contact with the object involved in prayer was essential— the practice of covering the hands in the handling of sacred objects, so prevalent in early Christianity, was virtually unknown to early Roman religion.[52]

Public religious practice is reflected in the pharmaceutical tracts that describe the rituals by which medicinal plants are collected.[53] Here our texts provide a special perspective on ways in which the body participated in nature. In addition to prescribing the most advantageous time of the day or month for collection, extant texts also repeatedly detail how and with which hand herbs should be plucked for best efficacy. This type of knowledge was so essential to the final outcome of a spell or cure that Ovid can refer to the hand that picks the herbs as a synecdoche for the sorcerer who manipulates them.[54] Surely the precision with which these texts preserve through the ages such details on digits indicates the importance tradition placed in the practitioners'

[48] Scrib. Larg. *praef.* 1: *Herophilus fertur dixisse medicamenta divinas manus esse. . . . prorsus enim, quod tactus divinus efficere potest, id praestant medicamenta usu experientiaque probata*; Weinreich 1909.37.

[49] Cumont 1923 starts with Eastern origins to trace how the raised hands develop from representing the act of prayer to a sign of protection; see, too, L'Orange 1953.153–59. The left hand seems to be an apotropaic sign only when appearing together with the right: Ucelli 1940.212–14 (on hands from Nemi; other examples of apotropaic hands appearing in tandem may be found in: Breccia 1911 no. 480 [Plate 52, 126]); Crawford 1974.21/4, 27/8. For the infernal associations of the left hand, see Sen. *Med.* 680 and Sittl 1890.189 n. 1.

[50] Appel 1909.185–86 gathers the evidence. He hypothesizes that originally the entire body was washed and that then this requirement was limited symbolically to the head and hands.

[51] Eitrem 1915.127.

[52] Dieterich 1911, who attributes the practice at Rome to the influence of the cult of Isis, which in turn inherited the practice ultimately from Persia. He notes the cult of *Fides* as an exception (447 n. 10); further Boyancé 1964.101–3.

[53] Stannard 1987.99 estimates that approximately forty descriptions occur in "Roman writers."

[54] Ov. *medic.* 35–36: *fortibus herbis / quas maga terribili subsecat arte manus*. For specified hands and fingers, see, for example, Plin. *nat.* 21.176, 23.110; Marcell. *med.* 14.65, 31.33; Köves-Zulauf 1972.159 n. 25.

relationship with their natural surroundings. One particularly full account of a collection ritual preserved by Marcellus Empiricus in the fifth century CE supports this suspicion. Marcellus enjoins the forager to pluck the plant *brittanice* with the "medicinal fingers" (i.e., the ring finger and thumb). Before removing the plant from its natural environment, however, Marcellus recommends reciting the following charm:

> terram teneo, herbam lego, in nomine Christi prosit ad quod te colligo. (Marcell. *med.* 25.13)

> I hold the earth, I pluck the herb; in the name of Christ may the purpose for which I collect you be advantageous.

We are to envision the forager holding the plant in one hand, the earth in the other, while praying for an auspicious outcome to these actions. This is, of course, not a practice introduced together with the Christian addition *in nomine Christi*. As I shall demonstrate in the next section, the special treatment of the plant grows out of a perceived special relationship between the human body—as represented in this instance by the two fingers—and the productive earth.

ROMANS AND EARTH

Roman bodies spoke not only to each other with their head nods and handshakes; they also reached out beyond the human. The perceived power of the earth underfoot reunites the realms we separate into the medical, the religious, and the political. Latin texts document with clarity the relationship between the Roman—whether acting as citizen, magistrate, or priest—and the earth itself. Saserna, a writer on agriculture of the second century BCE, shares the elder Cato's practice of including home remedies in his work. To relieve sore feet the author prescribes, among other things, touching the earth and asking that the ground take the pain from his feet.[55] The conception extends into the area of state religion. Numerous texts attest how dedicatory ceremonies by priests and magistrates depend on the human body drawing power from the earth; the ceremonial sanctity of touching altars in reverence and holding doorposts to create religious boundaries is respected even by self-professed skeptics such as Cicero and could be alluded to by Ovid in the context of seduction.[56] This Roman view of the sacredness of the earth can be traced back, according to Livy, at least to the reign of the king Tullus Hostilius, where

---

[55] Sasern. apud Varro *rust.* 1.2.27: "*ego tui memini, medere meis pedibus, terra pestem teneto, salus hic maneto in meis pedibus.*" hoc ter noviens cantare iubet, terram tangere, despuere, ieiunum cantare.

[56] Wagenvoort 1947.12–58; Wenger 1953.889–90; Latte 1960.200–1; for Cicero, see, for example, *dom.* 120–21; Ovid: *am.* 1.4.27 (*tange manu mensam, tangunt quo more precantes*).

an herb with earth attached is used to ratify a peace treaty.[57] This earth-bound, still-living plant was called a *sagmen*, a formation that seems literally to signify a "thing that renders one sacred" (*sac[er]* + *-men*). Pliny amplifies the significance of the *sagmen*: the founders of Rome used it for public cures and sacred rites as well as for official embassies.[58] This sacredness of the earth also explains an odd digression in which Pliny criticizes others for doubting that the honorific *corona graminea* was made of just grass. This honor, which Pliny identifies as the most important crown the Romans could bestow on a soldier (*nat.* 22.6), deceives his contemporaries by its sheer simplicity. It is the surrounding natural environs and not the plant itself that is most important, for the grass must be removed from the very site where the army achieved its victory. Pliny relates at length the moral to be drawn from this misrecognition of the value of the *corona graminea*: nature has already presented humans with the means for taking care of themselves and we show contempt for nature in not recognizing this (*nat.* 22.14–17). For Pliny's moral vision, in which his contemporaries threaten to lose all respect for the natural world, proper appreciation of the environment becomes a moral necessity.

This power associated with the earth is exploited as well in the search for the curative properties of plants. If a plant is not used for food or adornment, then it must, in Pliny's pharmacology, have a medicinal use, since "nothing is produced by nature without some hidden cause."[59] The clear implication is that eventually human investigation will reveal the purpose of all plants.[60] As a corollary to this emphasis on the efficiency of the natural, Pliny observes that remedies derived from a single source are more reliable than artificial mixtures and that wild plants are more effective than domesticated.[61] This feeds into the prevalent moral attitude in the early Empire about imitating nature: a plant removed from its environment, like a fish transplanted into a senator's fish pond, is no longer itself.

---

[57] Liv.1.24.4–6, with Wagenvoort 1947.19.

[58] Plin. *nat.* 22.5: *auctores imperii Romani conditoresque immensum quiddam et hinc [ex ignobilibus herbis] sumpsere, quoniam non aliunde sagmina in remediis publicis fuere et in sacris legationibusque verbenae. certe utroque nomine idem significatur, hoc est gramen ex arce cum sua terra evolsum, ac semper e legatis, cum ad hostes clarigatumque mitterentur, id est res raptas clare repetitum, unus utique verbenarius vocabatur.* See, too, Fest. p. 321; Serv. Aen. 12.120, who says *sagmen* comes not from the *arx*, but from the south hill of the Capitoline.

[59] Plin. *nat.* 22.1: *[herbarum] reliquarum potentia adprobat nihil ab rerum natura sine aliqua occultiore causa gigni.*

[60] Plin. *nat.* 21.2: *quippe reliqua usus alimentique gratia genuit [natura]* (he goes on to say that even ornamental flowers serve a function by reminding humans that "what blooms most spectacularly wastes away the quickest"); see Stannard 1982.10–11. Evans-Pritchard 1937.482 estimates that the Azande used over one thousand different plants as drugs, without suggesting a reason for this proliferation.

[61] Simple cures: Plin. *nat.* 22.106; wild plants: Plin. *nat.* 20.131; 20.76, 124; Verg. *georg.* 2.47–49; Stannard 1982.16.

PHYSICALITY OF PRAYER

Prayer, rooted in the earth through language, also participated physically in the way the external world was perceived. Each of the etymological manifestations of bodily desire I have discussed—*gestus, gestire, vultus, facies*—finds a further physical analog in the common prayer stance, by which the hands and gaze are extended in whatever direction the gods are thought to reside. This does not simply mean that prayers were directed by stretching both hands toward the sky, a practice that, an ancient Greek text asserts, all human beings share.[62] Rather, Greeks and Romans could also aim prayers toward the ground, or in the direction of an appropriate temple or statue in the vicinity.[63] To fail to realize the variations in this prayer type was to invite derision: the second-century Greek declaimer Polemon, upon seeing an actor pointing to the ground while addressing Zeus, but to the sky when addressing Earth, accused the man of committing a "solecism of the hand."[64] As with many other cultural phenomena, however, we find the Romans adapting to their own outlook cultural practices that they share with the Greeks. The act of prayer, for instance, shows the body of the Roman more overtly involved in worship than that of the Greek. A sensitivity to spatial relationships is indicated by the non-Greek practice of worshipping *capite velato*; with the head covered, the worshipper avoids meeting signs of ill omen.[65] Nigidius's speaking lips also seem to find a place in addressing divinities—perhaps even the frequent repetition of *tu* (you) in prayers is informed in part by a need to point literally to the deity with the lips. In any event, the lips are central to the Roman act of *adoratio*. In this display, the suppliant used gesture to extend the reach of the lips, in this case by using the hand to throw kisses toward the object of adoration. Again, the Greeks seem to have identified the posture of *adoratio* as particularly non-Greek, if Hesychius's mention of a certain "barbarian" practice refers to the Roman *adoratio*.[66] In this act of "adoration," the bodily

---

[62] Ps. Arist. Mun. 6.400A16: πάντες ἄνθρωποι ἀνατείνομεν τὰς χεῖρας εἰς τὸν οὐρανὸν εὐχὰς ποιούμενοι; Ohm 1948.251–65 attests to the widespread use of the gesture among ancient and modern peoples. Aubriot 1992.125–93 surveys in detail the prayer gestures of the Greeks.

[63] For Roman practice see, for example, Sen. *epist.* 41.1; Liv. 5.22.4 (statue); Apul. *met.* 6.3 (embrace altar); Serv. auct. *Aen.* 4.205 (*inferi*); Appel 1909.195–96; Severus 1152–62. For Greek gestures to chthonic deities, see Picard 1936.

[64] Philostr. VS 1.25.23: "οὗτος τῇ χειρὶ ἐσολοίκισεν. . . ."

[65] Varro apud Macr. *Sat.* 3.6.17; Verg. *Aen.* 3.405–7 (Helenus).

[66] Hesych. s.v. ἀντίχειρε· ἔνια τῶν βαρβάρων ἐθνῶν τοὺς ἀντίχειρας ὑποτιθέντα τοῖς γενείοις, καὶ τοὺς δακτύλους ἐκτείνοντα προσκυνεῖ τοὺς ἡγουμένους αὐτῶν; compare with this the Roman testimonia for throwing a kiss: Plin. *nat.* 28.25; Apul. *apol.* 56, *met.* 4.28; Min. Fel. 2.4 (to Serapis); Dio 63.8.1 (Otho to audience); Hier. *Apol. adv. Ruf.* 1.19 (*qui adorant solent deosculari manum*); Wolters 1935.72. Three late-Greek passages in Lucian also describe kiss-throwing—Luc. *de sacr.* 12, *de salt.* 17, *enc. Dem.* 49 (of Demosthenes)—and Saglio 80 offers possible visual examples in Greek art. Full bibliography in Severus 1159.

attitude signified respect, not subservience. Even the Roman practice of kneeling or prostrating oneself before a divinity, a practice condemned in Greek sources as superstitious or effeminate, was generally viewed by Roman writers as originating from piety, not fear.[67] Similarly, the Roman custom of sitting in prayer was probably intended to bring the worshipper in contact with earth.[68] It is with Christianity that Roman prayer stances begin to reflect subservience to, rather than unity with, a single god. When Tertullian boasts that, in contrast with pagans, Christians spread out their arms in prayer as a sign of their innocence ("with our hands spread out, since they are harmless;" *manibus expansis, quia innocuis*), he refers to the early Christian attitude of prayer—with hands out and palms showing—that suggested the normal position of surrender to a superior.[69] Christians also seem to have introduced the similarly subservient practice of bowing the head in prayer.[70] The Romans, on the contrary, tended to stress confrontation and physical contact in their communication with the divine.

The immanence of the deity in tangible objects and the ability for the worshipper to affect that immanence is especially evident in an odd ritual performed before the cult statue of Jupiter Optimus Maximus on Rome's Capitoline hill. Seneca describes as a common sight the following proceedings.

> alius nomina deo subicit, alius horas Iovi nuntiat; alius lutor[71] est, alius unctor qui vano motu bracchiorum imitatur unguentem. sunt quae Iunoni ac Minervae capillos disponant (longe a templo, non tantum a simulacro stantes digitos movent ornantium modo), sunt quae speculum teneant; sunt qui ad vadimonia sua deos advocent, sunt qui libellos offerant et illos causam suam doceant. (Sen. apud Aug. *civ.* 6.10)

> One man supplies names to the god while another tells Jupiter the time; another bathes him while another acts as perfumer, pretending with a show of his arms that he is applying unguents. There are women whose job is to arrange the hair of Juno and Minerva—standing far from the temple, not just from the statue, they move their fingers as if in the act of adorning while other women hold up a mirror. Men are present to call the gods to court to act as sureties on their behalf, or they offer up documents to instruct the gods about their particular suit.

It is striking how, in the very act of describing the scene, Seneca seems to become caught up in the ritual he intends to ridicule. He refers to the divine

[67] Sittl 1890.177–79; Eitrem 1953.605–6 shows that the practice was restricted among the Greeks to women and the poor; Brandt 1965.70.

[68] Macr. *Sat.* 1.10.21 (prayer to Ops).

[69] Tert. *apol.* 30.4: *illuc sursum suspicientes manibus expansis, quia innocuis, capite nudato, quia non erubescimus, denique sine monitore, quia de pectore oramus*; Eitrem 1953.598 and n. 2.

[70] Sittl 1890.147–48; Eitrem 1953.602.

[71] The reading of the codices is *lictor*, which ill suits the context; another plausible conjecture is *litor* (masseur). I thank Nicholas Purcell for drawing my attention to this passage.

icons not as "statues" or "images of the gods," but as "god" and "Jupiter" and "Juno" and "Minerva"; the legal practitioners address not piles of inert material but "gods." Following what seems to be a popular mode of expression, Seneca names the image as if it were the divinity itself.[72] The power of the god has become such an integral part of its representation that the two cannot be named as linguistically separate entities.

The temple of Jupiter Optimus Maximus dated, according to Roman tradition, to the late sixth century BCE. Given the inherent conservatism of Roman religion, it is not improbable that the practices described by Seneca date back to soon after the formal introduction of the cult. And yet Seneca clearly does not describe here the public ceremonies of state cult. Rather, he introduces his account by saying that these rituals do not take place during specific festivals but throughout the year. Indeed, the appeals made to the gods to assist in legal proceedings are out of place in a festival context (when the courts were closed) and imply that private individuals visited the gods as the need arose. Yet despite the peculiar idiosyncrasies of these visitors, each group does share a common goal: the manipulation of their own body to create a more intimate bond with the deity. Whether that activity consists of bathing the gods or fixing their hairstyles, its common efficacy depends upon the idea that these bodily movements can have a real effect on the god, that successful participation with the more-than-human can effect desirable outcomes in daily life.

An equally vivid, but more widespread, example of the body participating in worship is a practice the Romans seemed to have shared with the Celts, although not with the Greeks.[73] In the presence of a temple or other sacred object, the worshipper spun clockwise in a complete circle, marking most probably the completion of prayer.[74] The precise symbolism of this action suggested different explanations already in antiquity. Plutarch relates that the movement is commonly thought to mimic the circular motion of the universe, but prefers himself to believe that the rite allowed the worshipper to address a prayer simultaneously to the sun and the god in the temple, which would normally have faced east, or, alternatively, that the practice represents symbolically the uncertainty inherent in human affairs.[75] Spinning in prayer, how-

---

[72] On this mode of expression, see Gordon 1979.7–8 (on Pausanias and Pliny).

[73] Ath. 4.152D (Poseidonios); cf. Plin. nat. 28.25.

[74] Plaut. Curc. 169; Lucr. 5.1198–99; Liv. 5.21.16; Ov. fast. 3.283; Dion. Hal. 12.23; Val. Flacc. 8.246; Plin. nat. 28.25; Plut. Vit. Cam. 5.7, Vit. Marc. 6, Vit. Num. 14.3; Sittl 1890.194; Appel 1909.213–14, who compares the spinning at tombs of ancestors (Suet. Vit. 2.5; Plut. Quaest. Rom. 14 [Varro]). Koch 1933.19–22 connects the rite with worship of the Sun in archaic Italy. The suggestion of H. J. Rose 1923.86 that the worshipper thereby avoids confronting the divinity (cited approvingly by Latte 1960.41 n. 3), contradicts the otherwise direct tendencies of Roman prayer mentioned above.

[75] Plut. Vit. Num. 14.

ever, fits in with other aspects of Roman ritual that must predate such rationalization. The circular processions conducted at regular city festivals are likely
to date back as early as the first settlements on the Palatine, and to perform
the same function as the circumambulation of tombs. In the act of rotating,
the worshipper either becomes enclosed in a circle of protection, much as a
Christian wards off potential misfortune with the sign of the cross, or actively
encloses the object of veneration, be it a city or a gravesite or a farmer's field.[76]
A possibly related type of sympathetic circling takes place upon granting a
slave freedom. The master grabs the slave's right hand and turns the slave
around in a complete revolution. The full circle seems symbolically to pass
the newly freed slave on to the next stage of life.[77]

These extant descriptions of a ubiquitous ritual movement remind us of
what our text-based sources tend to make us forget: that for the Romans an
effective prayer or incantation required physical as well as verbal activity.
Numerous authors, to be discussed below, testify to the interdependence of
action and word in Roman appeals to the more-than-human. Studies in anthropology seem to provide historical support for this testimony: before developing complex spoken language, human beings already partook of rudimentary
ritual acts, such as simple burial and sacrifice.[78] An understanding of ritual
gesture is, therefore, a necessary part of understanding the earliest attempts at
communication with the more-than-human.[79]

J. G. Frazer, in his *Golden Bough*, identified one aspect of this nonverbal
communication as an element of what he termed "homeopathic magic," by
which the practitioner "infers that he can produce any effect he desires merely
by imitating it."[80] This imitation can be effected in a number of ways: either
by the creation of concrete images (such as voodoo dolls) or by the use of
language (as in the cure for venereal disease discussed above) or by bodily
enactment of what is desired. Frazer finds his favorite example of bodily enactment in the "leaping" festivals once practiced throughout Europe. In these
rites men perform leaps in the vicinity of their crops to ensure that they grow
sufficiently high.[81] In this third realm of homeopathic magic, that involving
bodily movement, Frazer has been criticized for not distinguishing between
gestures that are thought to contribute to a successful outcome and those that
simply illustrate what the desired outcome is.[82] In the latter case of "dramatized
petition," it is claimed that "far from believing (as Frazer supposes) that their

---

[76] Wolters 1935.76; lustration in festivals: Scullard 1981.26; Davies 1997.54–60 surveys the
magical properties of circles and circular movement in other aspects of Roman ritual.

[77] App. *B. Civ.* 4.135, with explanation and other citations in Sittl 1890.132 n. 7.

[78] Burkert 1983.29, citing the work of P. Lieberman.

[79] See the general discussion in Vorwahl 1932.

[80] Frazer (1911) 1.52.

[81] Ibid. 1.137–38.

[82] Gaster 1959.xvii, who distinguishes between "magical procedure" and "dramatized petition."

acts will be automatically effective, [the performers] usually accompany them by express invocation of superior beings."[83] However, this notion that words recited in accompaniment with physical movement somehow lessen the importance of that movement raises its own set of problems. First, it valorizes unduly the role of spoken language—not only do reconstructions of the evolutionary relationship between language and gesture indicate the primacy of action, but contemporary studies in cognitive science also point to the inseparability of gesture and voice in all types of human communication, from the most basic to the complex.[84] Second, and more to the point here, in the particular case of Rome, privileging the spoken word contradicts the ways in which ancient Roman authors depict prayer.

In the most extensive extant discussion of the power of the word in Roman prayer and incantation, chapters 10–29 of Book 28 of Pliny the Elder's *Natural History* (*polleantne aliquid verba et incantamenta carminum*; 28.10), the gestures meant to accompany these powerful words are either explicitly mentioned or known from other sources to be an indispensable part of the words' efficacy.[85] One story, for example, in which the Etruscan seer Olenus attempts to usurp Rome's power through a deceptive ritual, clearly demonstrates gesture and words acting hand in hand. During the preparation of the foundations for a temple on what was to be Rome's Capitoline hill, a human head was found. Uncertain of the meaning of this discovery, legates were sent to Olenus in Etruria. Olenus, recognizing that the head symbolized Rome's future superiority, traced a temple precinct on the ground and inquired of the envoys as follows:

> *hoc* ergo dicitis, Romani? *hic* templum Iovis optimi maximi futurum est, *hic* caput invenimus? (Plin. *nat.* 28.15; italics added)

> "Is *this* what you are saying, Romans? *Here* will be the temple of Jupiter Optimus Maximus, *here* we have found a head?"

The envoys, who have learned that Olenus was attempting through this ruse to transfer power to Etruria, responded, "Not *here* of course but *at Rome* we say the head was found" (*non plane* hic *sed* Romae *inventum caput dicimus*). Although Pliny categorizes this as an example of trying to alter destiny through the manipulation of language (*magnarum rerum fata et ostenta verbis permutari*; 28.14), the presence of the deictic adverb *hic* in both Olenus's query and the Roman response indicates what other sources for the anecdote make explicit, that Olenus's act of pointing to the ground (and, conversely, the unwillingness of the envoys to imitate this action) was at least as essential as

---

[83] Ibid.

[84] McNeill 1992 *passim*, for example, "we should regard the gesture and the spoken utterance as different sides of a single underlying mental process" (1).

[85] Gestures mentioned: Plin. *nat.* 28.12, 14, 15, 19; gestures integral to Pliny's source: 28.12 (*devotio*), 21 (Cato; Varro).

his words in ensuring the efficacy of his foiled ruse.[86] This anecdote has particular resonance for a consideration of the Roman legal sphere, where the importance of pointing supports my conclusions about the Pliny passage. In fixing a claim to property, the use of the finger to point out an object was deemed of equal validity as the naming or verbal description of that object.[87]

Pliny's discussion of the power of word in prayer and incantation concludes with a section appended as an apparent afterthought. Changes in the natural world can in fact be effected even without the use of words (28.24–29). Pliny prefaces this section by remarking "it is clear that, even without words, scrupulous religious activity has power" (28.24: *etiam mutas religiones pollere manifestum est*). Should someone inauspiciously mention fire at a banquet, Pliny tells us that the omen is avoided by pouring water under the table. The physical movement has the ability to countermand the unlucky utterance.[88] The apparent change of emphasis in Pliny's discussion, from words to gesture, has puzzled at least one historian of Roman religion, but it is clear that Pliny's own discussion and the examples he evinces has prompted him to realize that, in Roman prayer and incantation, words and gesture are often inseparable.[89] Implicit in Pliny's thought is the belief made explicit by Servius. In explaining why dance plays a role in Roman ritual, Servius asserted that "there is no part of the body that our ancestors did not want to feel religious activity" (Serv. *ecl.* 5.73: *nullam maiores nostri partem corporis esse voluerunt quae non sentiret religionem*).

In order to describe this inseparability of the body and the external world, I have been borrowing from anthropological writings the concept of "participatory" gesture.[90] The term is more accurate than Frazer's "homeopathic," which relies upon a notion of observable resemblances and has, at any rate, developed its own specialized connotations outside the area of ritual. The concept of "participation" places appropriate stress on the interpenetration of human gesture and physical reality. Everything "takes part" in everything, everyone, else. I have also consciously been avoiding terms such as "magical" or "supernatural." The activities I describe throughout this book do not represent an attempt

---

[86] Other sources include Dion. Hal. 4.60.4 (ταῦτα τῷ σκήπωνι δεικνύς), Serv. auct. *Aen.* 8.345 (*suum locum ostendens*). For a similar use of a deictic indicating gesture, see Plin. *nat.* 28.23: *cur ad primitias pomorum haec vetera esse dicimus, alia nova optamus?* Aldrete 1999.17–34 treats examples in oratory where pointing with the finger seems to have had significance.

[87] Paul. *dig.* 12.1.6: *nihil referre ait [Pedius] proprio nomine res appelletur an digito ostendatur an vocabulis quibusdam demonstretur.*

[88] Plin. *nat.* 28.26; for Trimalchio's appropriately exaggerated practice of this custom (Petron. 74.1), see Wolters 1935.84–85.

[89] Köves-Zulauf 1972.27 on Plin. *nat.* 28.22–29: "Der formale Aufbau erscheint . . . nicht unlogisch, obwohl man sich fragen muß, was die Gesten mit dem zur Diskussion gestellten Grundproblem zu tun haben." He later comments (34): "Wie störend all dies auch sein mag, ein Zufall ist es nicht."

[90] Lévy-Bruhl 1925.69–104; for this reference, I am indebted to David Abram.

to transcend nature—as the word "supernatural" implies—but to engage actively in its functioning. It is difficult to view these activities, in a Roman context, as anything but natural.

Roman authors offer explicit testimony concerning the inseparability of gesture and words in divine communication. A passage from an oration of Cicero describes the proper religious conduct to be observed during the procession that introduced a public festival. In addition to preserving proper words, the participants must follow proper physical procedures: any interruption of the procession or misuse of religious instruments requires a ritual of expiation in response.[91] The importance of bodily action implied in the Cicero passage is understood by Servius. In commenting on a religious rite carried out by the seer Helenus in Vergil's *Aeneid*, the commentator remarks that "in the system of sacred rites, the situation of both body and soul are equal" (3.370: *in ratione sacrorum par est et animae et corporis causa*). This equal valence of the physical and the spiritual, he goes on to say, should be attributed to the fact that each is able to perform, in a kind of symbiosis, functions that are impossible for the other; since the soul cannot be physically bound or loosened from binding, for example, the petitioner manipulates the body as a proxy for the soul whenever these types of ritual must be performed. It is through this bodily participation that "the soul can feel through affinity that which it cannot feel by itself."[92] A similar sympathetic relationship informs the gestures that a speaker uses when requesting the gods to avert some evil: every apotropaic prayer in Pliny includes a description of the gesture to be made.[93] The particular movement involved, Quintilian tells us, provides an exception to Servius's desire that the physical and spiritual act in tandem. For this is one case in which the speaker's gaze and gesture do not correspond. Rather, the object of the curse (*di, talem avertite pestem*) is symbolically pushed away by the hand as the gaze is averted.[94]

A passage from Macrobius provides another example of the centrality of physical activity to communication with the more-than-human. After providing the text of a long prayer by which a holder of *imperium* can curse an enemy, Macrobius adds a description of the speaker's movement:

cum tellurem dicit, manibus terram tangit; cum Iovem dicit, manus ad caelum tollit; cum votum recipere dicit, manibus pectus tangit. (Macr. *Sat.* 3.9.12)[95]

---

[91] Cic. *har. resp.* 23 (Arnob. *nat.* 4.31 offers a critique of the practice); for details see Lenaghan 1969.118–21.

[92] Serv. *Aen.* 3.370: *nam plerumque quae non possunt circa animam fieri, fiunt circa corpus, ut solvere vel ligare, quo possit anima, quod per se non potest, ex cognatione sentire.*

[93] Köves-Zulauf 1972.154 n. 160; compare the same gesture in curses: Eitrem 1953.602.

[94] Quint. *inst.* 11.3.70.

[95] Compare the actions of Curtius at Liv. 7.6.4.

When he says "earth," he touches the ground with his hands; when he says "Jupiter," he lifts his hands to the sky; when he says that he is taking a vow, he touches his chest with his hands.

As the general prays for the conquest of his opponent, the most important components of the plea—the gods and his own will—are gestured toward. In uniting his physical self with the natural world that encompasses him, the victim becomes "at the same time subject and object, consecrator and consecrated."[96] And just as proper gesture ensured the efficacy of this plea, improper gesture, by contrast, could be disastrous. Roman legend has it that the king Tullus Hostilius met his death while attempting to call down lightning from the sky. Having allegedly learned of the rite in the priestly books of his predecessor Numa, our sources indicate that his error was to be attributed at least as much to improper action as to misspoken words.[97] Hence the body technique of ritual, in mimicking a prayer or incantation's goal, presumes that physical movement, like words, "participate" in the natural world.

I would like to close this survey of the body's role in prayer with a Roman joke. In Plautus's play *Menaechmi*, the behavior of the "true" Menaechmus has prompted other characters to assume that he has gone insane. To prove this a doctor is summoned, who tests for madness by squeezing Menaechmus's arm. "Feel that?" the doctor asks. "Why shouldn't I?" Menaechmus replies.[98] The exchange represents one of many situations in the play in which Menaechmus's reasoned and dead-serious reaction contributes to the comedy of mistaken identity. Accordingly, he does not understand at this moment the doctor's intention. The joke depends upon the notion that insanity is signaled by disequilibrium in the body. The body plays so active a role in life's rituals that to lose physical sensation becomes a symptom of mental instability. If not *sanus* in body, the Roman cannot be *sanus* in mind.

PHYSICALITY OF CURES

The attempted diagnosis of the doctor in Plautus raises the expectation that physical ailments also receive treatment based on a notion of bodily participation in the world. Unfortunately, scientific descriptions of physical cures from the Roman era are far from numerous, presumably because this is the kind of learning passed down in an apprentice-style situation and hence there would

---

[96] Wagenvoort 1947.34, discussing the analogous prayer in Liv. 8.9.5.

[97] Liv. 1.31.8 (*operatum*); Plin. *nat.* 2.140 (*imitatum parum rite*); see, too, Ov. *fast.* 3.323 (*quid agant*).

[98] Plaut. *Men.* 912: MEDICUS: *ecquid sentis?* MENAECHMUS: *quidni sentiam?* I follow the interpretation of Gratwick 1993 ad loc.

never have been many writers on the subject.[99] Less direct evidence shows,
nevertheless, that the curative role of the human body was well recognized.
In the introductory remarks to his discussion of medical remedies, Pliny says
he will refrain from mentioning the many impious cures (*piacula*) that have
been suggested in the past. Among the legitimate aids for insuring good health
he specifies only three items: mother's milk, saliva, and contact with a human
body (*tactus . . . corporis; nat.* 28.8). The body and its natural fluids are the
only elements of the folk practitioner's pharmacy that Pliny will recommend.
I have already mentioned how Marcellus Empiricus, in the fifth century CE,
provides precise instructions concerning which fingers to use in gathering medicinal herbs. The same care extends to the use of the fingers and the hands
in general treatment of the body—nose bleed is prevented, for example, by
gliding the thumb and ring finger of the right hand from the forehead to the
back of the neck while reciting a charm (10.56). By Marcellus's time, there
has developed a complicated lexicon of the healing properties of the respective
fingers.[100]

The earliest extant description of a cure relying on participatory movement
dates to the second century BCE. In his treatise *On Agriculture*, the elder Cato
demonstrates how mending a twig can mend a fractured leg. The detailed
description warrants a lengthy quotation:

> luxum si quod est, hac cantione sanum fiet: harundinem prende tibi viridem p.
> IIII aut quinque longam, mediam diffinde, et duo homines teneant ad coxendices;
> incipe cantare "[*the text of the charm is corrupt*]" usque dum coeant. ferrum insuper
> iactato. ubi coierint et altera alteram tetigerint, id manu prehende et dextera
> sinistra praecide; ad luxum aut ad fracturam alliga; sanum fiet. et tamen cotidie
> cantato et luxato vel hoc modo: "[*the text of the charm is corrupt*]." (Cato *agr.* 160)

I will provide a paraphrase of the passage. "Proceed as follows: after having
split a long green reed down the middle, have two men bring each half together while a chant is recited; when the pieces are rejoined, fasten the now
trimmed-down reed to the fracture or dislocation.[101] This will ensure that the
leg will heal."[102] The symbolism is clear. The fracture of the human leg and

---

[99] See Edelstein 1967.361: "medicine . . . was the only art or science about which everybody
knew something."

[100] Fingers: Marcell. *med.* 8.170, 172, 190 (eye problems); 8.191, 193 (stye); 10.55 (stop bleeding); 12.46 (toothache); 15.11 (*evocatio*); 15.101–2 (*glandulae*); 18.30 (hangnail). Hands: 14.24
(stones), 20.78 (stomach), 34.100 (pimples), 36.70 (gout).

[101] The interpretation of Laughton 1938 concerning how the reed is cut ignores the precise
senses of *diffinde* and *praecide*.

[102] Frazer (1911) 1.205 includes a twentieth-century parallel: "It is said that when one of his
pigs or sheep breaks its leg, a farmer of Rhenish Bavaria or Hesse will bind up the leg of a chair
with bandages and splints in due form." See, too, Plin. *nat.* 28.201 (among the Magi a split spleen
tied to the sides of the patient and allowed to dry will cure a diseased spleen); Serv. *Aen.* 12.173
(the conventional gesture made with a sacrificial knife anticipates the slaughter of the victim).

the healing process envisioned are imitated in the manipulation of the reed. The performance of the cure visually enacts its goal, and depends on the interpenetration of the human body with the natural world.

The same mechanics of physical participation seem to operate in one of Pliny's cures for fever:

> buglosso inarescente, si quis medullam e caule eximat dicatque ad quem liberandum febri id faciat . . . aiunt febri liberari. (Plin. nat. 26.116)

> When ox-tongue [a plant] is drying, if someone removes the pith (medulla) from its stem and speaks the name of the one whom he intends to free from fever, . . . they say that [the sufferer] is freed from fever.

Removing the core from a plant-stalk while naming the sufferer from fever causes the malady to disappear. Presumably not by accident the word for the pith of the plant is medulla, the same word for bone marrow, where the person's fever is imagined to be residing.[103] As is usual in Pliny and other compilers of cures, the connection between the affliction and the remedy recommended is not made explicit. A similar case where the efficacy needs to be reconstructed occurs in the binding of the plant heliotrope around a feverish part of the human body; presumably the fact that the plant follows the sun contributes to the heat escaping from the sufferer (22.61). Once again, a plant's name, physical characteristics, and curative properties interact in a way for which it would be improper—and unnecessary—to seek a first cause.

A related set of examples of curative gesturing can be found among the numerous instances of binding ritual that have survived from antiquity.[104] The Roman tradition of folk remedies advises a man to alternately bind and loosen a woman's clothing to facilitate childbirth. I have found allusions to the connection between binding and successful conception in six different Roman or Greek sources, and it is a practice shared by a number of societies throughout the world.[105] Pliny offers our fullest account of unbinding at birth:

> partus accelerat hic mas ex quo quaeque conceperit, si cinctu suo soluto feminam cinxerit, dein solverit adiecta precatione se vinxisse, eundem et soluturum, atque abierit. (Plin. nat. 28.42)

> The man from whom the woman has conceived can speed up birth if he takes off his belt, binds the woman, and then releases it while praying that the one who has bound will also release. He should then leave.

---

[103] The roots of buglossos provide a source for red dye, which may further connect the two different senses of medulla.

[104] For a full assemblage, see Heckenbach 1911.

[105] Other sources not mentioned below in the text include: Plac. med. 17.11 (fifth century CE?): ut mulier concipiat. homo vir si solvat semicinctium suum et eam praecingat et dicat "ego de hoc

The prayer that accompanies the act of unbinding makes the meaning of the action clear. In binding the belt and chanting over the pregnant woman, the man expresses responsibility for the pregnancy on both a physical and verbal level. Then, as in Cato's cure for fracture, the man's physical action of loosening the belt replicates the act that will correct the present circumstances. With his participation replicated he is no longer necessary. The man leaves the room and—presumably—the birth takes place. This practical application of unbinding is symbolically represented in cult practice, as well, in this instance by women. In the rites of Juno Lucina, the Roman deity attendant at births, worshippers participate with unbound hair and clothing loosened.[106]

The role of binding in birth affords a glimpse at possible differences with which the Greeks and Romans viewed the role of participatory gestures in medicine. The Greek doctor Soranus mentions in his second-century treatise *Gynaecia* the practice both of loosening a pregnant woman's clothing to facilitate breathing and of unbinding the hair to promote relaxation. He stresses, however, that he does not advise this practice "on account of the folk practice" that recommends avoiding physical bonds, a remark that clearly refers to the practice preserved in Roman texts of the period.[107] His clarification offers an interesting example of a written authority rationalizing a folk practice and thereby sanctioning its continuance. When Soranus's treatise came to be translated four centuries later into a Latin paraphrase, however, the critique of folk practice is glossed over and becomes simply, and ambiguously, "first of all, [the pregnant woman's] clothing and hair should be loosened, since this usually promotes relaxation (*propter laxamentum*)."[108] A second instance of rationalizing folk practice seems to occur in Soranus. A passage of Ovid's *Metamorphoses* depicts the goddess Lucina laying hands on the pregnant Myrrha to assist childbirth; she accompanies the action with a verbal incantation. Soranus advises the same use of the hands but, as one would expect, does not mention the accompanying prayer.[109] In both these instances, Soranus seems to endorse examples of participatory treatment, but only because of their proven efficacy.

Many other examples survive in which the physical act of unbinding brings about a desired result: Festus mentions husbands who loosen a knot of their

---

explico te laborantem"; compare the Greek epithet "belt-loosening" (λυσίζωνος) for the moon goddess (Aubert 1989.444 and n.48).

[106] Serv. auct. *Aen.* 4.518; compare Ov. *fast.* 3.255. The practice of unbinding the hair and clothing is discussed more fully in chapter 3.

[107] Soranus *gyn.* 2.6: οὐ κατὰ τὴν ἰδιωτικὴν πρόληψιν, καθ' ἣν τὰ γυναίκια δεσμὸν οὐδένα βούλεται τυγχάνειν.

[108] Soran. p. 23, 13–14: *ante tamen omnia ligaturis et capillis solutis, quod propter laxamentum fieri solet*; see, too, Ps. Soran. *epit.* 66a.

[109] Soranus *gyn.* 2.6; Ov. *met.* 10.511: *admovitque manus et verba puerpera dixit* (Myrrha has been transformed into a tree); Weinreich 1909.14–16. For remarks on Soranus's reputation among the Romans, see Temkin 1991.xxix.

new bride to guarantee the birth of many children.[110] Conversely, just as the gestures of a man unbinding can ease childbirth, so, too, can the opposite action effect a desired outcome in preventing premature birth. A Latin medical treatise from the fifth century advises that a woman who has had trouble carrying a fetus to term should bind her stomach for nine months with a belt of lamb's wool; this will prevent any possibility of spontaneously aborting.[111] Perhaps the most familiar example of this role of binding and loosening occurs in Ovid's *Metamorphoses*, when the goddess Lucina crosses her knees and fingers in a foiled attempt to prevent the birth of Hercules.[112]

The means by which Lucina tried to block Hercules' birth did not exist solely in the realm of myth. In the context of this same story, Pliny informs us that this correspondence between human gesture and more-than-human effects reaches outside the boundaries of Roman fable, medicine, and folklore. Because of the recognized importance of binding actions, he tells us, "our ancestors forbade them in meetings of generals and magistrates since they hinder all action. They also forbade them for similar reasons whenever rites and vows were being performed" (Plin. *nat.* 28.59: *ideo haec in consiliis ducum potestatiumve fieri vetuere maiores velut omnem actum inpedientia, vetuere vero et sacris votisve simili modo interesse*). The *maiores*, the hallowed Roman ancestors, did not permit the interlacing of fingers, the clasping of the knee, or the crossing of the legs either at war councils, in the presence of magistrates, or at sacred rites. No binding gestures could be made at any important gathering. The ancient Romans, even while sitting or standing rigidly at assembly, participate continually in the natural world that surrounds them.

CONCLUSION

I am well aware that this chapter may simplify in its attempt to systematize such a vast variety of topics drawn from witnesses who lived centuries apart. And yet simplification is in many ways my principal point. What unites these disparate fields of Roman endeavor—medicine, science, religion—is precisely the notion that each is predicated on bodily participation in the world. The programmatic statement with which Pliny begins his investigations into nature reflects this participation in its tortuous syntax and self-conscious display of paradox.[113]

---

[110] Paul. Fest. p. 63.

[111] Ps. Theod. Prisc. *add.* p. 351: *lanam de ove quam lupus comederit collige <et fac eam tribus sororibus lavari, carminari, pectinari, et filari, et texant inde cingulum et per novem menses ad ventrem mulier eum deportat, ita ut numquam eum in aliquo loco deponat, nec faciet abortum>*; compare *add.* p. 352 for controlling menstrual bleeding; see too Marcell. *med.* 10.70, 10.82.

[112] Ov. *met.* 9.298–99; see, too, Paus. 9.11.3 with Frazer (1898) 5.45–46 for non-Western parallels.

[113] For the context of this sentence, see Beagon 1992, esp. 26–54, and 26 n. 1 for further bibliography.

[mundus est] totus in toto, immo vero ipse totum, finitus et infinito similis, omnium rerum certus et similis incerto, extra intra cuncta complexus in se, idemque
rerum naturae opus et rerum natura ipsa. (Plin. *nat.* 2.2)

[This universe is] whole in wholeness, or rather is itself the wholeness, bounded
and resembling the unbounded, fixed in all things but resembling the unfixed,
embracing in itself everything within and without, at the same time a work of
nature and nature itself.

The world of nature, in other words, is in the constant process of creating
itself, with neither beginning nor end. Pliny's nature, so conceived, is an example in the world at large of the phenomenon we observed in the case of
obtaining *lepos* by eating a *lepus*, or of personal pronouns literally growing out
of the body's involvement in the world, a case of what Bourdieu has called a
"structuring structure," a condition of existence "objectively 'regulated' and
'regular' without being in any way the product of obedience to rules."[114] Unable to be gotten outside of, the universe, which includes its human participants, renders any human objectivity impossible or meaningless. In such a
closely knit universe, the interpenetration of the human with the divine assumes that everything participates in the activity of everything else and hence
everything is an active subject. It is within such a dynamic but self-contained
system that I hope to have situated Roman ritual behavior. With no transcen-
dent power outside the observable world to consider, the relationship between
nature and human beings relies on understanding the universe as a closed
system. Realization of this aspect of nature places scholars such as Pliny in a
privileged place in their society. Unlike "wise men" or "big men" in most
traditional societies—such as shamans and healers—who use secret knowledge to empower themselves as mediators between their own communities
and the divine,[115] Pliny displays an extraordinary willingness to share knowledge with his readers. By presenting knowledge as based on his own scholarly
"mediation" of the feared forces of nature, Pliny makes all his readers into "big
men." In their self-acknowledged awe and ignorance, the Romans of Pliny's
text in fact are far superior to the overconfident *magi*, who come under constant rebuke in Pliny for their unwillingness to systematize their practice.

Pliny is not the only Roman to find strength in awe. Throughout the second
book of the treatise *On Divination*, the interlocutor Marcus Cicero systemati-
cally dismantles the possibility that human beings can read divine meaning
into the apparently random ruptures of the natural world. An incongruous
preface, however, precedes the attack: "If I were able to speak with certainty,
then I would be divining in the very act of denying the existence of divina-

[114] Bourdieu 1990.
[115] Lindstrom 1984.299–300.

tion."[116] This apparent attempt to win over the good will of his audience is echoed at the close of the work when Marcus chooses to leave open the possibility of true divination.[117] This kind of cautious ambiguity has troubled commentators but is not unparalleled; it also characterizes Livy's remarks about the possibility of divine intervention (e.g., 21.62.1). Ultimately, it would seem, awe before the uncertainty of the world takes precedence over dogma, however allegedly enlightened such dogma may be. A striking passage of the agricultural writer Columella proves especially illuminating in this context. A farm owner should not consider it a prodigy, he tells his reader, if a sow eats her young, since such an occurrence is not uncommon.[118] Precedent in nature, in other words, rescues this act from being labeled deviant. Odd rituals certainly invite mockery, as in the case of Petronius's confused Trimalchio (74.1–2), for whom a cock's crow initiates a confused flurry of preventative measures: he has wine poured under the table, extinguishes a lamp with unmixed wine, changes the ring on his hand, and orders the guilty bird cooked in a bronze pot. Petronius's mockery of superstition is apparent, but the very existence of the joke attests to the widespread practice as well as the abuse of the kinds of rituals catalogued by Pliny. Nature is a text to be carefully considered. Any odd phenomenon has potential for meaning, just as every tremor of the earth in Rome necessarily presaged a future event.[119] Proper attention to the more-than-human can transform even the most bizarre and frightening occurrence into, paradoxically, an indication of normalcy.[120]

A gesture, properly deployed and understood, can provide access to the workings of nature. Everything that is natural is divine; in other words, everything natural is supernatural—a paradox to us but not to the Romans.[121] Yet to repeat the point with which I began this chapter: there is a difference between the supernatural and the more-than-human. The former—"supernatural"—implies mysticism, whereas the latter—"more-than-human"—confesses to an awareness that nature includes the non-human in its workings. Nothing, that is, is beyond nature. This conception explains Roman fear of *adynata*—if the impossible can happen, then any trust in the world at large is lost.[122] What, on the other hand, may strike us as the impossible can be

---

[116] Cic. *div.* 2.8: *si enim aliquid certi haberem quod dicerem, ego ipse divinarem, qui esse divinationem nego.*

[117] Cic. *div.* 2.150. For Cicero's alleged views on divination, see Cic. *div.* 1.68 (Quintus describing Marcus); Linderski 1982; Schofield 1986.63.

[118] Colum. 7.11.3, cited at Rosenberger 1998.10–11.

[119] Plin. *nat.* 2.200: *numquam urbs Roma tremuit ut non futuri eventus alicuius id praenuntium esset.*

[120] M. Douglas 1960.136–37; Conte 1994.88–89 (on Pliny).

[121] Edelstein 1967 offers a similar explanation, in kind if not degree, in his discussion of "contradictions" in the writings of Hippocrates; these are only apparent because to Hippocrates "everything is natural, but in being so it is divine too" (214).

[122] Rosenberger 1998.103–7.

accepted if it derives from authority or experience. In one particularly compelling passage, Pliny's thought moves from the natural cleansing of the seas to the death of animals. The professed link depends upon the authority of a now-lost work attributed to Aristotle:

> omnia pleno fluctu maria purgantur, quaedam et stato tempore. . . . his addit—ut nihil, quod equidem noverim, praeteream—Aristoteles nullum animal nisi aestu recedente expirare. observatum id multum in Gallico oceano et dumtaxat in homine compertum. (Plin. *nat*. 2.220)[123]

> All seas are cleansed at high tide, some even at fixed intervals. . . . To this Aristotle adds (so as not to omit anything I have learned) that animals breathe their last only at receding tide. This has often been observed on the ocean coast of Gaul, and has been confirmed as far as human beings are concerned.

The sequence here shows succinctly the ways in which nature can gradually unveil its secrets to human beings: a claim of Aristotle is supported by observation of the phenomenon in the Atlantic, and then its application is broadened to cover human beings. The system has its own determinism, but one in which the thoughtful human agent, as part of the system, is able to play an active role. There is a tide in our lives, and one that matches the sea tides not as a simple metaphor, but as an actual manifestation of nature in the human body.

---

[123] For parallels, see Plin. *nat*. 7.43 (abortion caused by extinguishing a lamp), 18.321 (cutting and harvesting under a waning moon); H. J. Rose 1933.62–64.

Chapter 2

THE POWER OF THUMBS

With Thumbs bent back, they popularly kill.
—John Dryden, *The Third Satyr of Juvenal*, line 68

IN TREATING the various ways in which Roman bodies were thought to participate in the world around them, chapter 1 included a separate section on the
human hand. Playing a prevalent role in legal transactions, having special
power as an apotropaic icon, and performing a recognized function in pharmaceutical and medical practice, the hand offers an example of how the multiple
functions of one part of the body belong to a single coherent system of belief.
In this chapter I would like to offer a more extended analysis of this sort,
focusing on one part of the hand—the thumb. I will pay special attention to
the ways in which the gestural manifestations of the thumb retain stable
meanings across space and time.

The thumb—the *digitus pollex* or most often simply *pollex*—emerges across
Roman culture in familiar contexts. It can be used to wish someone good luck,
or it can possess an apotropaic function, as in the well-known "fig" gesture.
And of course, in the Roman manifestation most familiar to the modern
world, the thumb was employed by the crowd at the gladiatorial games to
indicate whether a defeated fighter should be killed or spared. But despite
what most people would suppose from later artistic renditions or from any of
a number of Hollywood films, scholarly reference works offer either conflicting
assertions or candid uncertainty regarding both the appearance and significance of the thumb in this gesture. It has been lifted up, pointed down, hidden
in the hand, directed at the chest, and squeezed between the middle and index
finger.[1] I would like to resolve this uncertainty, or at least try to systematize

---

[1] Only Echtermeyer 1835 and Post 1892 offer extended discussions of the sign from the arena
and, except for Post's discussion of the "médaillon de Cavillargues," both scholars restrict themselves to textual sources. Elsewhere, a wide variety of possible interpretations is found confidently
expressed in such standard works of classical studies as Forcellini 1828, s.v. *premere* (spare = thumb
in fist; death = thumb up); Otto 1890.283 (spare = "fig"); Friedländer (1928) 2.61, 4.520 (spare =
thumb up; death = thumb down); W. Smith et al., eds., (1914) 1.917 (spare = waving handkerchiefs; death = thumb up); Courtney 1980.161–62 ("the actual gesture is hard to establish");
Röhrich (1991) 1.305 assumes that the sign for sparing must have been equivalent to the German
Daumenhalten (thumb enclosed in fist). The only discussion I have found that corresponds with
my own conclusions is, if I interpret him correctly, that of Montaigne 1967.284 (spare = "de

it, by foregrounding the thumb's role in the symbolic system of bodily gesture, by isolating it as a thing in itself with independent properties, properties that allow it to participate with the natural world in ways not encountered in the case of other body parts. Latin texts repeatedly acknowledge the thumb's significance as an independent entity, and the digit's importance as expressed in these texts is unique to the Romans. Neglected visual evidence, illustrating the thumb's perceived power, can be shown to support the philological claims made by Roman authors. In particular, I conclude by returning to the arena to demonstrate that, contrary to the fullest scholarly discussion of the thumb gesture (Post 1892), the sign for death to a fallen gladiator was made not by pointing the thumbs down toward the ground, but toward the sky. In the opposite circumstance, when the fallen gladiator was deemed to have fought with sufficient courage to justify retaining his life, the Roman gestured in a way that resembles a closed fist.

TEXTUAL APPEARANCES

My analysis of representations of the thumb in both texts and art spans several centuries. As a result, I must depend on the connotations of the thumb remaining stable. Such an assumption is not unjustified; numerous examples attest to gestural language outlasting spoken language. For Roman antiquity, consider the relatively unchanged connotations in Europe of the "fig" or of the outstretched middle finger. Even sets of gesture seem to survive the centuries virtually intact: recent studies document how a number of ritual acts, including standardized physical movements, have crossed the boundaries of language and centuries in their westward transmission.[2] Similarly, finger-gestures mentioned in European folktales, such as crossing the fingers for luck or making the "horns" of the cuckold, continue to retain their meanings across millennia.[3] Since gestures can maintain such stability across cultures, it appears intuitively even more likely that a particular gesture would be preserved within the culturally coherent environment of the pre-Christian Roman Empire. One noteworthy example explicitly illustrates that some Romans, in any case, unquestionably believed that gestures contained a stable essence. The rhetorician Quintilian, writing toward the close of the first century CE, is certain of both the position and motion of Demosthenes' hand when the Greek orator began his speech for Ctesiphon four hundred years earlier. Quintilian's confidence could not rely upon any external evidence; instead it is informed by the inherent essence of the particular gesture of bringing together the tips of

---

comprimer et baisser les pouces;" death = "de les hausser et contourner au-dehors," from "Des pouces" [*Essai* 2.26]).

    [2] Burkert 1992.41–87.
    [3] Klíma (1975–) 4.1141.

the thumb and the adjacent three fingers. Such a formation strikes Quintilian as the most appropriate for Demosthenes' situation and, as a great orator, he could not disappoint Quintilian's future expectations.[4]

In the case of the solo thumb, the inquiries of etymologists from Roman antiquity support the notion of a continuity in significations. During the early Empire, the jurist Ateius Capito, in the middle of a moral diatribe against the wearing of precious rings, asserted that the Latin word for thumb (*pollex*), derives from the fact that this finger "has power" (*pollet*).[5] Capito's contention has met with the approval of most modern authorities, who are inclined to accept that the earliest speakers of the Latin language recognized a semantic link between thumbs and power.[6] The implied dominance of the thumb over the other fingers may be reflected in Latin poetry, as well, where *pollex* frequently appears in synecdoche for the entire hand to describe such diverse and complex activities as spinning, lyre-playing, writing, and masturbation.[7] No other single digit performs this function with comparable frequency. Yet in the same way that the first chapter showed how Nigidius Figulus's etymologies belong to a wider context, so, too, do Capito's claims about the origins of *pollex* form part of a larger argument. His remarks on the thumb, which Macrobius quotes from a work entitled *On Pontifical Law*, represent this finger as exhibiting a kind of moral superiority, as well as a physical one, since, unlike the rest of the hand, the thumb disdains rings and other forms of luxurious ornamentation. The ethical implications of this statement seem to have survived the six centuries separating Capito from Isidore, who remarks in his own etymology that "the first finger is called *pollex* because it holds sway (*polleat*) over the remaining [fingers] through its power and manly virtue (*virtus*)."[8]

---

[4] Quint. *inst.* 11.3.96–97: *hoc modo coepisse Demosthenen credo in illo pro Ctesiphonte timido summissoque principio.*

[5] Ateius Capito frg. 12 Strzelecki (= Macr. *Sat.* 7.13.14): *nam pollex, qui nomen ab eo, quod pollet, accepit, nec in sinistra cessat nec minus quam tota manus semper in officio est.* Rosetti 1928.161 attributes the etymology to Varro; see, too, Strzelecki 1967.xiv.

[6] Lewis and Short accept the relationship of the two words without comment, while Walde-Hofmann, s.v. *pollex*, declare that the connection is secure ("wohl sicher"); see too Groß (1968) 7.927. Less certain verdicts are rendered by OLD (the etymology is probable) and by Ernout, Meillet, and André 1985, s.v. *pollex*, who regard the ancient explanation as "only a pun" ("L'explication . . . n'est pas que un calembour"). For the supernatural associations of the thumb in later Europe, see Grimm 1860, s.v. *Daume, Daumen*: "die alpartige natur des daumens erklärt mancherlei sitten und gebräuche und sonst unverständliche bildliche redensarten"; further examples in Grimm (1875) 3.457, 460, 500.

[7] Spinning (e.g., Ov. *met.* 4.34–36); lyre-playing (e.g., Hor. *carm.* 4.6.36); writing (e.g., Ov. *epist.* 17.266); masturbation (Mart. 11.29.2, 12.97.9); for a more complete list, see Echtermeyer 1835.1–6. Most occurrences of *pollex* in poetry, I should note, are in the ablative singular (*pollice*), which provides the poet with a metrically convenient dactyl (twenty-seven of the twenty-eight examples of the word in Ovid occur in this form).

[8] Isid. *orig.* 11.1.70 (see, too, Isid. *diff.* 2.63). Isidore is echoed in a Latin gloss from the ninth– or tenth–century codex Cassinensis 402 (Goetz [1888–1923] 5.556, 8) and, in the early thirteenth

The odd assertion that the thumb is endowed with particular virtues setting
it at the head of the hand is also found in Lactantius, a writer of the early
fourth century and Isidore's apparent source. In treating the divine creation
of human body parts, the Christian Lactantius includes the following eulogy:
"the thumb, either as the primary agent or acting by itself, has complete control over grasping and controlling, as if it were the guide and moderator of all
[the fingers]."[9] The phrase "the guide and moderator of all [the fingers]" (*rector
omnium atque moderator*) may seem an innocent, if perhaps overenthusiastic,
formulation, yet Lactantius uses the words *rector* and *moderator* on no less than
thirteen other occasions in his writings, in each case to describe only the
Christian god.[10] The two nouns are used in tandem solely in this passage—to
describe the thumb. The etymology of *pollex* again supports its function in the
world. Common to the etymologies of all three writers—Capito, Isidore, and
Lactantius—is the notion that the thumb's power encompasses otherworldly
features we would not commonly associate with individual body parts.

These connotations of power distinguish the *pollex* from its Greek counterpart, ἀντίχειρ. Ancient Greek writers on the language understood ἀντίχειρ
as simply identifying the physical location of the thumb—it is "opposite the
hand" (ἀντί + χείρ)—and these ancient opinions are echoed in the modern
authorities.[11] It was apparently only under Roman influence that writers in
Greek began to construe the prefix ἀντί- as meaning not "opposite" but "instead of" the hand, with the result that the thumb became identified as a
"second hand."[12] The powerful thumb is absent from the other ancient Indo-
European languages, as well. The pre-Teutonic *tûmon- (as in German *Daumen* and English *thumb*) and Sanskrit *añgustha-* simply describe the thickness

---

century, in John of Ford, *Sermo* 27.4, where the thumb of the spouse in *Song of Songs* prophesies
Christ's arrival on earth.

[9] I cite more fully Lact. *opif*. 10.24: [*pollex*] *qui se velut obvium ceteris praebens omnem tenendi
faciendique rationem vel solus vel praecipue possidet tamquam rector omnium atque moderator; unde
etiam pollicis nomen accepit, quod vi et potestate inter ceteros polleat*; see the similar remarks of Theo-
doretus, *De providentia* 4.55–57.

[10] *Rector*: Lact. *inst*. 1.3.21, 1.11.14, 2.16.8, 3.15.5, 3.20.14, 5.1.1, 7.22.5; *ira* 10.51 and 53; *epit*.
1.1. *Moderator*: *inst*. 3.20.13, 7.27.2 add. 16; *epit*. 2.5 (citations are from Perrin 1981.83, who can
cite no other ancient text that assigns to the thumb a divine symbolism).

[11] LSJ s.v.; Groß (1968) 7.926–27. Among ancient writers, see Meletius (7th–9th c. CE), *De
natura hominis*, p. 121, l. 19 ("it is called ἀντίχειρ because it lies opposite the other fingers;"
ἀντίχειρ . . . , ὅτι ἀντίκειται τοῖς ἄλλοις [δακτύλοις]) and compare the remarks of Arist. *Hist.
an*. 2.11. The earliest Greek references to the digit given by LSJ employ not ἀντίχειρ but the
periphrasis ὁ μέγας δάκτυλος ("the big finger:" Hdt. 3.8; Diogenes of Apollonia 6); the earliest
use of ἀντίχειρ I have found in a computer search of *Thesaurus linguae Graecae* is by Poseidonios
the philosopher (2d–1st c. BCE).

[12] Ateius Capito frg. 12 Strzelecki (= Macr. *Sat*. 7.13.14): *apud Graecos vocatur* ἀντίχειρ *quasi
manus alter*; see, too, Galen, *De usu partium* 3.79, 9 (Kühn), Ps.-Galen, *Introductio seu medicus*
14.704, 9 (Kühn). For ἀντί as a synonym for ἴσος, see Ammonius, *In Aristotelis categorias com-
mentarius*, p. 71, 4.

of this finger.[13] Extant evidence, therefore, indicates that the Romans were unique among Indo-European peoples in identifying at an early stage of their language's development the thumb's singularity as a digit.

Uses of the thumb in the Roman world indicate that its implied power extended outside the etymological tradition. The following references, although scattered, help to provide the cultural background necessary for understanding the uses of the thumb in nonverbal communication. Often it appears as a curative agent or as an accompaniment to medical and magical incantation. An obscure tradition that one source dates back to Orpheus suggests a possible source of its efficacy: certain veins, it was said, ran directly from the sexual organs to the thumb, thereby endowing this finger with regenerative powers.[14] Traces of this belief may be found in the statement of Melampus, a Greek writer of the third century BCE, that the thumb is the finger sacred to Aphrodite (Περὶ παλμῶν μαντική vers. A 94). In any case, notions of sexual energy would seem to underlie Pliny's attestation that the right thumb of a virgin can cause a fallen epileptic to recover (nat. 28.43; see, too, 23.110). Four centuries later, Marcellus Empiricus prescribes using the thumb as a transferring agent to relieve stomach ailments: in this case he provides a verbal formula that is designed to accompany the physical action of the thumb pressing the stomach and then touching the ground; elsewhere in Marcellus, the thumb and ring finger are used in conjunction as the "medicinal fingers" (med. 28.72; e.g., 2.9, 25.13, 32.5). In the "Great Magical Papyrus" in Paris, for the charm to work the speaker must gain control over the thumb of Selene.[15] In Roman practice the thumb lived up to its etymological reputation. It could both bestow and withhold favor, grant and deprive life.

The conception that the thumb has access to more-than-human powers also elucidates an apparently common gesture that is attested by only a single aside in the elder Pliny. Pliny reminds his readers that "when we approve of something, a proverbial expression bids us to press the thumbs (pollices premere)."[16] The reference occurs in a section of his encyclopedia where the author lists how certain types of physical movement, even when performed without words, possess power (nat. 28.24: etiam mutas religiones pollere). In using the verb pollere to represent the category of "silent scrupulous actions" (mutae religiones), Pliny seems to play on the familiar etymology of pollex,

---

[13] Buck 1949.240–41 conjectures that pollere may have originally derived from a notion of swelling (as Sanskrit phala-).

[14] Fulg. myth. 3.7 (see, too, Mythogr. 3.11.24). Whitbread 1971.91 incorrectly translates pollex in the Fulgentius passage as "great toe;" cf. Onians 1954.528 n. 2.

[15] PGM 4.2328–30 with commentary of Bonner 1930.180–83; see, too, PGM 36.163, 69.3, 70.6; examples not from antiquity are listed in Drechsler (1906) 2.44, 294. I am unconvinced by the attempts of Volkmann 1935.188–91 to find magical significance in the Spartan practice of thumb-biting mentioned by Plutarch (Vit. Lyc. 18).

[16] Plin. nat. 28.25: pollices, cum faveamus, premere etiam proverbio iubemur.

thereby indicating that the power in the thumb-pressing gesture resides in the thumb itself.[17] The thumb once again acts as agent. Yet despite its apparent familiarity to Pliny's original readers, this proverbial gesture appears in no other extant text and the precise appearance of the ancient Roman manifestation is disputed. In modern Italy, Pliny's gesture of goodwill seems to have disappeared; an absence that, as we shall see, may have particular relevance in determining the gesture's cultural associations.[18] Elsewhere in Europe, variations on thumb-pressing survive in at least three different forms. In German-speaking regions, a gesture often does not accompany the popular wish of good luck expressed by "pressing the thumbs" (*drücken die Daumen*);[19] when a hand sign does supplement the words, the thumb is enclosed in the four remaining fingers and held tightly (or, less frequently, the thumb is pressed upon the closed fist). The similarity of meaning between the prevailing German gesture and that of ancient Rome has led Germanic scholars to assume that their own "thumb-holding" (*Daumenhalten*) is identical with *pollices premere*.[20] In modern Romania, by contrast, the equivalent expression for extending good-will translates as "to hold the fists for someone" (*a tine pumni*) and is expressed with the thumb lying on top of the clenched fist or fists. A third use of the thumb in granting favor survives in Switzerland, where an apotropaic gesture is used that resembles the popular American "thumbs-up" sign: "I raise my thumbs for you" (*I hed dr de Duume*).[21] In each of these instances, it is impossible to decide which, if any, of the twentieth-century gestures is the direct descendant of a Roman ancestor. Their diversity, however, suggests that each instance represents a later manifestation, perhaps one that tried to make sense of the Latin expression *pollices premere*. Comparative evidence, therefore, provides no sure help in discovering what Pliny and his audience would have understood by the phrase *pollices premere*.

Attempts to recover Pliny's gesture from philological arguments also prove vain. In the recently completed entry on the verb *premo* in the *Thesaurus linguae Latinae*, the expression *pollices premere* has been taken to mean "to press the thumbs *with* something (namely, with or inside the fingers of the closed

[17] For other examples of Pliny exploiting etymological links to account for function, see chapter 1 and McCartney 1927.

[18] Sittl 1890.125 remarks on the abandonment of this gesture in Italy, and it is not included in Munari 1994. My own research in libraries and via personal communication supports Sittl's claim.

[19] Röhrich 1967.34.

[20] For the thumb enclosed in the fist in Germany, see Drechsler (1906) 2.266 on nineteenth-century Schlesien; Heckenbach 1911.99; Stemplinger (1927–1942) 2.174; analogous gestures are also recognized in Poland and parts of England, presumably as a result of German influence (personal communications). For Switzerland, see Wanner et al. 12.1825. Schrader 1894–1895.223–26 seems to be the first to connect the Roman proverb with the Germanic gesture.

[21] Niederer 1989.209; Niederer notes that in contemporary Switzerland the expression of "pressing the thumb for someone" is normally not accompanied by any gesture whatsoever (202).

fists)" (10.2: 1170.51). This view, however, is based upon the prevailing manifestation of this gesture in Central Europe and the editors, referring to TLL 10.2: 1175.14–56, admit that Latin usage equally allows for an interpretation "to press the thumbs *on* something (namely, on the top of the hands)."[22] In the two relevant parallels I have found for this collocation of *pollex* and *premere*, the thumb clearly plays the active role as "the presser." The poet Propertius bids his lover to arrange her hair by pressing her thumb upon it (*presso pollice*) and the stomach cure of Marcellus Empiricus that I mentioned earlier advises "pressing the thumb on the stomach" (*pollicem supra ventrem premes*).[23] These verbal parallels show that the sense of *pollices premere* as "press down with the thumbs" is acceptable Latin, although they are by no means numerous enough to allow us to interpret with certainty what the phrase describes in Pliny.

Another common use of the thumb in Rome provides more concrete indications that Pliny's phrase *policies premere* refers to the thumb pressing down upon the fist. At least three extant Roman texts mention the peculiar but apparently well-known oratorical gesture distinguished by the epithet of the "hostile thumb" (*infestus pollex*). The most complete exposition of this sign occurs in Quintilian's discussion of rhetorical gesture in Book 11 of his *Institutio oratoria*: "with the head inclined toward the right shoulder the arm is stretched out from the ear and the hand is extended 'with the hostile thumb.' This gesture," he continues, "is most pleasing to those who boast that they speak with an uplifted hand."[24] While most commentators interpret Quintilian as describing a gesture in which the thumb points downward, their arguments rest primarily not on Quintilian's language but on the assumption, either explicit or implicit, that the ultimate position of the thumb should resemble the sign given for death following gladiatorial combat. It is clear why this particular gesture would aptly be termed "a hostile thumb," and indeed in the Latin Anthology it is a gesture "with a hostile thumb" (*infesto pollice*) that the conquered gladiator fears from the unfriendly crowd: "Even in the fierce arena the conquered gladiator has hope, although the crowd threatens

[22] E-mail communication 10 April 1997; the entry on "premo" is in TLL 10.2: 1167–81 (M. Pade). Courtney 1980.161–62 also chooses not to commit to a precise gesture, stating that *premere* "would naturally mean turn down the thumb or cover it beneath the fingers."

[23] Prop. 3.10.14; Marcell. *med.* 28.72; see also *inpresso . . . sub pollice* at Prudent. *apoth.* 1026 (to describe the molding of clay) and *pollice impresso* at Scrib. Larg. 37 (for massaging in eye ointment). I discuss an occurrence of *pollice depresso* in the closing section of this article. In the third example of *presso pollice*, Repos. 98, *pollex* means "big toe."

[24] Quint. *inst.* 11.3.119: *fit et ille* [gestus] *qui inclinato in umerum dextrum capite bracchio ab aure protenso, manum infesto pollice extendit: qui quidem maxime placet iis qui se dicere sublata manu iactant.* Manuscript *b* contains after *fit et ille* the apparent gloss *qui esse in statuis pacificator solet ille*, which Winterbottom 1970a, ad loc. assigns to the *apparatus criticus* of his edition; see his evaluation of *b* in Winterbottom 1970b.16–17. "Most commentators" in the next sentence includes J. Watson (1905) 2.373 (following Spalding and Buttmann); Post 1892.219; Maier-Eichhorn 1989.126.

with its hostile thumb."[25] While I do agree that the phrase *infesto pollice* in both Quintilian and the Anthology describes the same thumb position and that that position is in fact the sign prescribing death to a vanquished opponent in the arena, I do not agree with the conclusion commonly reached from these facts. The sign for death is not rendered by the thumb turned down. Indeed, upon closer examination, the description in Quintilian points in the opposite direction. First, when one adopts the stance he describes—with the arm extended to the side—the natural position of the thumb is pointing *upward*. This is especially the case if this movement accompanies an extension of the remaining fingers (as implied by *manum . . . extendit*). The opposing movements of lifting the hand *up* and pointing the thumb *down* produces a pose that both looks clumsy and feels uncomfortable. Second, an upwardly erect thumb suits Quintilian's dismissal of those who are fans of the gesture. Those who speak "with uplifted hand" (*sublata manu*) boast about their attraction to using the hostile thumb. The phrase *sublata manu* or its variations (e.g., *tollens manus*) is the normal way to describe a Roman with the hands lifted in prayer, palms raised toward the sky. If Quintilian had indeed wished to describe a thumb pointed downward, it is difficult to imagine why he would have described the accompanying hand as *sublata*. A raised hand and a downward thumb militate against each other both physiologically and culturally. Hence a careful reading of Quintilian's description indicates that the hostile thumb points toward the sky. The *infesto pollice* of the Latin Anthology, in turn, identifies this gesture with death in the arena.

The only remaining ancient occurrence of the phrase *infesto pollice* is contained in Apuleius's *Golden Ass*. Apuleius's text demands with even greater clarity than Quintilian's that the phrase describe an upturned thumb. The narrator is meticulously describing a speaker lying on a couch, propped on his left elbow as he prepares to tell a story. The speaker shapes his right hand, we are told, "like an orator, shutting in the two lowest fingers, extending the rest straight out, and beginning calmly with *infesto pollice* (*infesto pollice clementer*)."[26] As in Quintilian's description, the thumb pointing upward, yielding a natural and comfortable gesture, seems the most likely possibility for *infesto pollice*. Furthermore, the oxymoronic juxtaposition of *infesto pollice* and *clementer* ("calmly") would seem to indicate that Apuleius intends to parody his recumbent orator, who ineptly combines a conventional oratorical hand gesture—index and middle fingers extended—with a thumb that is

---

[25] Anth. Lat. 415 (413 Shackleton Bailey).27–28: *sperat et in saeva victus gladiator arena, / sit licet infesto pollice turba minax.*

[26] Apul. met. 2.21: *effultus in cubitum suberectusque in torum porrigit dexteram et ad instar oratorum conformat articulum duobusque infimis conclusis digitis ceteros eminens et infesto pollice clementer subrigens infit Thelyphron* (there are minor textual problems here). Walsh 1994.31 renders the words *infesto pollice clementer* as "with the thumb gently but accusingly pointed upward."

incongruously obtrusive and whose formation connotes potential violence.[27] Indeed, the entire discourse of this speaker, Thelyphron ("Feminine-minded"), represents a gradual revelation to the reader of his impaired judg-ment.[28] By having a weak-minded character needlessly assert the hostility of his thumb, Apuleius uses Thelyphron's opening gesture to anticipate the mis-prision that becomes the theme of his subsequent narrative. The silence of his upright *pollex* speaks for him.

Comparative evidence from outside the Roman context suggests that the hostility of the thumb in the upright position resides in its uninhibited erect-ness. The folklorist Archer Taylor, in his monograph on the "Shanghai Ges-ture" (thumb to nose, with remaining fingers extended and usually wiggling), also identifies the *pollex infestus* as resembling the modern "thumbs-up." He bases his argument not on a reading of the Latin sources, but on the fact that the hostility of the gesture is the same as that behind the extended middle finger, the "wanton finger" of the Romans (*digitus impudicus*): in its upright position, in other words, the thumb suggests an erect phallus.[29] Similar sexual connotations of the thumb survive in a regional American insult whereby the upwardly extended thumb is moved up and down in a suggestion of inter-course.[30] The notion of the thumb as phallus certainly lies behind the well-attested occurrences of the "fig" gesture in antiquity, by which the thumb inserted between the index and middle finger is meant to represent the penis entering the vagina.[31] In parallel to the representations of the phallus in Roman antiquity, the originally apotropaic significations of the thumb came to be perceived as hostile and threatening.[32]

A less confrontational use of the extended thumb has survived in Italy from antiquity to the present and may be related to the use of the thumb in the gladiatorial arena. In these manifestations the thumb is used to point in scorn. It may either point toward the object of derision or, more often, it is directed dismissively to the side or over the shoulder of the person gesturing. Quintilian indicates that the gesture was in everyday use in the early Empire—"to point to something with the thumb turned away I consider more a traditional usage than one fitting for an orator"—a stricture repeated three centuries later by the rhetorician Julius Victor.[33] The same gesture continues to carry connota-

---

[27] I discuss more fully at the end of this section the conventional speaking gesture here parodied.

[28] Winkler 1985.110–15.

[29] A. Taylor 1956.53; cf. Onians 1954.139–40 n. 4, D. Morris et al. 1979.186–96.

[30] Saitz and Cervenka 1972.78.

[31] Sittl 1890.102–3, 123.

[32] On the phallus as both protective and aggressive, see Barton 1993.95–96. Röhrich 1967.20–24 traces a similar course of development for the gestures of the "fig" and "horns" (index and little finger extended and held vertically).

[33] Quint. *inst.* 11.3.104: *averso pollice demonstrare aliquid, receptum magis puto quam oratori deco-rum*; Iul. Vict. *rhet.* p. 98, 29.

tions of scorn or deprecation from the age of Dante to nineteenth-century Naples to twentieth-century Rome.[34] The erect thumb, either upright or pointing, was a gesture avoided in respectable situations. And in antiquity there seems to have been no chance of confusion in the interpretation of this sign. It is only in the twentieth century that this gesture could have been mistaken for the "thumbs-up" of approval that is now ubiquitous in the United States. A study of gesture by Desmond Morris demonstrates that the Italians consider the "thumbs-up" with positive connotations to be "a new thing imported by the American G.I.s during the war," a contention that receives support from the *Oxford English Dictionary*.[35] Morris hypothesizes that it is this now-common sign of approval that has led contemporary Westerners to believe that the sign for sparing in the arena was represented by an equivalent thumb gesture.[36] There is no indication that the optimistic "thumbs-up" has its antecedent in antiquity. Rather, all evidence points to this thumb as connoting disapprobation and hostility among the ancient Romans.

One final oratorical gesture leads back to the thumb-pressing in Pliny. In Fulgentius's fifth-century treatise on Vergil, the spirit of the poet appears to the narrator to elucidate the allegorical aspects of his *Aeneid*. As Vergil prepares to deliver his exposition, Fulgentius describes the poet's hand position as follows: "with two fingers sticking out in the shape of an iota and pressing together against them a third, the thumb (*tertium pollicem comprimens*)."[37] The gesture is identical with that of the speaker in Apuleius, except that the thumb is—in an unhostile and rhetorically appropriate way—pressed down on the two adjacent fingers. Vergil addresses the narrator Fulgentius with what was the canonical speaking gesture employed in the visual arts. Repeatedly depicted in two illustrated codices of (coincidentally) Vergil's texts, also from the fifth century, the pressed thumb indicates to the viewer which persons in a given

---

[34] Dante and Naples: De Jorio [1832] 2000.73–74; contemporary Rome: Graham 1969.26. At Claud. 27.574, the virgin "points with her thumb" (*pollice monstrat*) in an apparent expression of naiveté: see Dewar 1996, ad loc. I have not been able to discover if this thumb-pointing gesture has any relation to the umpire's "out" sign in American baseball.

[35] D. Morris et al. 1979.193; OED s.v. "thumb" 5.h.: "1939 *War Illustr.* 4 Nov. p. iii/1 French peasants now return the 'thumbs up' gesture with which they are greeted by British troops on their way to the front;" for the recent appearance of this meaning in Switzerland, see Niederer 1989.209.

[36] Similarly, Ackerman 1986.94 attributes to Gérôme's painting *Pollice Verso* the popular association of "thumbs down" with death: "thanks to the popularity of the picture, since 1872 *pollice verso* has meant 'thumbs down.' "

[37] Fulg. *Virg. cont.* p. 86, 21: *itaque compositus in dicendi modum erectis in iotam duobus digitis tertium pollicem comprimens ita verbis exorsus est.* Whitbread 1971.145 unnecessarily construes *pollicem* as *pollice*, thereby having Vergil use the common Christian sign of blessing (thumb pressing on ring finger). Besides being an unnatural way of construing the Latin, the ring finger is, according to Roman nomenclature, the fourth and not the third finger (*digitus quartus*; TLL 5.1: 1127.21 and 38 [J. Rubenbauer]).

scene are speaking.[38] Examples of this gesture also occur with the same meaning on Italian vases, sarcophagi, and in early Christian painting and mosaic.[39] Finally, this configuration of the fingers, I suggest, represents a variation on Pliny's pressed thumb. The speaker elicits the goodwill of his audience as he begins to speak by calmly pressing down the thumb.

A sampling of the textual evidence provides a consistent picture of the importance of the thumb in Roman culture. The Latin thumb clearly has access to supernatural power and is in this respect unique among other early Indo-European societies. The gesture *infesto pollice*, in particular, which seems certain to refer to the erect thumb, was indecorous for the orator and demanded death for the gladiator. By contrast with the hostile connotations of the directly opposite *infesto pollice*, the gesture for goodwill seems in all likelihood to be conveyed by pressing the thumb down upon the enclosed fist.

VISUAL REPRESENTATIONS

Pliny's well-wishing thumb-pressing has sometimes been identified with the sign given to a gladiator to spare his fallen opponent.[40] The identification relies on an assumed economy of gestural vocabulary: if it is known that good favor is extended by the thumb in two contexts—in both the arena and day-to-day life—then it is reasonable to suppose that these two thumb gestures are visually equivalent. At this point the argument necessarily stops, for there survives no unambiguous textual evidence describing the thumb gesture for mercy. Texts do, however, describe alternative means available to the spectators in the arena to express compassion for a fallen gladiator. A line of Martial implies that, at least on some occasions, the crowd appealed for mercy by waving handkerchiefs.[41] Under other circumstances, the audience could express its will simply through shouting.[42] Yet none of these possible forms of appeal—handkerchiefs, shouting crowds, or gesticulating thumbs—has yet been found in the extant visual material.[43] This lack is not the result of a lack of evidence, however, but of beginning with the wrong assumptions. If we

[38] For illustrations, see Wright 1992.56–57, 62–63, and passim, and Wright 1993.14–15, 46–47, 130.

[39] Vases and sarcophagi: Weickert 1925.11; painting: Bourguet 1966, fig. 95; mosaic: Stevenson 1983.96.

[40] Politian, in the fifteenth century, is the earliest scholar I have found who associates the proverb with the arena, but it is not clear what he thinks the gesture looked like (*Miscellanea* 42). For other early scholars who have made the association, see note 1 in the present chapter (Montaigne, Forcellini).

[41] Mart. 12.29.7–8: *nuper cum Myrino peteretur missio laeso, / subduxit mappas quattuor Hermogenes*; see Post 1892.222–24.

[42] Mart. *epigr.* 29.3: *missio . . . viris magno clamore petita est.*

[43] The suggestions of Friedländer (1928) 4.520, have been convincingly refuted by Post 1892.224–25.

assume that the crowd is the key decision maker in these contexts, then we look in vain for artistic representations of gesturing spectators. Two ancient reliefs, however, cast doubt on this assumption and provide evidence for the thumb gesture that complements the information found in our texts. A hand-signal was used during gladiatorial contests not simply by the audience, but also as a means for the *editor*, the person in charge of the games, to communicate the symbol for reprieve directly to the pair of combatants. We need not look into the stands for a gesticulating thumb; the gesture lies closer at hand.

Before turning to artistic representations of this merciful thumb, I begin with a hand gesture so well attested in the textual and material sources that its meaning seems beyond doubt. When a conquered gladiator wished to admit defeat, he requested mercy with an unambiguous gesture—the raising of the index finger, usually of the left hand, in the direction of his opponent or the attendant.[44] Depictions of this sign have been found throughout the Roman Empire, from Britain to Africa, during its first four centuries. The number of surviving examples of this long-lived gesture supports my claims regarding the durability of gestural language: this particular hand signal seems to have remained stable and intelligible wherever and whenever these matches occurred. Other aspects of the games, such as the musical instruments used and the types of gladiatorial equipment worn, also reveal such consistency in both literary and visual descriptions that a recent study of gladiators has stressed how the arena's rituals "represent a common culture uniting Italy, Africa, and the Celtic provinces in their Romanness."[45] The hand gestures also constituted part of this common culture.

The gesture made in assent to the raised index finger, to the vanquished fighter's plea for mercy, was identical with Pliny's gesture of goodwill. This gladiatorial signal appears in two material representations, both of which represent variations on the gesture as I have reconstructed it from textual evidence—thumb pressed on the closed fist. The first piece is a terra-cotta appliqué medallion found in Cavillargues, France, and now housed in the Musée Archéologique at Nîmes (fig. 2).[46] This relief was considered by both Friedländer and Post in their discussions of the sign for mercy, but lack of opportunity to study it first-hand has led both scholars to incorrect (and opposing)

---

[44] Textual sources: Schol. Pers. 5.119: [*gladiatores*] *victi ostensione digiti veniam a populo postulabant*; the practice seems alluded to at Mart. *epigr.* 29.5; Quint. *inst.* 8.5.20; Sidon. *carm.* 23.129–30; for a full list, see Lafaye 1595. Material sources: see the final set of combatants in my fig. 4; Wiedemann 1992.95. Competitors in the Greek *pankration* also signaled defeat by raising the index finger; S. Miller 1991.219.

[45] Wiedemann 1992.94.

[46] When found the medallion was already detached from its original setting. For appliqué medallions, see the catalogue of Wuilleumier and Audin 1952 (photographs of medallions still affixed to their ancient vases appear on Pl. 8).

2. "Médallion de Cavillargues," 16 cm in diameter, Musée
Archéologique, Nîmes, France, inv. GD 188 (photo Musée).

conclusions regarding important details of the medallion.[47] It will be worth-
while, therefore, to offer here a close analysis of the piece. The medallion,
dated on stylistic grounds to the late second or early third century, depicts the
crucial moment in a contest between two gladiators, identifiable from left to
right as a *retiarius* and a *secutor*. After having fought to a draw, both men are
granted a reprieve and their lives. Four distinct elements in the composition
of the piece make the moment clear to the viewer: 1) the inscribed phrase
STANTES MISSI; 2) the scene in the upper background; 3) the gaze of the official
standing between the two fighters in the foreground; and of most importance
to my discussion of the thumb, 4) the hand gesture of the attendant on the
far right of the main scene. Each of these four features will be discussed in
order, since each contributes to a coherent understanding of the narrative of
the relief.

[47] Friedländer (1928) 4.520; Post 1892.224–25.

The wording of the inscription STANTES MISSI (roughly rendered as, "released [while still] standing") is paralleled elsewhere and unquestionably describes the *missio* or release of two combatants after a draw. A poem of Martial narrates just such an outcome:[48]

> cum traheret Priscus, traheret certamina Verus,
>   esset et aequalis Mars utriusque diu,
> missio saepe viris magno clamore petita est.

> When Priscus was pulling the contest one way and Verus the other,
>   and for a long time each man's strength was equal,
> a release (*missio*) was repeatedly sought for the men with a great shout.

On the Nîmes medallion the two fighters, whom placards carried in the background identify as Xantus and Eros, show no indications of an immediate cessation of activity.[49] As a result, commentators have supposed that the inscription STANTES MISSI is meant to represent the shouts of the crowd, much as we hear of in the Martial poem, shouts that have yet to be heeded by those officiating. These spectators, moreover, are thought to be represented by the four smaller figures in the upper part of the medallion.[50] Another interpretation of these secondary figures regards them as four gladiators who have already obtained their reprieve from the crowd. According to this latter reading, the inscription describes the current situation of these finished gladiators, and not the imminent position of the fighters in the foreground.[51]

A close analysis of these secondary figures, however, provides a third option: the background scene depicts the aftermath of the principal match, during which the two released gladiators, Eros and Xantus, are attended to by their assistants. From a detail of the scene (fig. 3), it is clear that the two central figures are wearing characteristic armor, identifiable with the type portrayed in detail in the main scene below: among the smaller figures, the second one from the left, Xantus, wears the protection of the left upper-arm characteristic

---

[48] Mart. *epigr.* 29.1–3. Lafaye 1595–1596 cites parallels to the phrase *stantes missi* (including CIL 6.10194, 33983; 10.7297); see, too, Ville 1981.421–22, Wuilleumier and Audin 1952, figs. 111–12, and Héron de Villefosse 1895, who discusses a lamp depicting a scene of gladiatorial combat similar to that of the Nîmes medallion and accompanied by the abbreviated inscription S MIS.

[49] The texts of each placard are still legible. The inscription on the far left reads XANTVS / CAESXV ("Xantus, [servant] of Caesar, [victor in] fifteen contests"), that on the right EROS / CAESXVI ("Eros, [servant] of Caesar, [victor in] sixteen contests"). The two fighters are evenly matched before the contest begins.

[50] Pelet 1851.39; Golvin and Landes 1990.198. Henzen 1853.130 describes one of the spectators as a woman, raising her thumb to request that the fighters be spared; he is followed by Friedländer (1928) 4.520. Viewing the piece in 1997, I see no evidence for such claims.

[51] Germer-Durand et al. 1893.444. Héron de Villefosse 1895.98, followed by Wuilleumier and Audin 1952.39, proposes that the figures depict Xantus and Eros invoking their respective guardian deities before the fight.

3. First detail of figure 2 (photo Musée).

of the *retiarius* and seems to be otherwise scantily clad, whereas the third figure, the *secutor* Eros, retains his helmet and the protective guards on his right arm and left leg. The fighters turn their backs to each other to face their attendants. These attendants, portrayed as smaller to indicate their subordinate importance in the scene, are clothed in knee-length tunics and are perhaps to be identified with the figures carrying placards in the main field. They assist the gladiators in a manner that must have been clear to the intended viewers of the medallion: perhaps they are disarming the fighters, or rewarding them with an object—a garland or palm—that would signify their shared victory.[52] A parallel for this mode of dual representation, with the fighter being simultaneously portrayed in combat and in victory, appears in the figure of Astacius in the Galleria Borghese mosaics.[53] By this interpretation the four

[52] For the palm and garland, see Lafaye 1596–1597; Wuilleumeier and Audin 1952, cat. no. 110.
[53] Rocchetti 1961.93 identifies the unarmed Astacius, who holds a kind of pennant, as an *incitator* designated to stir up the fighters. He offers parallels neither for the Latin term nor the associated function. The rarity of the name Astacius (the onomastica cite only this example for Latin) suggests that it is unlikely that two unrelated Astacii would be represented simultaneously, especially in two very different functions. Hence, I assume that this unarmed Astacius represents the gladiator celebrating the victory depicted beneath him. For similar celebrations after a conquest, compare the victor's customary circuit of the arena (Suet. *Cal.* 32.2).

background figures unite with the inscription and the central scene to become an integral part of a coherent narrative: the welcome release of tired and valiant fighters.

No crowd on the medallion demands the release of the combatants. Nevertheless, a group of spectators is imagined. The barricade in the lower foreground invites the viewer to read the scene as if in attendance, sitting in the front row with the elite.[54] We become part of the central narrative, on the receiving end of any gestures directed toward the crowd. From this vantage point the active poses of the two officials, apparently dressed in short togas, make clear that a decisive moment has been reached: the time when the decision is made whether to spare the vanquished or allow them to die. This is the moment often depicted in art and at the movies, where the imagination has created a dramatic situation but hardly a realistic one: is the victorious gladiator, exhausted and perhaps even wounded, expected to assess for himself how many thumbs he can see in the crowd, and in what direction the majority of the thumbs are pointing? The Nîmes relief provides an easier alternative: the single *editor* of the games has made the decision—presumably by taking into account the reactions of the spectators—and this decision is conveyed to the pair fighting in the arena.[55] In this way the *editor* can publicly reassert his authority as the presenter of the spectacle while at the same time win favor from his audience by choosing (or pretending) to yield to its wishes. This reconstructed scenario also explains an otherwise odd feature of the Nîmes medallion. Between the combatants stands an umpire who, despite the vigorous fighting taking place directly in front of him, has his attention distracted by something out of the picture to the viewer's left (see fig. 2). The pose, present on other medallions depicting the release of combatants,[56] would of course not require explanation to the Roman who frequented the gladiatorial shows. The umpire looks to see the verdict of the *editor*, either as given by the producer of the games himself or as conveyed by an assistant. His attention would have been secured, I believe, by the use of musical instruments, a feature commonly found in visual and textual depictions of the arena.[57] The use of instruments to halt the gladiatorial action explains a similarly odd pose from

[54] For a similarly styled barricade, see Rouquette and Sintès 1989.73; the ivory diptych from 506 CE features spectators behind such a barricade (Wiedemann 1992, fig. 8).

[55] For this scenario, see Cic. *Tusc.* 2.41: "the gladiators, even when done in with wounds, send someone to discover their masters' wishes" (*mittunt etiam vulneribus confecti [gladiatores] ad dominos, qui quaerant quid velint*); Lafaye 1595; Post 1892.215 n. 1; Robert (1948) 5.84–86, discusses the role of the attendant, with numerous visual examples.

[56] See Wuilleumeier and Audin 1952, cat. nos. 111–12, accompanied by the inscriptions MISSI and STA[N]T[ES] MISSI respectively.

[57] Wille 1967.202–4 contains a full list of sources for the use of music in the arena. For other works in which a referee gazes at something outside the field represented, see Wuilleumier and Audin 1952, cat. nos. 18 and 112.

4. Zliten mosaic, northern sequence. Archeological Museum, Tripoli
(after Hönle and Henze 1981.33)

the famous depictions of the arena found in the Zliten mosaics of Northern
Africa (fig. 4). A brief examination of the narrative of this mosaic will help
clarify the action depicted on the Nîmes medallion.

The iconography of the Zliten mosaics has caused problems in dating the
piece.[58] Although I do not wish to enter into this controversy, I would like to
comment on the apparent eclecticism of the work, for it provides further evidence that the gestures and conventions observed in the gladiatorial shows
contained certain constants throughout antiquity. The components of this
North African ensemble have parallels that have been found as far away as
Germany and that span the first three centuries of the common era.[59] Not
only the costumes, equipment, and musical instruments, but the gestures and
mechanics alluded to in the mosaic would have been familiar to all who had
witnessed gladiatorial combat. The sequence shown in figure 4 depicts gladiators in various stages of battle: in the lower panel, beginning from the left, a
retiarius has just received a leg wound from his opponent; the next pair is

---

[58] The attribution of the ensemble to the Flavian period by Aurigemma 1926.199–201, 267–
78 is further refined by Dunbabin 1978.235–37; Parrish 1985.137–58 places the work in the late
second–mid-third century.

[59] Parrish 1985.153–55.

actively engaged in fighting, while the third pair has finished, with one of the gladiators giving the attendant the raised index finger that admits defeat. It is the first pair, in the upper register of the figure, that is of importance for interpreting the Nîmes medallion. Here an umpire prevents a fighter from delivering the deathblow to his fallen opponent. And yet despite his imagined exertions this official seems strangely occupied with something to his right. The standing gladiator, too, seems to be looking away from the task at hand, in striking contrast to his body's dynamic. Following the gaze of the official, we see that it is directed beyond the water organ toward a lone horn player from whom, as I shall argue below, will come a gesture that will continue the action that has been frozen here for eternity. The Nîmes medallion provides one of the alternative endings to the Zliten narrative. If the referee is bidden that the victim be spared, he will continue to intervene until he has stopped the battle.

The potential for mercy returns us to the second referee on the Nîmes piece and the use of the thumb in the arena (fig. 2). With a spirited gesture the official on the viewer's right underscores the text STANTES MISSI inscribed above his balled-up fist. Post assumed that the peculiar pose of this attendant must carry specific representational meaning, and has proposed that he makes the gesture *pollices premere*. So far I agree with Post, although I cannot accept his claim concerning the appearance of the gesture that this Latin phrase describes. Having available only a photograph of the Nîmes medallion, Post believed that "the hand is represented with the four fingers bent down over the thumb."[60] I have had the opportunity to examine the medallion first-hand, and it is clear that the thumb lies *atop* the clenched fingers (fig. 5). This observation confirms my arguments from philological evidence concerning *pollices premere* that, in the act of pressing, the thumb acts as agent and not as object. Once we recognize the connection between this gesture and the overall narrative of the piece, most earlier interpretations of the man's stance are easily dispensed with.[61]

One reading of his pose, however, deserves further consideration. Héron de Villefosse has construed the vertical line rising behind the official's raised fist as a baton that he holds should it become necessary to separate the two fighters, an eventuality for which there exist many artistic parallels.[62] Close examination of the piece, however, shows that this line is clearly rising behind the fist and that, furthermore, the position of the thumb is not such as one would use for clutching a long baton. I have two possible explanations for this anom-

[60] Post 1892.225.

[61] Pelet 1851.6, followed by Henzen 1853.130, believes that the attendant is bestowing a wooden sword (*rudis*) as a sign of manumission. Germer-Durand et al. 1893.443 interpret the gesture as an expression of triumph.

[62] Héron de Villefosse 1895.98; other parallels he does not mention include the Zliten mosaic (fig. 4); Lafaye, figs. 3573, 3581; Hönle and Henze 1981, figs. 15, 27.

5. Second detail of figure 2 (photo Musée).

alous line: either it is an artistic device meant to separate the smaller scene above (depicting the victorious pair after the fight) from the main action (especially the attendant to the right, who is carrying a placard in the imagined arena) or that it is in fact a baton, but we are meant to imagine that it is being held not by the referee gesturing but by the one who gazes to our left. I am inclined to accept the latter possibility, despite the distance of the baton from the attendant, for two reasons. First, it provides this attendant with his subsequent action in the implied narrative of the scene, that is, to intervene between the two fighters, just like the umpire on the Zliten mosaic. Second, when representations depict two attendants at a gladiatorial contest, we find that it is the one closest to the action who holds the baton.[63] If, then, the left-hand attendant on the medallion wields the baton, there remains only one reasonable explanation for the outstretched arm and closed fist of the figure on the right. In granting mercy, the official employs the proverbial wish of goodwill described by Pliny. In this case mercy effects an honorable outcome. The two gladiators, nearly equally matched as the placards proclaim—Xantus has fifteen victories, Eros sixteen—share eternal glory in the space above. The associations of this gesture with the arena may also explain an anomaly already mentioned, namely the fact that this "proverbial" gesture of goodwill seems

[63] Rocchetti 1961.107, fig. 23 (a mosaic now in Madrid); Lafaye, fig. 3577.

6. Gladiatorial relief, Glyptothek, Munich, Germany, cat.
no. 364 (photo author).

not to have survived Roman antiquity. Just as early Christians strove to
cleanse liturgical Latin of associations with pagan religion, so, too, they may
have avoided gestures linked with the site of frequent Christian persecution.[64]
The pressed thumb of the pagan yields to the raised index and middle fingers
of the compassionate Christ.

One other relief from the Roman era clearly depicts the sign of *missio* and
corresponds to a version of the pressed thumb (fig. 6). This relief, found in
Germany and now in Munich's Glyptothek, depicts the same decisive moment as the Nîmes medallion, except that here the gladiatorial pair is frozen
as it awaits judgment concerning the fate of the fallen fighter. As in the Zliten
mosaic, the sound of horns calls their attention to where the sign will be

[64] For early Christian vocabulary, see especially Mohrmann 1958–1965.

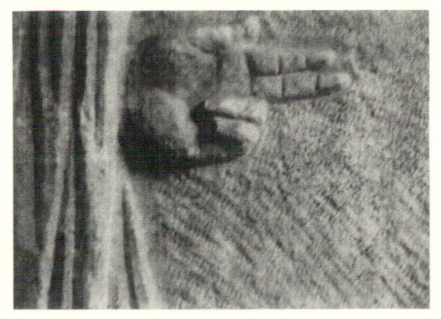

7. Detail of figure 6 (photo author).

displayed. One of the horn players, presumably at the request of the person sponsoring the games, gives what every scholar has agreed must be a gesture entreating mercy (fig. 7). Again we see someone pressing the thumb, here with the addition of the extension of the two adjacent fingers. The result is identical with the hand of Vergil as he begins his allegorical discourse in Fulgentius's treatise. It seems likely that the thumb pressed in a proverbial expression of goodwill, the opening gesture of the calm speaker, and the granting of mercy in the arena share a common feature: the essence of the gesture resides in the thumb, pressed firmly on the hand.

The thumb's prominence in the arena is likely linked to its perceived power, a power that is most clearly reflected in the etymological speculations concerning the word *pollex*. Scattered artistic precedents that survive for the thumb-pressing gesture in nongladiatorial contexts indicate the ways in which human beings tried to harness this power: pressing the thumb neutralized any potential bad luck surrounding the person toward whom the gesture is directed.[65] Deubner has traced the gesture to one found on archaic Greek reliefs that depict a suppliant approaching a hero or chthonic deity.[66] The pointing of the

[65] Contrast Meschke (1929/1930) 3.331, who proposes that the thumb *in fist* allows the gesturer to transfer luck to the object of the gesture, a suggestion that runs counter to the function of binding the thumb that frequently occurs in the magical papyri (see n. 15).

[66] Deubner 1943, where three of his five examples are illustrated.

thumb as it lies atop the fist, he claims, is meant to put pressure on the deity at whom the thumb is directed and, as a result, protects the suppliant who is making the gesture.[67] Deubner's interpretation surely makes less sense than that the pressed thumb sends a positive message to the deity; in other words, it acts contrary to an opposite gesture found in magical papyri. To restrain a potentially harmful deity, the speaker performs a gesture that metaphorically binds a deity's thumb; in this way the divinity's powers are controlled and constrained.[68] The unencumbered and pressed thumb, by contrast, transmits and shares its power. This expression of goodwill found in the pressed thumb may be compared with other ways the ancient Greeks and Romans approached gods: in the traditional interpretation of the familiar *orans* gesture, the hands lifted up in prayer signify adoration and greeting of the deity addressed;[69] in reliefs depicting the welcoming of a god or important human being, the standard gesture is again the raised and extended arm.[70] Physical forms of greeting in other European cultures also originate from the perceived metaphysical power of the gesture performed.[71] If the Greek and Roman reliefs discussed by Deubner do indeed share functional features with the gladiatorial gesture, the action of the thumb then possesses a clear goal. It arose as a means of transmitting protective powers to the fallen fighter.

THE SIGN FOR THE DEATHBLOW IN THE ARENA

It remains to return to the gesture that would have encouraged the deathblow. The first section of this chapter has indicated that the sign was made by the thumb extending upwards and was identical with the gesture known as the "hostile thumb" (*infestus pollex*). Unlike the signal for mercy, I know of no visual illustrations of this gesture. The death sign does, however, receive explicit mention twice in the extant textual sources. In the poetry of Juvenal and Prudentius, spectators demand the deathblow by "turning the thumb" (*verso pollice* in Juvenal, *converso pollice* in Prudentius).[72] That much is clear

---

[67] Deubner 1926.412 makes it clear that he does not identify the gesture on these Greek reliefs with Pliny's *pollices premere*, which he believes involved the thumb in the fist. For the notion of supernatural particles moving through space, see the discussion of the Evil Eye in Dunbabin and Dickie 1983.10–11.

[68] Bonner 1930.180–83; Betz 1980.290 conjectures that the gesture allows the person to identify with the deity.

[69] Ohm 1948.264–65 assembles references to this prayer gesture in numerous ancient and modern cultures.

[70] Sittl 1890.292–94.

[71] Röhrich 1967.15.

[72] Juv. 3.36–37: *munera nunc edunt, et verso pollice vulgus / cum iubet occidunt populariter*; Prud. c. Symm. 2.1097–99: *et quotiens victor ferrum iugulo inserit, illa [virgo Vestalis] / delicias ait esse suas pectusque iacentis / virgo modesta iubet converso pollice rumpi* (other references to the thumb in

and well known; it is the direction in which the thumb turns that the sources do not reveal and scholars have suggested many variations, the commonest three being to the sky, the gesturer's chest, or the ground. One reasonable approach to deciding among these possibilities is to think of the gesture as arising *per contrarium*—that is, the thumb is turned *away from* the direction commonly indicating goodwill. The notion of gestures opposing one another to give opposite meanings is commonly attested; the best parallel to the thumb movement is in the Greek and Roman head nods of assent and denial mentioned in the previous chapter: *ad-nuere* / κατα - νεύειν (to nod *toward* or down in granting a favor) is opposed to *ab-nuere* / ἀνα - νεύειν (to nod away *from* or up in denial).[73] A direct contrast to the assenting position of thumbs flat (*pollices premere*) would be thumbs back, directly corresponding to "the hostile thumb" whose vestiges still survive in modern Italy. As this chapter's epigram from John Dryden attests, this was a common interpretation of Juvenal's "turned thumb" in seventeenth-century Europe.[74] The thumb bent toward a person grants assent, while one bent back and away symbolizes denial.

Linguistic arguments further support the hypothesis that *(con)verso pollice* describes the erect thumb pointing upward. A root meaning of the verb *verto* is "to turn as on a pivot." In describing the movement of the thumb from its place at rest atop the hand (*pollicem premere*) to its threatening position (*infestus pollex*), the phrase *verso pollice* would then denote the thumb turning upward from the closed fist in the way a door turns on its hinges. The verb functions thus in the poet Tibullus—*didicit . . . / cardine tunc tacito vertere posse fores* ("then did she learn how to be able to turn [*vertere*] the door on a silent hinge")—and Pliny uses *vertere* to describe the movement of the legs in the hip joint.[75] Indeed, understanding *verso pollice* as a pivoting thumb yields a much more apt description of thumbs up than down (the commonest interpretation of the phrase), since pointing the thumb down requires a greater twisting of the hand than of the thumb, and our textual sources do not specify that the hand be moved in any way. Furthermore, if *vertere* means "to turn on a pivot," then thumb up is also the most efficient gesture to make when the thumb is resting in its neutral position, flat on the fist. The very action of the thumb pivoting upward in its socket is described explicitly by one author with

either granting or denying favor occur at Hor. *epist.* 1.18.67 and Stat. *Theb.* 8.26; their precise relation to the gladiatorial games is much disputed and I shall not consider them here).

[73] See Onians 1954.139 n. 4, who cites more such oppositions in the Greek and Roman world. For a general discussion of metaphorical gestures arising by contraries, see Sittl 1890.81–116.

[74] Dryden's own note on Juvenal's line reads as follows: "In a Prize of Sword-Players, when one of the Fencers had the other at his Mercy, the Vanquish'd Party implor'd the Clemency of the Spectators. If they thought he deserv'd it not, they held up their Thumbs and bent them backwards, in sign of Death" (in Swedenberg et al. [1974] 4.142; see further the editors' note at 4.608).

[75] Tib. 1.6.11–12; Plin. *nat.* 28.179; more examples in OLD, s.v. *verto* 2. I am indebted to Brian Krostenko for suggesting this use of *vertere*.

the compound verb *a-vertere* ("to turn away"). Quintilian uses the phrase *averso pollice*, a close parallel to the *(con)verso pollice* of Juvenal and Prudentius, to describe the thumb moving away from the hand to point to an object (*inst.* 11.3.104). An analysis of the motion attested by the verb *vertere* supports my earlier conclusions concerning the probable position of the hostile thumb. It turns aggressively upward.

A RIDDLE

Although I hope my preceding arguments and lists of parallels have succeeded in convincing, perhaps the positions of the Roman thumb will remain to some a riddle. It is appropriate, then, to end with a riddle from the Latin Anthology. This ancient puzzle has a clear solution and provides surprising support for my conclusions. The genre of the riddling poem in Latin begins with Symphosius, a writer of the fourth or fifth century CE. In this genre, each riddle consists of a brief poem in either quantitative or stress-based verse, often spoken in the first person by the poem's subject (i.e., in the familiar form "What am I?"). In one of these poems, the pressing and raising of thumbs provides a clue to solving the puzzle. Many problems exist in this short piece—of manuscript readings, rhythm, and vocabulary—but scholars agree on the solution to the riddle. The poem describes the qualities of a siphon (Latin *sipho*). I cite the complete text according to the edition of Glorie and offer a free translation (*Anthologia latina* 481.181–86 Riese; emphasis added):[76]

> ore mihi nulla petenti pocula dantur
> ebrius nec ullum reddo perinde fluorem.
> versa mihi datur vice bibendi facultas
> et vacuo ventri potus ab ima defertur.
> *pollice depresso* conceptas denego limphas
> et *sublato* rursum diffusos confero nimbos.

> No cups are given to my desirous mouth,
> Nor when full of drink do I give back very much flow.
> And yet I have the means to drink
> And drink is brought to my empty stomach from the depths.
> *With the thumb pressed down* I deny the collected waters
> And, *with it raised*, I gather again the scattered storm clouds.

The solution to the poem is confirmed by the puns on *venter* (both "stomach," and the technical term for describing the expanded portion of a siphon) and *conceptas* (the verb used for measuring and storing water in a particular

---

[76] Glorie 1968.577. Glorie's text relies on a superior manuscript unknown to Riese 1894, the previously standard edition of these riddles; see Finch 1961. The recent edition of Shackleton Bailey 1982 does not include this poem (see his remarks at 1.iii).

place: Sen. *nat*. 2.16.1, Frontin. *aq*. 1.11). But when the riddle turns in its final two lines to describing how the siphon functions, we are meant to imagine not the monumental type used in aqueducts but a hand-held pipette for measuring liquids, resembling a modern drinking straw.[77] It is the familiar use of the thumb with this instrument—a diversion that still occupies children every day—that the final couplet plays on. By pressing the thumb on the upper end of the *sipho*, the liquids inside are kept in place ("I deny the collected waters"); when the thumb is lifted, the liquids are released, a circumstance that the poet expresses hyperbolically with the phrase "I gather again the scattered storm clouds."

The expression used in this riddle for pressing the thumb—*pollice depresso*—is what draws our attention. Recalling the proverbial phrase "to press the thumbs" (*pollices premere*), the collocation provides additional linguistic evidence that it is the thumb in this expression that acts as agent; just as the pressing down of the thumb displays goodwill, so, too, does it retain water in the siphon. The lifting of the thumb from the instrument—*[pollice] sublato*—matches another gesture discussed above, the *infestus pollex*, or erect thumb, which, I have argued, was the sign in the arena given for the deathblow. The coexistence of these pairs both in the arena and the epigram is hardly a coincidence; on the contrary, a reference to gladiatorial combat increases the playful nature of the riddle. Riese dates the poem to at least the fifth century CE on the basis of the resemblance between its nonquantitative rhythm and that of the poetry of Commodianus.[78] Hence the riddle seems to have been composed when gladiatorial contests were still an active part of Roman society. When the allusion is recognized, the hyperbolic metaphors of the final two lines become understandable. Pressing the thumb, the gesture of sparing, brings about a cessation of activity, a period of calm. By lifting the thumb, the storm clouds gather: down comes the rain, down comes the sword.

CONCLUSION

"Is the thumb a finger?" A German doctor in the 1996 movie *The English Patient* poses this question before ordering the thumbs severed from the hands of a captured spy. The amputee, it becomes clear, would not have hesitated to answer "No" or, at least, "Not only." Throughout the film, he is haunted by the loss of his thumbs. He has been deprived of more than two fingers; he has lost some part of his essence as a human being. The Romans, too, had a marked respect for the opposable digit. The power they invested in the thumb in

---

[77] For an illustration and explanation of the type, see Dorigny 4:2.1349; Roman references include Cels. 1.8.3 and Colum. 9.14.15.

[78] Riese (1894) 1.xlvii. Finch 1961.146 dates the earliest extant manuscript to before 820 CE.

etymology (it is *pollex* because it is powerful) and in magic and healing (it accompanies verbal incantations and controls access to the gods) extended as well to the granting of good favor to combatants in the arena. A thumb pressed to the fist conveys mercy, perhaps by transmitting goodwill to the fallen opponent, while the erect threat of an upraised thumb requests the deathblow. Herein lay the most awful authority of the *pollex*, the powerful digit.

Chapter 3

BLOOD, MILK, AND TEARS:
THE GESTURES OF
MOURNING WOMEN

A Hamilton, Ontario, lifeguard ordered Shannon Wray,
25, out of a municipal pool in February when she began
to breast-feed her 9-month-old daughter. Wray assumed
it was because she was offending swimmers, but the lifeguard
pointed to the "no food in the pool" rule.
—C. Shepherd, *News of the Weird* (as reported in
Pitch Weekly, 1–7 April 1999)

THIS ANECDOTE appeared in the syndicated column *News of the Weird*, a
weekly collection of unusual stories compiled from legitimate newspapers
throughout the world. Often the "weirdness" of a selection depends upon it
being incongruent with the sensibilities of the column's projected readership,
which seems to be middle-class North Americans with left-leaning political
tendencies. This anecdote about pool behavior provokes a response because
the lifeguard (whose sex, interestingly, is not specified) has hedged around a
potential dilemma regarding political correctness by appealing directly to the
rule of law: "no food in the pool." The irony that entertains—or perhaps
angers—the reader stems from our recognition that the lifeguard is so obviously correct. Breast-feeding provides nourishment; mother's milk is our most
basic food.

This chapter receives its inspiration from an equally startling bit of reasoning preserved in one of the ancient Roman approximations of *News of the
Weird*—a scholiast to Vergil's *Aeneid*. Beginning from the Servian tradition, I
will demonstrate how breast-feeding joins with other features of the Roman
birth process to act as rejuvenating forces in death ritual. Care for the newborn
and treatment of the corpse are two processes gendered as female in Roman
society. In both these areas, I will argue, breast-feeding is prominent and this
prominence offers a new perspective on the violent ways women greeted
death. In Roman antiquity, it seems, the child at the breast did not prompt
embarrassment. On the contrary, the depiction of the subject in art becomes
a metaphor for celebrating nature's abundance, while in literary texts mothers
allude to breast-feeding in appeals for pity. The act had not become detached

from its primary associations with the origins of life and the fertility of nature, as appears to have been the case, if only momentarily, even for the twentieth-century mother in our swimming pool.

GENDERED FUNERALS

Chapter 1 sketched ways in which gesture enabled Romans to participate in the natural world that surrounded them. In chapter 2 I showed how one specific part of the Roman body interacted with the world in a manner both powerful and self-consistent. In the symbiosis between human bodies and nature, gesture was also thought to derive from and strengthen deeper structures of gender and status. In this chapter I will examine one particular case of gender-specific bodily movement. My test case treats the respective roles of men and women in the mourning process as these roles are depicted in the legal, written, and visual evidence.

Research on death rituals in a number of societies has revealed the ways in which funerary practice reflects both the social identity of the deceased and the moral and civic values of the society left behind, and this claim is no less valid for Roman practice.[1] I shall focus, therefore, not on what ritual says about the dead, but about the living, who wear the signs of grief on their bodies. Mourning gesture in antiquity involved not the inward contemplation and quiet solemnity familiar in modern American practice. Grief found expression that was both visible and audible. The common Latin words that describe states of mourning focus not on internal emotions but on external manifestations. *Luctus, planctus, squalor*—words all synonymous in Roman texts with the mourning process in general—describe, respectively, the sound of wailing, of the mourner's body struck by self-inflicted blows, and the disheveled and dirty appearance of the living mourner.[2] The act of mourning was public expression.

Anthropologists have documented for communities throughout the world consistent patterns in how the rituals surrounding death develop. As the form of society grows more complex, mortuary practice correspondingly changes in ways that directly correlate with its society's evolving systems of status.[3] Vergil, for example, in his evocation of the heroic past in the *Aeneid*, follows his Homeric model in depicting men undergoing self-degradation in grief—beating chests, rending cheeks, and rolling in the dirt—behavior that, we shall see, would have been deemed excessive and hence unacceptable for

---

[1] Among studies outside ancient Greece and Rome, I have found most helpful Hertz [1907] 1960; D'Agostino 1987; Watson 1988; Metcalf and Huntington 1991. See, too, the bibliography discussed in I. Morris 1992, esp. 1–30, 205–10.

[2] *Maeror*, in describing the expression of internal grief, provides an apparent exception.

[3] Binford 1971.18–21, with statistical tables.

men living in the poet's own age.[4] From the perspective of extant Roman sources, the differentiation of status in the evolution of Roman mourning is most marked in the division of sex roles: women take on themselves the public self-degradation that accompanies funerary rites, a role that could involve physical pain and blood-letting, while men normally avoid such extremes. This public use of the body accompanies another dichotomy in the conception of how each sex cares for the dead. Roman funerals, like Greek, were modeled on the sequence of private display in the home, followed by public procession and burial. In this sequence, the woman's function tends to concentrate on ensuring the destiny of the individual corpse, while men use grieving to maintain the continuity of the community and the status of families within the community.

Two related explanations can be brought to bear in explaining the male role in death rites. First, there is the well-documented aversion to displaying emotional extremes publicly. As we shall see in detail in the next chapter, such displays undermine the *gravitas* of elite males, for whom control of the body not merely concerns the realm of the physical but allows the observer to read a person's internal moral makeup. The Roman historical tradition preserves numerous instances of elite males struggling to preserve their dignity even when learning of the death of their own children, often returning to public duties quickly or, in extreme cases, not leaving their duties at all.[5] This valorization of state over family informs the second explanation for the male avoidance of extreme emotions: proper maintenance of the cult of the dead, which in Rome includes the cult of the ancestors, dictates that men participate not in overt expressions of grief but in the procession of ancestral portraits that culminates in the male-dominated funeral oration.[6] To use the terms of one anthropologist of death, the males appropriate that half of the funerary cult devoted to maintaining the collectivity upon the loss of one of its members: "in establishing a society of the dead, the society of the living regularly recreates itself."[7] A vivid passage in the second-century BCE historian Polybius describes the effectiveness with which Roman public funerals achieved this goal. He describes as follows the effects that the funeral oration and its accompanying display could have on an audience: "the masses, recalling the achievements [of the deceased] and perceiving them on display, end up feeling sympathy whether they had a share in these deeds or not; so much so that the loss

---

[4] Verg. *Aen.* 11.86–87: *pectora nunc foedans pugnis, nunc unguibus ora; / sternitur et toto proiectus corpore terrae* (Acoetes for Pallas); 12.611: *canitiem immundo perfusam pulvere turpans* (Latinus for Amata).

[5] Prescendi 1995 offers a convenient collection of such incidents; he ignores, however, how visual evidence for mourning men often violates this ideal.

[6] See the famous description of the Roman funeral at Polyb. 6.53–54; for Roman funeral orations, see Kierdorf 1980, esp. 135–36; Maurin 1984.201–2.

[7] Hertz [1907] 1960.72.

seems not the sole property of the mourners, but shared by all the people."[8] Such ceremony enables society to continue without apparent interruption while allowing the elite to preserve the preexistent hierarchy.[9] The spectacle of the procession, in which individuals impersonate the hallowed ancestors of the deceased, visually enacts the past and present stature of the family.[10] The importance of maintaining the status quo at Rome even in death is further reflected in the dress adopted by the deceased members of society. Polybius devotes special attention to this feature of the funeral, noting that the style of the toga worn by the deceased corresponds to the highest political office held during his lifetime (6.53.7). Indeed, even if the family has little or no political importance, the civic status of the dead is still stressed through dress—at a minimum, the deceased Roman citizen wears the toga that marks his civic status.[11]

With women, on the contrary, belongs the task not of praise but of lamentation, a lamentation in which dramatic gestures and bodily abuse on the part of the bereaved play a key role. Female activity does not, however, simply invert this male role, focusing on the negative loss as opposed to the positive contributions the deceased made while still alive. Rather, female mourning practice has its own end in effecting the successful separation of the corpse from the surviving society. Women's ritual, I shall argue, replicates the birth process in a dual form that first ushers the deceased out of the community of the living and then guides it into its new phase of existence. In this replication, standardized female roles in mourning both in antiquity and elsewhere— tearing cheeks, baring and beating breasts, unbinding the hair—become adapted to a new function in the Roman context. The resultant Romanization of the inherited structures of ritual mourning originates from the pervasive Roman belief I analyzed in chapter 1: physical movement, properly deployed, can be used to influence and manipulate the more-than-human world.

GENDERED GESTURES

In areas of Roman ritual other than mourning, it is not surprising to find men and women performing respectively different functions. As Bourdieu has shown in his classic analysis of the Kabyle, societies readily organize themselves around the division of gendered roles, a division that informs every level of activity, from the way meals are eaten to the understanding of metaphorical

---

[8] Polyb. 6.53.3: συμβαίνει τοὺς πολλοὺς ἀναμιμνησκομένους καὶ λαμβάνοντας ὑπὸ τὴν ὄψιν τὰ γεγονότα, μὴ μόνον τοὺς κεκοινωνηκότας τῶν ἔργων, ἀλλὰ καὶ τοὺς ἐκτός, τοσοῦ ἐπὶ τον γίνεσθαι συμπαθεῖς ὥστε μὴ τῶν κηδευόντων ἴδιον, ἀλλὰ κοινὸν τοῦ δήμου φαίνεσθαι τὸ σύμπτωμα.

[9] Hertz [1907] 1960.74; D'Agostino 1987.50 (citing Saxe 1970).

[10] On the political manipulation of elite funerals, see Flower 1996.91–127, esp. 122–26.

[11] Maurin 1984.193 and n. 5.

language to the interpretation of prodigies.[12] A similar case could be made for Rome, but it is important to stress at the outset that this gender division need not correspond to a dichotomy of dominance and subordination. During times when danger threatens the city, for example, numerous texts attest that Roman *matronae* were ordered to sweep out the temples and altars of the gods with their unbound hair.[13] There is no sense in these texts that the women are performing an essentially degrading act; indeed, on these desperate occasions, when men were occupied with military affairs, one could even argue that this extraordinarily pious behavior shows the women as the most capable of influencing divine favor. This use of the female body parallels other aspects of Roman religion. Despite the fact that the state religion is largely controlled by politically powerful men, this all-male contingent has frequent recourse to women's roles in religious performance, so much so that these roles can aptly be regarded as "the feminine complement of masculine action or debate."[14]

The sexing of Roman society reaches beyond religious roles and into constructions of moral and social decorum.[15] Cicero, in authoring his *On Duties*, a treatise that purports to provide his son Marcus with the "principles for leading a consistently decorous life" (*constanter honesteque vivendi praecepta*; 3.5), supplies a clear example of how behavior could naturally divide into gendered categories. He points out that in the display of public decorum there are two types of beauty: the womanly (*venustas*) and the masculine (*dignitas*). The womanly, which is marked by lovely ornamentation, can threaten to become detectable in a man's gesture and bodily movements, and therefore men should avoid such slippage by paying special attention to the care of the body.[16] Cicero was well aware of how a manipulation of such boundaries could provide a powerful tool for rhetorical invective by making his male enemies into visible manifestations of deviance.[17]

It is not surprising, then, to find Cicero explicitly instructing members of his family on proper carriage, and doing so along gender lines. When he saw that his son-in-law walked rather gently (*mollius*), while his daughter Tullia had too much bustle, he jokingly advised Tullia to "Walk like *vir*."[18] The remark plays ironically on the double sense of *vir*: Tullia should walk like her

---

[12] Bourdieu 1990.271–83 (a revised version of Bourdieu 1970), further elaborated at Bourdieu 1990.70–71.

[13] For example, Liv. 3.7.7–8, 26.9.7; Appel 1909.203; Heckenbach 1911.71.

[14] Wardman 1982.39; further discussion in Scheid 1992.

[15] The essays in Hallett and Skinner 1997 offer numerous examples of how Romans gendered decorum; see, too, Edwards 1993.63–97.

[16] Cic. *off.* 1.130: *cum autem pulchritudinis duo genera sint, quorum in altero venustas sit, in altero dignitas, venustatem muliebrem ducere debemus, dignitatem virilem. ergo et a forma removeatur omnis viro non dignus ornatus, et huic simile vitium in gestu motuque caveatur.*

[17] Corbeill 1996.128–73.

[18] Macr. *Sat.* 2.3.16: *Cicero . . . cum Piso gener eius mollius incederet, filia autem concitatius, ait filiae: "ambula tamquam vir."*

husband (*vir*), who seems effeminate because he violates the proper carriage of a man (*vir*). Both husband and wife transgress movement appropriate for their sex. Roman tradition repeatedly offers examples of how morality hinges on proper respect for this boundary. Seneca, for example, remarks how Roman men of old were able to exhibit masculine dignity even while dancing (*virilem in modum tripudiare*), and to do so in such a way that they would not lose face should they be seen by their enemies; Seneca's own male contemporaries, on the contrary, could not help from appearing womanish even when they walked.[19] In the next chapter I shall explore further how the sexual associations of ways of walking in Roman society could be exploited in a political context to maintain the elite status quo. For now I wish merely to point out how a person's sex implied a certain decorum in bodily movement. For each sex certain gestures are considered appropriate. The division of sex roles in mourning, then, should not simply offer a negative example of what men did *not* do, but rather a positive interpretation of a woman's relationship with death and dying.

GREEK AND ETRUSCAN MOURNING GESTURES

Beginning with the earliest extant representations of mourning ritual in the western Mediterranean world, both the textual and the visual material attest to a male-female division of labor.[20] In the iconography of Greek Geometric vases, the raising of both arms to the head marks the gestural domain of mourning women; in only one certain example does a man employ this two-handed gesture.[21] The gesture can represent the rending of the hair and possibly also the beating of the head; the scratching of cheeks by women seems also to have been depicted in this early period.[22] Men, by contrast, do not normally adopt emotionally demonstrative attitudes while mourning; occasionally they are represented as having one hand to the head, a gesture that seems to represent the beating of the head.[23] Far more often male figures are depicted extending one arm outward in what appears to be a gesture of farewell to the deceased.[24] These conventionalized renderings tone down the emotional content of grief expressed in the Homeric poems, where men roll on the ground and women add the action of violently beating their breasts.[25]

---

[19] Sen. *dial.* 9.17.4.

[20] Brandt 1965.72–88 offers a hypothetical reconstruction of how Greek mourning gestures developed from Minoan ritual.

[21] Ahlberg 1971.76–78, 227.

[22] Zschietzschmann 1928.20; Ahlberg 1971.263–65 believes these depictions represent only the rending of the hair.

[23] Ahlberg 1971.265.

[24] Zschietzschmann 1928.27; Ahlberg 1971.265–66.

[25] Holst-Warhaft 1992.105–14.

Nevertheless, despite differences in degree, both the visual and textual record agree in assigning different roles to each sex.[26]

More than eighty depictions of persons lamenting the dead survive on black- and red-figure Attic vase paintings of the sixth and fifth centuries.[27] A division of roles similar to that found in Geometric depictions continues in these artistic representations from Athens, but the representations have become increasingly conventionalized as depictions of women scratching cheeks now disappear from the visual record.[28] In scenes of the body lying in state (*prothesis*), men are normally depicted entering in procession, greeting the dead with voice and gesture, while women lament around the corpse, holding its head or touching its hand while wailing and exhibiting the now-standard gestures of grief, tearing the hair and striking the head.[29] On the rare occasions when men are depicted near the corpse they most likely represent close male relatives.[30] These dichotomous duties pertaining to the corpse match descriptions found in contemporary literary sources.[31] In Etruria as well, where funerary ritual seems to have developed independently of Greek influence, the roles of the sexes depicted deviate little from those in Greece, at least insofar as we can tell from the material evidence available.[32] Visual representations show Etruscan women engaged in preparing and anointing the corpse.[33] Women also are depicted displaying the expected signs of mourning—disheveled and torn hair, scratching of cheeks, overt gestures of distress—while men greet the dead with a salute.[34] The division of lament in both the Greek and Etruscan worlds mirrors the respective roles of the sexes as I have outlined them above: women take on the role of grieving loss in the domestic sphere while male behavior demonstrates public recognition of the deceased's passing.

Recent studies of the city-state of classical Athens have added nuance to this generalization by placing mourning practice in its specific historical context. Shapiro notes that, over the course of the fifth century, scenes of *prothesis* depicted on vases move from the privacy of the home to the public spaces of the city. This shift in modes of representation, he argues, corresponds to a change in how Athenians perceived the relationship between the deceased

---

[26] Neumann 1965.85–86; Reiner 1938.42–49 provides a concise selection of the relevant material.

[27] McNiven 1982.92.

[28] Neumann 1965.89.

[29] Shapiro 1991.631–44.

[30] Ibid., 639.

[31] Alexiou 1974.5–7; Lizzi 1995.51–52.

[32] Camporeale 1959 attempts to distinguish Etruscan elements from Greek in visual representations of *prothesis*.

[33] Lizzi 1995.50.

[34] Women: Monceaux 1382–83; Sittl 1890.69. Men: Camporeale 1959.34–36.

and society.[35] As Athens becomes a major military force, the warrior dead move from symbolizing the loss experienced by a single family to one affecting the entire community. Artistic representations, accordingly, begin to figure the dead hero as the property of the state. With this shift away from the family, women are no longer portrayed in art as playing the leading role in mourning; representations of women as principals become confined largely to the more personal scenes depicted on *lekythoi*, private vases placed directly in the tomb by the deceased's nearest relatives. According to Holst-Warhaft, this increasing separation of men into the public sphere and women into the domestic develops in additional areas during this century, when the male-dominated funeral oration (*epitaphios logos*) displaces female mourning as the dominant public expression of grief.[36] Stears has further demonstrated the ways in which the division of gender roles in Greek funerary practice reflects the division of civic and domestic roles in the city. But rather than seeing women's roles as the necessary result of the politicization of male roles, she regards the changes as having relevance to the position of both sexes. In adopting the women's perspective, Stears is able to claim that "participation in funerals . . . served in fact as a means for the construction and display of women's powers."[37]

Only recently have these kinds of studies of the pre-Roman material begun to suggest that women in mourning ritual occupied something other than a space for the containment of immoderate grief. Closest to the body as it is bathed, anointed, and lamented, women express openly and dramatically the human loss felt by the family and community. Simultaneously, however, it is normally claimed that close contact with the decaying body created in women a potential locus of pollution. This common reading of the evidence fits in with the role of mourning in a wide variety of cultures throughout the world, past and present, where the most vocal mourners are perceived as taking upon themselves the dirt—both literal and symbolic—of death. Yet by contextualizing the situation in Rome along the lines of what has been done for Athens, a new reading of the Roman evidence emerges, one that accords with the more traditional relationship perceived between the body and the external world that I discussed in the first chapter. Rather than being perceived as transcending the phenomenal world, women's gestures—like the movement of priests and healers—actively participate in their surroundings. In the mourning ritual of Roman society, the persistent dichotomy between male and female roles creates not conflict, but distinct spaces for embodying coexistent ways of maintaining both social and psychic order. Let us now turn to the evidence for how Roman women grieved, and how the male-dominated political and literary elite evaluated that grief.

[35] Shapiro 1991.646–55.
[36] Holst-Warhaft 1992.119–21.
[37] Stears 1998, esp. 117–26; quotation is from 118.

LEGAL EVIDENCE

From our earliest recorded evidence, Roman legislation deemed it important to control excessive display at funerals.[38] Of most relevance to the use of the body in lament is a specific prohibition contained in the Twelve Tables, a law code collected in the fifth century BCE.[39] Cicero records in his treatise *On the Laws* that the Tables included legislation barring women from practicing self-mutilation: "Women shall not tear their cheeks, nor shall they have a *lessum* for the purpose of a funeral."[40] This prohibition was thought by Cicero to derive from the Greek precedent of the legislation of Solon, who created a set of laws forbidding women at funerals from lacerating flesh, as well as from reciting set dirges and lamenting the dead when they are not close relatives.[41] Our ancient sources do not cite the reasons for either set of prohibitions, but the link between the Greek and Roman codes and the occurrence of the mysterious word *lessum* indicate a possibility. As Cicero argues by citing parallels in the Solonic laws—the word *lessum* was already unknown to him— the Table seems to refer here to a ban on certain types of public lamentation. Moreover, the placement of these laws in the code indicates that they belong to a larger set of sumptuary legislation that included restrictions on the use of unguents for the corpse and on supplementing the adornment of the pyre with gold. Hence, it is clear that the early Romans implemented restrictions against female self-mutilation and public lament as a means of controlling competition among the elite in society, who intended to advertise their self-importance through elaborate funerals that involved not only expensive accouterments, but also sensational demonstrations of grief.[42] In its attempts to oversee relations among the elite, legislation controlled what we have identified as the male province of death ritual—the maintenance of the community. Accordingly, these laws were aimed not at controlling beliefs about the dead and the afterlife, but at regulating public practice.[43] The legal tradition, therefore,

[38] Baltrusch 1989.44–50 summarizes the tradition, with bibliography.

[39] Sources, translation, and commentary conveniently collected in Crawford (1996) 2.555–721.

[40] Cic. *leg.* 2.59: "*mulieres genas ne radunto neve lessum funeris ergo habento*"; FIRA 1.67.

[41] Cic. *leg* 2.64–65. For Solon's funerary legislation, see [Dem.] 43.62, Plut. *Vit. Sol.* 21; Humphreys 1983.85–87. For the controversy over to what extent, if any, Athenian law codes influenced the Twelve Tables, see Crawford (1996) 2.560–61, with literature; Ducos 1978.37–41 evaluates Cicero's testimony in particular.

[42] Lizzi 1995.58–60. Holst-Warhaft 1992.114–19, following Alexiou 1974, similarly assesses funerary restrictions in ancient Greece; her remarks that the legislation indicates "a belief in women's laments or lamenting women as a force to be reckoned with" (26) do not, I believe, apply in the Roman case.

[43] See the similar remarks of Watson 1988, esp. 10–11, regarding modern China ("Chinese imperial authorities were content to control and legislate actions, not beliefs").

does not assign any extrapolitical significance to the grieving gestures of women. These fifth-century Roman legislators, in their concern to pass sumptuary measures, show no concern for understanding the more-than-human mechanics of female grief. The effectiveness of this legislation in Rome, moreover, appears to be dubious. As we shall see, the laceration of the cheeks was not banished from the literary tradition nor probably even from lived experience. This continuity of the tradition further indicates that the gestures of mourning had significance for the women involved that went beyond the boundaries of elite competition.

Lamentation received criticism outside the legal sphere as well. Dominant voices in society spoke out against excessive mourning. These strictures, like legislation, separated propriety along gender lines. Beginning from the fourth century BCE, legal theoreticians begin to reevaluate why statutory limits, such as those in the Solonic code and the Twelve Tables, had come to be placed upon women's participation in funerary ritual. Rather than seeing the cause in sumptuary restrictions, as clearly seems to have been the primary motivation, ancient writers use the restrictions as a starting point from which to evaluate differences in the ways men and women react to grief.[44] From these considerations arose an insistence upon a dichotomy between emotional control in men and uncontrolled and uncontrollable display in women, a distinction that has a bearing not so much on real practice as on moral evaluations of practice. As often, the category of "natural" behavior arises from making sense of culturally determined actions. Seneca, for example, argues that mourning is intended to teach forbearance, and that therefore the cessation of mourning should come about as the result of a conscious decision, not on account of fatigue or loss of interest. Energetic displays of grief preclude such conscious self-examination, he argues, since they arise for purposes of ostentation rather than as true expressions of emotion. These considerations, he concludes, determined why the ancient Romans set a legal limit of one year to a woman's period of mourning; for men, contrarily, "there is no time set by law, since none is honorable."[45] Using underlying logic such as this, Roman texts follow Greek tradition in marking it as particularly unusual for men to display their grief publicly.[46] When Agrippina arrived in Rome with the ashes of her dead husband Germanicus, the historian Tacitus underlines the uniqueness of the spectacle by remarking that "one could not distinguish the laments of the men from the women."[47] Normally, it is implied, the loud cries of women would

[44] Lizzi 1995.61–64, with abundant ancient evidence.

[45] Sen. epist. 63.13: annum feminis ad lugendum constituere maiores, non ut tam diu lugerent, sed ne diutius; viris nullum legitimum tempus est, quia nullum honestum. The limit to female mourning seems in fact to have arisen from more pragmatic considerations; see Frazer (1929) 2.30–32.

[46] Lizzi 1995.61–64.

[47] Tac. ann. 3.1.5: neque discerneres . . . virorum feminarumque planctus. Néraudau 1987.205–8 argues that during the early Empire it became acceptable for men to lament children, a change he attributes to the new political climate.

dominate such scenes. As in other parts of Tacitus's narrative, Germanicus's death produced here a notable effect in its capacity to allow grief to conquer propriety.

Further indications of the predominance of women in mourning ritual can be found in a practice that Aristotle apparently considered to have no Greek precedent: the employment of women as praise-singers for the dead.[48] These women, called by the Latin name *praeficae*, seem originally to have led songs that included praise of the deceased, and their functions later came to include other public expressions of grief.[49] This professional role clearly finds women depicted not as violating decorum through the display of excess emotion, but as channeling the disorder of the community's grief into controlled lamentation.[50] This interpretation gains further support from visual representations, most famously on the tomb of the Haterii and the Amiternum relief, that show women taking the lead in the expression of grief (see figs. 8 and 13). It is impossible, however, to determine what kinds of factors—the economic status or civic importance of the deceased, the emotional needs of the family— were considered in deciding the role or even the presence of *praeficae* at funerals; it is at any rate reasonably clear that the *praefica* did not always displace female relatives as mourners.[51] What the rise of professional mourners at Rome does indicate is the importance attached to female display, both in the private realm of the *collocatio* and the public procession. As a result, when I refer to the role of mourning women in my subsequent remarks, I shall understand "woman" as a gendered category whose role in mourning does not necessarily depend on any personal relationship with the corpse.

ROMAN MOURNING GESTURES

Gestures employed in the immediate vicinity of the deceased fall into two types: static and self-directed postures that both men and women exhibit, and vividly expressive displays that tend to be restricted to women.

Texts and images depict male Roman bodies expressing grief by directing the self inward in postures that appear contemplative and self-focused. The principal two attitudes involve raising the hand to meet the cheek or chin in a kind of "thinker" pose, or clasping the knee or knees. Both these forms of expressing grief are demonstrated by women as well, usually those who have

---

[48] Arist. apud Varro *ling.* 7.70, with Fraenkel 1960.19–20; Stählin 1965.834 provides parallels from ancient Egypt and Babylon.

[49] Kierdorf 1980.104–5.

[50] Lizzi 1995.52–53 reconstructs the role of the *praefica* as a type of chorus leader.

[51] Jensen 1978.46–47 cites Luc. 2.23–24 as the strongest evidence in support of his claim (following Mau) that the female mourners behind the bed in the Haterii relief are relatives and not *praeficae*. I do not see how certainty is possible.

8. Relief with lying-in-state from tomb of the Haterii. Vatican
Museum Ex-Lateranense, inv. 9999 (photo Schwanke; Deutsches
Archäologisches Institut Rom, inst. neg. 81.2858).

a close attachment to the corpse, such as mothers and grandmothers.[52] The
former act, of resting one's own chin or cheek on the hand, has a long history
in Western art, and seems primarily to evoke connotations of pensiveness and
uncertainty. In a mournful or abject context, this pose of pensive reflection
carried additional overtones of repentance or lamentation.[53] If it is correct to
connect this entire range of attitudes with one posture, the earliest reference
in Latin to the pose appears in Plautus, where one character describes a "foreign poet" (*poeta barbarus*) sitting in prison with his "mouth on a column" (*os
columnatum*). The poet, in other words, seems to be sitting with his elbow
propped on his knee, resting his chin on his hand, with the forearm acting as

[52] Standard works on mourning, stressing differences between the sexes, tend to neglect these
shared characteristics (e.g., Sittl 1890.69–70, Stählin 1965.835, Nußbaum 1976.938).
    [53] Settis 1984, esp. 205–8.

9. Relief from an altar showing two caryatids and a seated woman; detail
of the seated woman, a personification of conquered territory
(copyright Alinari / Art Resource, NY).

the supporting "column." The elliptical nature of the description indicates
that the pose must have been well-known to Plautus's audience as a way of
expressing a combination of contemplation and grief.[54] This bodily pose came
to be part of the standard visual repertoire for representing the vanquished
underdog, as is attested by its frequent use in Roman art in personified representations of conquered provinces (see fig. 9).[55] In funerary contexts, the pose
is frequently found in depictions of the deceased lying-in-state primarily on
Roman sarcophagi, where it is employed by those seated closest to the corpse.[56]
There seems to be no distinction between the poses of men and women in

[54] Plaut. Mil. 211–12: nam os columnatum poetae esse inaudivi barbaro, / quoi bini custodes semper
totis horis occubant. For the traditional identification of the poet with Naevius, imprisoned for
publicly slandering the Metelli, see Gruen 1990.96–104. Allen 1896 and Killeen 1973 offer less
likely interpretations of the phrase os columnatum.

[55] Conquered provinces: for example, Stuart Jones (1926) 1.1, 17 (Plate 8; Dacia); Zanker
1988a.183 (fig. 142).

[56] Amedick 1991, nos. 2, 47, 60, 215, 225, etc.; Müller 1994, figs. 11, 12.

these scenes—both sexes have their heads covered and bowed, with hunched shoulders. Standing figures are also found in the pose, in which case the arm supporting the chin rests its elbow either on a supporting horizontal arm or on a piece of furniture, such as the back of the deathbed.[57]

The second closed-in position commonly depicted shows the mourner clasping his or her own knee. The grasping of parts of the body so as to create a fetal-like position seems to be an inherent human reaction to sadness and grief, and one exhibited by primates when dejected. In Apuleius's *Golden Ass* the narrator Lucius describes himself in such a position. He believes, incorrectly as it turns out, that he has just committed murder. As Lucius contemplates his action and its legal consequences, he positions himself in a gesture that reflects his despair: "with my feet woven together and my palms joined over my knees with alternating fingers, I wept copiously as I sat squatting on the bed."[58] By embracing the knees in this fashion Lucius employs a type of gesture familiar from chapter 1: the formation of the feet, hands, and fingers creates a multiple binding gesture intended, like the ancient practice of circumambulation or the modern crossing of the fingers, to ward off any further misfortune. In light of Durkheim's arguments that funerary ritual originates in human fear of the unknown consequences of death, it is not surprising that Lucius's posture is clearly to be read in other contexts as an expression of grief.[59] In Augustine's *Confessions*, for example, the embrace of the knee with woven fingers combines with unambiguous reactions of despair such as striking the forehead and tearing at the hair.[60] The connection between the knee embrace and mourning is also apparent from extant material depictions in which the bereaved adopts the pose of embracing one knee. The most familiar example, from the tomb of the Haterii, depicts three individuals, marked as freedpersons by their distinctive headgear, seated below and to the right of the funeral bed with both arms clasping a folded right knee (see fig. 8 and compare fig. 10).[61]

There are numerous indications that the ancestors of the Romans attached significance to this knee embrace. Several cultural phenomena shared among Indo-European peoples presume a connection between the knee and the life-

---

[57] Amedick 1991, nos. 115, 121, 194.

[58] Apul. *met.* 3.1: *aestus invadit animum vespertini recordatione facinoris; complicitis denique pedibus ac palmulis in alternas digitorum vicissitudines super genua conexis sic grabattum cossim insidens ubertim flebam.*

[59] Durkheim 1965.434–55, discussed in the next section.

[60] Aug. *conf.* 8.8: *si vulsi capillum, si percussi frontem, si consertis digitis complexatus sum genu.* The only possible Greek example of this gesture as a sign of grief is described at Paus. 10.31.5, on which see Frazer (1898) 5.386–87 and the literature he cites (the examples of Sittl 1890.23 n. 5 are irrelevant; McNiven 1982.93–94 does not cite instances from Attic vase paintings).

[61] Toynbee 1971, fig. 9 (on the identification of these figures, see Samter 1903.252); Amedick 1991, no. 121; Saverkina 1979, no. 19.

10. Death of a Young Girl. Marble relief from a child's sarcophagus. Musée du Moyen Age (Cluny), Paris, France (copyright Réunion des Musées nationaux / Art Resource, NY).

giving forces in human beings: the nouns and verbs describing male procreation, for example, and the commonest words for "knee" appear to be cognate (for Latin, consider *genu, genus, genitor, gigno*); life in Homer and sexual desire in Hesiod are each represented as residing in the knees; suppliants appeal for pity by extending their hands toward or embracing the knees of their superiors.[62] Pliny provides the most explicit ancient testimony that recognizes a connection between knees and life. Having observed that all peoples adopt a similar posture when supplicating, he conjectures that this is because a certain life-force (*vitalitas*) resides in the principal leg joint.[63] Visual support for this claim that the force of supplication depends on the superior individual's knee can be found in a peculiar scene on a Roman sarcophagus now in Pisa's Campo Santo (see fig. 11). Here a young barbarian boy supplicates a Roman soldier not by submissively lowering himself to the ground, but by reaching *up* to the commander's knee.[64] By analogy, embracing the knees in grief may have been seen as a way of embracing one's own life-giving capabilities at the moment when one laments the death of another. If this type of universal reaction to grief was in fact interpreted along the lines suggested by Pliny, we have an example of the Romans constructing a rational explanation for a naturally occurring gesture of sorrow: the bowing of the body in the presence of death brings one closer to a source of life-energy (*vitalitas*). This means of rationalization anticipates my reconstruction of the female reaction to grief. Although the actions exhibited by women have parallels throughout the world, I will claim that they take on a new meaning when they come to share the space occupied by Roman conceptions of the body.

[62] Deonna 1939; Onians 1954.174–86.
[63] Plin. *nat.* 11.250; compare Serv. *Aen.* 3.607 (knee as seat of *misericordia*).
[64] For scenes of supplication on Roman sarcophagi, see Brilliant 1963. 154–61.

11. Battle sarcophagus, Campo Santo, Pisa, Italy; detail (photo Felbermeyer; Deutsches Archäologisches Institut Rom, inst. neg. 34.238).

In general, visual examples display men exhibiting grief in a controlled manner, in accordance with the surviving textual discussions that stress the need to restrict outward signs of mourning. Any betrayal of violent emotions, such as tearing out hair or rending cheeks, accordingly becomes the recognized province of women. This tendency toward greater mourning on the part of women could be documented in dozens of textual and visual examples. A passage in Petronius offers an almost complete list of the features of female mourning when the author describes the grief of the Widow of Ephesus. His description not only provides a convenient compendium of the actions expected of a grieving Roman wife, but the context also indicates that he is describing Roman lamentation as opposed to Greek. The narrator of the Widow's tale notes that her actions during the funeral procession follow "common custom" (*vulgari more*), actions that he explicitly contrasts with the placing of the corpse in an underground chamber, which he notes as following "Greek custom" (*Graeco more*). The Widow's behavior also accords with the conduct that Lucian ascribes to women in his treatise "On Mourning," written a century after Petronius and generally agreed to reflect contemporary attitudes in the eastern Roman empire.[65] I shall now briefly survey the gestures characteristic of female mourning by going through the Widow's actions in order.

The Widow follows the funeral procession of her husband with her hair unbound (*passis . . . crinibus*; Petron. 111.2). The practice of unbinding the hair in grief is particularly characteristic of women in Roman society, and dozens of textual and visual depictions of the practice survive.[66] The loose hair is accompanied in the funerary procession by beating the breast, which is often bared (*nudatum pectus*).[67] This practice also is normally performed by women, especially in the vicinity of the corpse; the one visual example known to me of men beating their (covered) chest occurs on the tomb of the Haterii (see fig. 8). Here two men, flanking two women, process to the right in the field below the funeral bed; their dress and lack of prominence on the relief make it probable that the men depicted are slaves or freedmen of the deceased.[68]

The Widow practices her most violent actions in the tomb itself where, weeping, she lacerates her face with her nails, causes her breasts to bleed, and tears out her hair (111.8–9).[69] These extreme actions were identified by the Romans with women in particular, as is clear from the wording of the Twelve Tables discussed above, where this behavior is restricted. There remains one final physical expression of grief for a woman, not mentioned in this Petronius passage. In Terence's *Phormio*, a girl in mourning is described. Among other characteristic elements—tears, disheveled hair, unkempt clothing—the description includes her bare feet (*nudus pes*).[70] The bareness of the feet is mentioned and depicted elsewhere in the Roman tradition, and may be a vestige of ritual nudity.[71] What is of immediate concern for us is the fact that the practice seems to have been gender-specific when performed during mourning and that it places the woman, shoeless, in a position more suited to domestic

---

[65] Sittl 1890.65; Stählin 1965.833.

[66] For textual references to women with hair unbound in mourning, see Heckenbach 1911.75, Nußbaum 1976.938; visual references include my figs. 8, 10, 12, 13, and Amedick 1991, nos. 60, 115, 198, passim.

[67] Beating of breast: Pease 1935.519; bared breasts: Heckenbach 1911.32–33. Visual representations include my figs. 8 and 12; Amedick 1991, nos. 115, 248; Sichtermann and Koch 1975, no. 44; Wright 1993.38, 40.

[68] Jensen 1978.47–49.

[69] Rending cheeks: Cic. *leg.* 2.59 (discussed above), *Tusc.* 3.62; Pease 1935.517–18. Tearing hair: Nußbaum 1976.938; Frazer (1918) 3.302–3.

[70] Ter. *Phorm.* 106–7: *capillus passus, nudus pes, ipsa horrida, / lacrumae, vestitus turpis.*

[71] Samter 1903.253–54; on bare feet in ritual generally, Heckenbach 1911.23–31. Parallels for this type of ritual substitution include sprinkling with water in place of ritual bathing (Eitrem 1915.126) or the washing before prayer of head and hands instead of the entire body (Appel 1909.185–86).

than public activity. That is, bare feet render her more suited to those spaces gendered female in Roman society. The *mos vulgaris*, then, the common method by which women expressed grief, involves two types of behavior—self-inflicted violence and the release of bonds—actions that create an appearance of physical and spiritual vulnerability. I shall now suggest ways in which this appearance is deceiving.

WOMEN AS SCAPEGOATS

According to the generally accepted interpretation, women throughout history have traditionally taken on violent, self-mutilating gestures as a way of appeasing the dead and preventing the recently deceased from somehow adversely affecting the surviving society.[72] Durkheim, in *The Elementary Forms of the Religious Life*, has provided the most influential formulation of how this practice may have developed.[73] Upon the death of a close relative or companion, Durkheim has observed, an abstract and nonrational fear of the unknown arises among the living, who then spontaneously respond to this fear with displays of grief designed to counteract the resultant anxiety that society itself will eventually dismantle. Among survivors, the discharge of the pain and anger arising from this fear takes the form of self-inflicted violence. Since women in traditional societies generally "have smaller social value" (447), they become perceived as the most efficient scapegoats, taking on the most violent manifestations of grief. Durkheim posits that the attempt of mourners to rationalize this type of violence gives rise to the notion of something akin to the "soul" of the deceased; rather than recognizing grief as a natural manifestation of their fear for the future of the community, mourners perceive their self-mutilation as a kind of offering for the dead. And since the decomposed body has no visible survival to which offerings could be made, something nonmaterial was posited to exist after death: the spirit.

If we accept this reconstruction at least in its rough outline, Roman society of the late Republic would seem to have adopted a conception by which it acknowledges some form of nonbodily existence after death, but has not found it necessary to formulate the precise nature of that existence. In fact, both literary texts and what survives of death ritual make it clear that the average Roman would have concurred with Cicero's assertion that "there is sensation in death, and people are not so nullified at the end of life that they perish utterly."[74] Nevertheless, repeated attempts by scholars to reconstruct what that

---

[72] The explanation occurs repeatedly in the anthropological literature; for Rome, see Samter 1911.179–81 (citing earlier scholars); Lizzi 1995.55.

[73] Durkheim 1965.434–55.

[74] Cic. *Tusc.* 1.27: *itaque unum illud erat insitum priscis illis, . . . esse in morte sensum, neque excessu vitae sic deleri hominem ut funditus interiret; idque cum multis aliis rebus tum e pontificio iure et e caerimoniis sepulcrorum intellegi licet.* The nature of the pagan Roman afterlife has, of

afterlife was thought to have entailed have met with no consensus. The conclusion seems inevitable. What is important in Roman funerary ritual is not
so much the precise status of the dead as their future relationship with the
living.[75] If survivors symbolically feed the dead at the funeral or subsequent
festivals, in other words, their primary concern is not with the dead's well-
being so much as with appeasing any possible wrath. The Roman antiquarian
Marcus Varro betrays precisely such a concern when he explains why women
tear their cheeks in grief: "by displaying blood," he contends, "women are
able to appease the spirits below."[76] The Romans did not, however—with the
possible exception of the rare practice of *devotio*—partake in expiatory acts
that involved self-mortification or self-sacrifice, preferring instead to sway the
gods through other means.[77] The notion of appeasing the divine dead through
self-inflicted violence was alien to the normal ritual activity conducted in
relation to the gods. Let us return then to the question that prompted Durkheim to see in mourning ritual a possible origin for the idea of the human
soul: why should the recently dead suddenly have become perceived as antago-
nistically demanding the self-mutilation of a relative or close companion? As
we have seen, the Greek and Roman philosophical tradition, dominated by
elite males, manufactured an explanation: overt expression of grief is a manifestation of the weakness of women in enduring pain and loss. But did women
think differently? There are cogent reasons to believe that their advertised
weakness served to conceal real power.

Woman's Work

It would be fascinating to know how women learned mourning ritual: was
the young widow, loosening her hair and beating her breast, unconsciously
reenacting what she had seen demonstrated countless times before, or did she
attach some additional significance to this performance? We of course will
never know what she was thinking—even the verbal content of the dirges
sung (if indeed there was any) has been permanently lost.[78] Parallels in contemporary anthropology, however, may help retrieve a possible context for an
ancient understanding of these gestures; namely, that death is an area gendered first *for* women and then *by* women until the tending of the dead

---

course, received much discussion; among chief works that treat the question from different perspectives, see Brelich 1937; Cumont 1949; Nock 1972; and Toynbee 1971.33–64.

[75] Nock 1972.626–41; Dumézil (1970) 1.363–69; Scheid 1984.118; Belayche 1995.156.

[76] Serv. auct. Aen. 3.67: *Varro . . . dicit mulieres in exsequiis et luctu ideo solitas ora lacerare ut
sanguine ostenso inferis satisfaciant.*

[77] Rosenberger 1998.168–69.

[78] On the low regard given *neniae* in antiquity, see Heller 1943, esp. 216–19; comparative
studies of dirges include Alexiou 1974.131–205 (ancient to modern Greece) and Johnson 1988
(Taiwan).

becomes uniquely marked as woman's work. Indeed, one scholar discussing modern Chinese mourning practice seems to be responding to Varro's characterization of the ritual of scratching the cheeks when she writes that the "emphasis [in violent mourning] is not so much on women's taking upon themselves the pollution of the dead as on their tending to the concrete, material, and emotional needs of the person who died." In doing so ritual recognizes "woman's contribution to the cycle and flow of existence."[79] From this perspective, mourning ritual may even recall a time in the early history of the community when familial concerns were more important than the social, in which case women would be not simply engaged in work, but also demonstrating their control in matters concerning death. In the area of Greek funerary ritual, Stears has recently proposed that female lamentation may have fulfilled a variety of social functions by promoting, through ritual, the well-being of each individual woman's *oikos*: "participation in funerary ritual would . . . have been one of the means of enhancing female status, rather than a way of emphasizing the social inferiority of women as a gender."[80]

The most significant contribution a woman makes to "the cycle and flow of existence" is, of course, her role in birth. This brings us to the ancient explanation of women's roles in mourning to which I have alluded in my opening remarks, an explanation preserved in the Servian tradition of commentary on Vergil's *Aeneid*. A consideration of the scholia suggests an alternative to Varro's scapegoat theory, by which women mutilate themselves to appease the shades. I would like to look at this explanation only briefly, then return to it more fully at the end of this chapter. It is well known that milk and blood are ritual offerings to the dead, intended to nourish the spirits.[81] As we have seen, Varro detects an echo of this type of gift in female mourning ritual: by scratching the cheeks women offer nourishment to the corpse as it prepares for its next existence; the blood also obviates the need for any sacrifice, either animal or human.[82] Such a claim of ritual substitution does not seem unusual. Parallels can be found in Roman practice and elsewhere in which a symbolic activity represents a more violent original action.[83] How then is the offering of milk supplied? It is produced, the scholiast writes, by the women "who follow the dead, beating their breasts."[84]

[79] Martin 1988.172–73.

[80] Stears 1998.126.

[81] Wyß 1914.25–32; Eitrem 1915.102–4 (milk), 416–23 (blood), 454–58 (blood and milk). For comparative studies, see Frazer (1918) 3.270–303 (blood and hair offerings), Deonna 1954. 156–66 (milk).

[82] Serv. auct. *Aen.* 3.67 (Varro) and more explicitly at Serv. *Aen.* 12.606 (with no mention of Varro), where the rending of the cheeks is understood as a vestige of human sacrifice; see, too, Hor. *epod.* 5.93; Tert. *spect.* 12.97.

[83] Burkert 1983.20–21.

[84] Serv. auct. *Aen.* 5.78: *umbrae autem sanguine et lacte satiantur: unde feminae, quae mortuos prosequuntur, ubera tundunt, ut lac exprimant, cuncti autem se lacerant, ut sanguinem effundant.*

It will not come as a surprise that the veracity of this evidence is normally rejected out of hand by scholars of Roman religion.[85] Beating the breast to produce milk does seem, if nothing else, an idea that is physiologically problematic. And yet the uniqueness of this interpretation—not to be found in either Greek or other parallel traditions—should not cause it to be rejected outright. Identical rituals often adopt different meanings in different societies. Sociologists have long recognized that rituals tend not to arise from the concrete display of ideas, but that ideas are actually born from the rationalization of virtual acts.[86] Just as Durkheim sees the notion of the immortal soul as arising from making sense of formalized acts, so, too, I would propose that the interpretation preserved in the Servian tradition—that women beat breasts to produce milk to feed corpses—arises from a context within which the fertile value of the female breast determines the understanding of an inherited funerary rite.

To begin with, the scholiast's apparently odd claim has linguistic support. When Roman women are described as beating their breasts in grief, the word most commonly used is *pectora*, which neutrally describes the chest area of a human being, either male or female. On approximately twenty occasions in our surviving sources, however, the noun *ubera* is used. The word *ubera* strictly denotes the breasts of women, and then only in direct reference or allusion to their function as the source of mother's milk.[87] To cite a familiar example: when Apuleius's Psyche bids her parents to desist from beating their chests in grief at her apparently impending death, she explicitly uses *pectora* in reference to her father, *ubera* for the mother.[88] The simultaneous perception of women as both mourners of the dead and givers of life is reflected in funerary inscriptions as well: one infant's epitaph, in particular, bids the mother not to tear at her womb in grief and, in an apparent oxymoron, many epitaphs address the earth (*terra*) both as fertile mother and as recipient of the corpse.[89] Although it is a common topos in Greek and Roman literature for mothers and nurses to grieve or appeal for pity in ways that recall their function as childbearers, especially by revealing their breasts, this only underscores the possibility for

---

[85] For example, Wyß 1914.27 ("Die Erklärung . . . ist kaum die zutreffende"); Eitrem 1915.454 ("freilich sinnlos"). In a discussion of the similarities between birth and death ritual, Maurin 1984.199–200 accepts Servius auctor's statement without discussion.

[86] Burkert 1983.17–18.

[87] This figure is based on a search in the PHI database of Latin authors. Some of the more striking examples: CLE 541.6 (3rd c. CE): *mater misera palmisque ubera tundens*; Apul. *met.* 7.27 (a mother). The only passages where I have found *uber* used outside an actual or implied context of lactation is in the Vulgate translations of Song of Solomon and Ezekiel; in both passages the word has sexual overtones.

[88] Apul. *met.* 4.34: *quid pectora, quid ubera sancta tunditis?*

[89] CLE 2155.5: *quid mater ventrem laceras?*; see, too, Sen. *Herc. O.* 1669–70, 1678–79; Brelich 1937.38–39.

12. Fragment of a Roman sarcophagus (Department of Classical and Near
Eastern Antiquities, National Museum of Denmark, inv. no. 2226).

construing breast-beating in the way the scholiast has, since it provides a
larger context within which the Romans connected birth with death.[90]

A peculiarity in the visual record invites further reflection. When funerary
scenes depict women baring breasts, these women are normally the mourners
depicted in closest proximity to the deceased. Depictions such as we see on
a mid-second-century sarcophagus fragment from Copenhagen are especially
tantalizing in this context (fig. 12). This relief portrays the bared breasts of
the woman, nearly touching the head of the corpse. Her attitude provides a
visual companion to a mother's lament for her dead son preserved in a text
from the same era. A declamation describes a mother crying over her son as
follows: "Now we are calling back the heat to his cold chest by placing our
breasts over him" (*iam frigidi pectoris calorem superpositis revocamus uberibus*).[91]
The Latin word denoting the mother's breasts in this passage is, again, *ubera*.

Women then, according to the Servian tradition, produce blood *and* milk
to appease the dead. In no other culture have I come across such an explanatory model for the breast-beating of mourning women. But the lack of a parallel should not cause us to ignore the scholiast's claim. Instead, I would like
now to examine the funerary process from the point of view of woman's role
in birth to see how a Roman context has adapted traditional mourning gestures. The scapegoat, we shall see, becomes a mother.

[90] Showing the breast: Denniston 1968.199; Sen. *Phaedr.* 247, *Herc. O.* 926. Compare Plut.
mor. 264F–65A, where a Greek man, thought to have died while abroad and so given a complete
funeral by his family, returns home alive. In order to reenter society he undergoes a ritual rebirth,
which includes being washed, swaddled, and suckled by women.

[91] Ps. Quint. *decl.* 8.5; other visual examples of bared breasts near the head of a corpse include
an illustration from the Vatican Vergil (Wright 1993.40); Sichtermann and Koch 1975, fig. 44;
Amedick 1991, figs. 115, 248.

ROMAN DEATH RITUAL AS DOUBLE-BIRTH

In 1907 the sociologist Robert Hertz observed among funerary cults in South-east Asia a practice he termed the "double funeral."[92] Hertz demonstrates that each phase in this dual rite has a distinct purpose. I wish to show in the remainder of this chapter how these two rites correspond with the ways in which the Romans represented their own care of the dead. The first funeral serves two major functions. First, it involves a provisional burial, by which the corpse is laid in a temporary resting place. For wealthy Romans this lying-in-state, or *collocatio*, took place in the atrium of the house. This period of provisional burial separates the individual deceased from the collectivity of the living; without the completion of this period the remains of the deceased reside on the margin of two worlds, that of the afterlife and of its former existence.[93] Second, this period also has a public aspect, intended to separate the particular individual from the collectivity of the community; the more important the deceased, the more elaborate the mourning period.[94] One finds a ready parallel for this aspect of the first funeral in the importance the Roman elite attached to the public procession and funeral oration. The second funeral follows either immediately upon the first or after an extended period of time, often depending upon whether the corpse is cremated or to be buried. This final portion of the rites serves primarily "to ensure the soul peace and access to the land of the dead, and finally to free the living from the obligations of mourning."[95] To this phase corresponds the Roman mourning period following cremation or burial.

I intend to demonstrate the particular features of these double-obsequies for the Roman case, concentrating on areas where the Romans shape their received ritual in accordance with Italic beliefs. One significant difference between Roman and Asian practice lies in the period that elapses between the two funerals. In the Southeast Asian examples studied by Hertz, eight months to five years can separate the two halves of the double-ceremony, since the celebrants of the ritual must wait for the body to decompose to bare bones. Since the Romans practiced cremation for most of the period I will be considering, such a delay is unnecessary and the secondary funeral can begin immediately after burning. The same contraction of the waiting period takes place in those societies studied by Hertz that practiced cremation, which indicates that the delay generally is of practical use in allowing time for loss of flesh, rather than of any significant symbolic value.[96]

---

[92] Hertz [1907] 1960.27–86 (notes on 117–54). His findings are supplemented by van Gennep [1908] 1960.146–65.

[93] Hertz [1907] 1960.30–37.

[94] Ibid., 76–77

[95] Ibid., 54.

[96] Ibid., 42–43 ("this interval may be reduced to such an extent that both ceremonies form a single continuous whole, which does not, however, prevent the cremation being a preliminary

Despite the difference in the method of corpse disposal, it is striking how the dichotomy of Roman funerary ritual matches the Asian—one half ensuring the future of the community, the other the future life of the deceased. At Rome this dichotomy, in addition to marking two distinct phases in death ritual, also corresponds, as we have seen, to male and female roles. In the case of Roman women, however, this dual process of separation, this double-funeral, is envisioned as a type of birth, a birth that is facilitated by female action in mourning. Parallels for the similarity between rites of birth and death survive in numerous societies.[97] The number of these parallels can be multiplied even further if one includes the cases of metaphorical birth and death that occur in ceremonies that mark a rite of passage.[98] Yet the Roman treatment of the dead is, as far as I can tell, unique in providing evidence for a kind of double-birth. First, an inverted birth process ushers the deceased out of the world; second, a simulated birth escorts the dead into its next existence. In what follows I shall rehearse the steps in the funerary ritual that seem relevant to my explanation. Sources are scattered, and no single source gives the ritual complete, but the order of events is generally agreed upon.[99] An outline of these events is provided in table 3.1.

FIRST FUNERAL

A.1. Role of Bare Earth

I begin with the role of the earth underfoot (step A.1 in table 3.1). Some time during the birth process at Rome, the newborn was placed upon the ground.[100] The meaning of this ritual—or even whether a ritual is involved—is disputed. There is little ancient evidence to support the long-standing notion that this action provided the father with the opportunity of deciding whether to accept the child by lifting it from the ground or whether to reject it by leaving it lie.[101] What the visual evidence does leave undisputed, however, is that the child was immediately laid on the bare earth—if the birth did not in fact take

---

operation and occupying, within the system of funeral rites, the same place as the temporary exposure").

[97] Bloch and Parry 1982 offer numerous non-Western parallels; Hertz [1907] 1960.80.

[98] Wagenvoort 1956, who includes an interesting case from the order of St. Benedict, where initiates are covered with a shroud and sung the *Miserere* before entering the order (135).

[99] Cuq 1386–1409 provides a full description, with citation of the relevant textual and visual evidence; more succinct are Toynbee 1971.43–55, Maurin 1984.193–96. In the following discussion I ignore parallels between birth and death rites that do not seem to be predicated on the idea of the corpse undergoing rebirth, such as the use of torches (Samter 1911.67–82) or the offering of hair (Samter 1901.65 with Samter 1911.179–81).

[100] Macr. *Sat.* 1.12.20: *vox nascenti homini terrae contactu datur.*

[101] Köves-Zulauf 1990.1–92 convincingly demolishes this notion, which he shows originates in a misconstrual of the common Latin phrases *liberos tollere/suscipere.*

TABLE 3.1: A Comparison of the Steps in Birth- and Death-Rituals

Death	Birth
A. Birth out of world	
1. Corpse on ground, followed by death (*depositio*)	1. Birth, on ground
2. Eyes closed	2. Test for life (eyes open)
3. Wash	3. Wash
4. Clothe, according to status	4. Clothe
5. Corpse in atrium	5. Infant in cradle
6. Lament	6. Feeding
7. Nine days before cremation/burial: (Serv. *Aen.* 5.64)	7. Nine days before child given name (*dies lustricus*)
8. Corpse leaves atrium feet first	
Exit from house; inversion of birth process	
B. Birth into afterlife	
1. Corpse head first in funeral procession	
2. Mourning increases (*neniae*)	
3. Eyes opened; toes bound. Pyre lit.	
4. Nine days after cremation/burial: changing of mourning garments (*dies denicales*), funerary feast (*novendialis*), and burial of *os resectum*.	

place there.[102] Using this certainty, Wagenvoort argues, from parallel passages in which the Romans saw the earth as a source of power, that this form of delivery allows the child, and in some cases the mother, to derive strength from mother earth.[103] If one accepts the hypothesis that funerary ritual imitates and replicates birth ritual, I believe we can strengthen Wagenvoort's interpretation of the treatment of the newborn. Delivery onto the bare ground resembles another controversial Roman practice, that of *depositio*, whereby a dying person, while still alive, is placed on the bare earth outside the home.[104] The

[102] Full citation of ancient testimonia and modern discussions at Köves-Zulauf 1990.4 n. 7; he does not discuss visual evidence, which seems without exception to depict the mother seated on a stool while an attendant places the newborn on the ground; see Kampen 1981.69–71, figs. 58, 60; Amedick 1991, passim.

[103] Wagenvoort 1947.17–18; medical writers also accept the utility of placing the newborn on the earth (Köves-Zulauf 1990.5).

[104] Relevant texts are evaluated at Samter 1903.249–51 (references include Lucil. apud Non. p. 279, 25; Ov. *Pont.* 2.2.45, *trist.* 3.3.40; Serv. *Aen.* 12.395). Dieterich 1925.6–35 finds in these two practices a vestige of the belief that human souls were thought to reside in "Mother Earth"; contra Samter 1911.10; Scheid 1984.120 n. 11.

dream interpreter Artemidorus notes the similarity between these two practices and offers an explanation: "Like infants, the dead are wrapped in torn
strips of cloth and put on the ground. The end has the same relation to the
beginning as the beginning does to the end."[105] Whatever the origins of the
practice of *depositio*, the symbolic closure inherent in the act is clear: contact
with earth marks the beginning and end of life. In funerary ritual, this union
of earth and death initiates a series of acts that invert the birth process, a
process that concluded with the union of earth and birth.

A.2–5. Preparation of Corpse

When the person dies following the *depositio* on the earth (as, according to
extant texts, invariably happened), the steps in preparing the corpse for subsequent ceremonies match those taken in the care of a child after birth (steps
2–5 in table 3.1). In analogy to the newborn opening its eyes, the eyes of the
corpse are deliberately closed. This familiar practice, employed now to preserve
the dignity of the dead, would seem not to require explanation, but we shall
see that this ritual, like many other Roman rituals of death, is in fact meant to
serve the survivors rather than the dead. After the eyes have been closed, the
corpse, like the newborn, is bathed, anointed, dressed, and put to bed.[106] As
already mentioned, the dress of the corpse was not a simple shroud, but intended
to convey the social rank of the deceased; male citizens wore togas, for example,
with additional trappings appropriate to the political importance they possessed
while alive, while victorious athletes were permitted to wear crowns.[107]

A.6. Female Lamentation

Having prepared and dressed the corpse, the women begin their lamentation
(step A.6 in table 3.1). As already noted, all types of knots or binding are
eliminated. The avoidance includes in this case the hair, breast, and feet. This
action is normally interpreted in the context of mourning as a way of exposing
women to the pollution of death or the malevolence of spirits. Such an explanation, however, fails to account for the fact that the avoidance of binding
was also expected of pregnant women. Festus mentions husbands who loosen
a knot of their new bride to guarantee the birth of many children and Ovid

---

[105] Artem. 1.13: οἱ ἀποθανόντες ἐσχισμένοις ἐνειλοῦνται ῥάκεσιν ὡς καὶ τὰ βρέφη καὶ
χαμαὶ τίθενται, καὶ οἷόν περ λόγον ἔχει ἡ ἀρχὴ πρὸς τὸ τέλος, τὸν αὐτὸν καὶ τὸ τέλος πρὸς
τὴν ἀρχήν.

[106] Closing of eyes: Verg. *Aen.* 9.486–87; Ov. *am.* 3.9.49, *epist.* 1.102, *trist.* 3.3.44, 4.3.44; Val.
Max. 2.6.8; Sen. *contr.* 9.4.5; Luc. 3.740; Plin. *nat.* 11.150. The practice seems to be represented
on an Etruscan urn from Volterra (Monceaux 1382 and fig. 3359). Bathing and anointing: Serv.
Aen. 6.218–19; Apul. *flor.* 19, *met.* 8.14.

[107] Dress: Liv. 5.41.2, 34.7.2–3; Marquardt 1886.347 n. 3. Crowns: Cic. *leg.* 2.60; Plin. *nat.*
21.7; Cuq 1388.

relates the famous story of Lucina, the goddess of childbirth, who crosses her knees and fingers in a foiled attempt to prevent the birth of Hercules. Outside the realm of myth and ritual, medical writers, too, advise that mothers avoid knots and bindings as birth nears.[108]

In Rome, the avoidance of binding at the time of a loved one's death is moreover a gender-specific practice. In his *Roman Questions*, Plutarch makes it clear that the practice does *not* apply to men. What is of especial interest is Plutarch's explanation for this distinction, which reaffirms my argument for women's role in mourning: by custom (*nomos*), men arrange for the worship of the dead as newly created divinities, while the women take up the domestic task of mourning the dead as formerly living human beings.[109] It is her personal relationship with the dead in this case that determines a woman's outer appearance, mimicking the physical process of birth.

A.7. Nine-Day Period after Death

Our textual sources indicate that the rites from death to cremation should last for a specific period. As usual, we are at the mercy of written sources, which presumably describe an ideal, and an ideal for the aristocracy. But this makes our information no less telling about Roman views of death and the relation of living human bodies to the afterlife of the corpse.[110] According to Servius, a nine-day period normally follows death, during which the deceased is successfully severed from the community: this includes seven days in the atrium of the house, an eighth at the cremation, and burial or entombment on the ninth.[111] We may contrast Classical Greece, where a three-day period is normally prescribed between death and burial.[112] The nine days among the Romans, I suggest, represent a collapsing of the normal nine-month gestation period into a corresponding number of days. Such a symbolic correspondence occurs elsewhere in mourning ritual. A Roman law attested as originating in the time of Numa prescribes that children over the age of three are mourned

---

[108] I provide a full discussion of this practice in chapter 1.

[109] Plut. *mor.* 267A. Although Plutarch specifically speaks of "sons" and "daughters," the textual and visual record demonstrates that this division applies to all men and women; see Heckenbach 1911.75.

[110] Belayche 1995.156–57.

[111] Serv. Aen. 5.64: *et illic [sedibus suis] septem erat diebus, octavo incendebatur, nono sepeliebatur*; see, too, 6.218: *servabantur cadavera septem diebus*. Belayche 1995 examines the evidence for what mourners may have done and why during this period, which he, for no clear reason, maintains lasted seven or eight days. Marquardt 1886.378–79 argues unnecessarily that Servius is confused here, and must be referring to the nine days after burial, not death (contra Samter RE 5.219–20, who uses Gell. 16.4.3–4 to support the evidence in Servius).

[112] Kurtz and Boardman 1971.144–46 (contra Rohde 1925.195 n. 83). The Homeric period varies, and is apparently dependent upon the status of the deceased; Hector is cremated on the tenth day following the recovery of his body (*Il.* 24.785), Achilles on the eighteenth (*Od.* 24.63–64).

for as many months as the years they lived: a three-year-old baby who dies, for example, receives three months of mourning.[113]

A significant objection to seeing in this nine-day period an intentional allusion to human gestation needs to be considered. The Romans, like the Greeks, normally described a human pregnancy as lasting "ten months" (*decem menses*, δέκα μῆνας) or as ending "in the tenth month" (*decimo mense*, δεκάτῳ μηνί).[114] Herescu has argued that these expressions date to an early historical period when time was kept by lunar months of twenty-seven to twenty-eight days. When, over time, the year in the annual calendar came to be reckoned by solar months, the previously accurate description of a "ten-month" (c. 270-day) pregnancy had already petrified as an idiomatic expression and did not change to rectify the relatively minor discrepancy.[115] That two systems of time-reckoning coexisted is supported by the fact that references to a nine-month gestation period also can be found, although less frequently. Ovid in fact recognizes both possibilities within the single text of *Metamorphoses*.[116] Other authors who refer to a nine-month period include Cicero, Censorinus, Lactantius, and Macrobius, while Gellius devotes an entire chapter of his *Attic Nights* to ancient opinions on which conception was more accurate.[117] It is significant that, in these passages where a nine-month period is specified, the designation is not simply being used as an idiomatic way of referring to the passage of time during pregnancy, but occurs in a context where the topic of discussion is human gestation as a biological phenomenon. Perhaps the clearest indication that the Romans associated the number nine with the female reproductive cycle is Varro's testimony to the existence of the deity *Nona* ("Ninth") who, together with *Decima* ("Tenth"), received her name "from the appropriate period for birth" (*a partus tempestivi tempore*).[118] At the level of popular religion as well as in scholarly discussion, then, the number nine would have had undeniable associations with the birth process.

A.8. Feet First

Finally, let us consider a well-known death ritual that further indicates the ways in which the first phase of death ritual was figured as inverted birth.

[113] Ulp.(?) frg.Vat. 321 (FIRA 2.536): *minores liberi tot mensibus elugeantur, quot annorum decesserint usque ad trimatum; minor trimo non lugetur, sed sublugetur*; Plut. *Vit. Num.* 12.

[114] References collected at Pease (1955) 2.731–32.

[115] Herescu 1946 (following Turnebus), with additional remarks in Herescu 1955.

[116] Ten months: Ov. *met.* 8.500, 9.286; nine months: *met.* 10.296, 479. I have collected seventeen references to nine-month gestation in Latin authors and in Greek authors writing in the Roman period.

[117] Cic. *nat.* 2.69; Censorin. 8.1.1–13; Lact. *opif.* 17.8; Macr. *somn.* 1.6.14; Gell. 3.16.

[118] Varro apud Gell. 3.16.9–10; Tert. *anim.* 37.1; Wissowa 1912.220; Tels-de Jong 1959, esp. 93–104, attempts to trace the origins of these mysterious goddesses.

When the corpse is removed from the atrium after the *collocatio*, it must always leave the home feet-first (step A.8 in table 3.1). Our clearest source for this custom records it while discussing, appropriately enough, human birth. In the seventh book of his *Natural History*, Pliny cites a number of counterexamples to prove that it is against nature (*contra naturam*) to be born feet-first. He then concludes as follows: "it is part of nature's ceremonial"—the unusual Latin phrase he uses is *ritus naturae*—"that humans are born head-first; it is human custom (*mos*) that they are carried out of the house by the feet."[119] The Romans, he implies, have consciously adopted this particular custom (*mos*) for disposing of the corpse as a complement to the ritual processes observed in nature. And in fact Pliny has no reason to mention death at this point in his discussion. He has already been discussing matters related to human birth for twelve chapters, and will continue to do so for seventeen more (7.33–62). It would seem that the way we come into the world is intimately linked in his mind with the way we make our exit.

Second Funeral

Birth ritual, replicated in funerary practice, removes the deceased from society. But where does it go? The remainder of death ritual assures that the spirit—or whatever we should choose to call what remains—enter into some afterlife. As I have said, modern scholarship has not been able to reconstruct precisely what the nature of this Roman afterworld is, and I tend to agree with those scholars who have argued that the Romans never formed a clear consensus themselves. Certainly this absence of a fixed form of the afterlife informs the arguments of Augustine, whose *City of God* uses this lack of certainty as one of his bases for a critique of pre-Christian beliefs.[120] Nevertheless, although these intricate funerary rites may not speak clearly to us of an afterlife, they do make clear that the afterworld is a place where you wanted the dead to go—and to stay.

B.1. Head First

Numerous societies take special care that bodies adopt a particular orientation when laid in their final resting place—toward the rising sun, for example, or in the direction of a building that held particular significance for the living. In each case, the orientation of the deceased seems to align with its presumed

---

[119] Plin. *nat.* 7.46: *ritus naturae capite hominem gigni, mos est pedibus efferri* (see, too, Pers. 3.105); Latte 1960.101 believes the custom is intended to prevent the dead from returning. Corpses in Greece also faced the door with their feet (and presumably were carried out in this way): Hsch. s.v. διὲκ θυρῶν.

[120] For example, Aug. *civ.* 6.4 (on Varro): *in hac tota serie pulcherrimae ac subtilissimae distributionis et distinctionis vitam aeternam frustra quaeri et sperari impudentissime vel optari.*

13. Funerary relief from Amiternum. National Museum of Abruzzo, L'Aquila, Italy
(photo Hutzel; Deutsches Archäologisches Institut Rom, inst. neg. 61.4).

existence after death.[121] At Rome, an unusual shifting in the orientation of
the deceased appears to introduce the ritual steps that follow cremation or
burial. The funerary relief from Amiternum makes visual a ritual inversion
(fig. 13). Text and image concur that the corpse leaves the home feet-first;
why then does the Amiternum relief portray it being conveyed in the procession head-first?[122] The artist may have chosen this rendering on the basis of
aesthetics: since reclining figures are normally portrayed leaning on the left
elbow, the corpse must point head-first here in order to face the viewer fron-
tally.[123] But surely it would be preferable to adopt an explanation for the portrayal that takes into account ritual practice rather than artistic convention.
A more attractive explanation suggests itself if we keep thinking along the
lines of Pliny, linking death with birth. In this context, the inversion of the
position of the corpse signals a new stage in the rite: in the proper, head-
first, position, the corpse is ready to be reborn. And indeed, the few surviving

[121] H. J. Rose 1922, esp. 129–30, 136.
[122] Franchi 1966.23–29 examines this relief in detail.
[123] Samter 1903.255, who first noted this inversion (also present in Greek ritual; see Lécrivain 2.2:
1374–76, figs. 3340–43), argues convincingly against it being simply a matter of artistic convention.

indications of how the rites proceed after the funeral procession *do* indicate that a new birth occurs, to allow entry into the afterlife.

This repositioning for birth *out of* the world offers an additional explanation for why, in the "first funeral" (i.e., in the ceremony preceding burial or cremation), emphasis falls on the relationship between the corpse and the public. Anthropologists, in fact, have aptly referred to the deceased during the period of the first burial as the "living dead." Rites before the disposal of the body concentrate on the achievements of the dead as alive, as Polybius makes so clear, because the corpse has not yet been ushered successfully from the world.[124]

B.2. *Lamentation and Nonbinding Continues*

As the female mourners approach the pyre or the tomb, vocal lament increases to its highest pitch, while nonbinding and beating of the breasts continue.[125] The presence of loud lamentation at the grave may be a practice particularly emphasized in Roman funerary ritual, as there is no evidence of such behavior in the Greek world.[126] If so, an explanation for the innovation suggests itself: as the body is born into the afterlife, the pain of the women who initiate this journey reaches its highest point. This pain is vocalized in part by incantations chanted at the pyre or tomb. These incantations are denoted in Latin by the odd word *neniae*, a word whose semantic field ranges from "dirge" to "incantation" to "jingle" to "silly things, rubbish."[127] The most thorough discussion of this mysterious word concludes that the original meaning of *neniae* was "childish things" and that the associated personification, Nenia, was the goddess who embodied children's playtime.[128] One particular allusion to Nenia's province of duties is relevant here. In his polemic against pre-Christian Roman religion, Arnobius describes the goddess as watching over the "extreme times" of life—our beginnings and our end.[129] Such a characterization fits in well with my reconstruction here: at the time of death, the songs sung recall the lullabies mothers sing to children.[130] Perhaps this association informs the peculiar imagery Lucretius uses in describing the cyclical nature of existence: "Now on this side, now on that, the vital force conquers and is conquered in turn; mixed in with the funeral dirge is the wail that children raise upon first seeing the

[124] On the "living dead," see Belayche 1995, esp. his analysis of the *pompa funebris* at 158–62.

[125] Maurin 1984.195.

[126] Sittl 1890.73, who notes of Greeks that "beim Begräbnisse selbst die Totenklage . . . ist nicht ausdrücklich überliefert."

[127] OLD, s.v.

[128] Heller 1943, esp. 263, who offers a different connection with funerary lamentation.

[129] Arnob. *nat.* 4.7; for *extremus* describing the beginning and end of a cycle or closed system, see Cic. *rep.* 6.18 (this meaning is overlooked in TLL s.v.).

[130] Maurin 1984.200 makes a similar suggestion, without argument.

shores of light" (*nunc hic nunc illic superant vitalia rerum / et superantur item: miscetur funere vagor / quem pueri tollunt visentis luminis oras*).[131]

B.3. Other Funerary Customs

Before the pyre is lit, two odd rituals are performed, two rituals that are each attested in only one ancient source (see B.3 in table 3.1). Each rite supports Cicero's contention that "there *is* sensation in death,"[132] since these aspects of funerary practice are best explained by the belief that the corpse is being prepared for a rebirth. The first practice represents an inversion of what occurs immediately upon death. When the corpse has been placed on the pyre, Pliny tells us, it is a Roman custom to open the eyes of the deceased before lighting the funerary fire.[133] The corpse, having been born out of the society of the living, apparently needs to see its way in the existence into which it has been newly born; "it is wrong," Pliny writes, "that the eyes not be shown the sky." The second custom is attested in a second-century imaginary dialogue between the emperor Hadrian and the philosopher Epictetus. "Why," Hadrian asks, "do we bind the big toes of a corpse?" "Because," the philosopher replies, "then it will realize it is different after death."[134] In other words it will, after its rebirth has been successfully effected, look down at its toes with newly open eyes and know that something significant has changed.

B.4 Nine-Day Period after Burial

After the burial or entombment—that is, after, in the normal order of things, nine days have passed since death—the corpse is thought to have been successfully "unborn" out of the society of the living. The second phase of the dual burial as outlined by Hertz must now follow. The ritual must work to "ensure the soul peace and access to the land of the dead, and finally to free the living from the obligations of mourning." This phase is initiated, as I have indicated, by switching the corpse into proper birthing position, by opening its eyes, by binding its toes, and by the increased lamentation of the women. Eventually, this intense period of lamentation, a period marked by private grief of the closest friends and relatives, will come to an end. Closure is marked by the mourners removing their mourning clothes (see B.4 in table 3.1). As in a number of societies, termination of mourning coincides with the imagined end

---

[131] Lucr. 2.575–77 (see, too, 2.579–80). I am indebted to Michael J. Clarke for this reference.

[132] Cic. *Tusc.* 1.27.

[133] Plin. *nat.* 11.150.

[134] So I interpret Alterc. Hadr. et Epict. 26: *H. quare mortuo pollices ligantur? E. ut parem post obitum esse se nesciat.* Daly and Suchier 1939 record other possible interpretations (87 [the exchange conceals an etymology of *pollinctor*], 108 [*pollex* = "thumb"; various textual emendations]).

of the transition of the deceased into the next world.[135] This closure occurs in Rome at the funeral feast, the *novendialis*, which occurs *nine days* after the cremation or burial.[136] The number nine reappears to mark the second stage of ritual. When this period has terminated, women no longer have a role in the rite except to cleanse themselves in the *denicales*, to remove death from their persons (*de + nex*). This is undoubtedly the point at which the corpse becomes divine, to be recognized and honored henceforth at the annual festivals for the dead. This also appears to be when ritual burial disposes of the last remaining physical part of the dead, a joint of the finger that had been removed before cremation (*os resectum*).[137] With the passage of this second period of nine days, the deceased has completely departed, both spiritually and physically.

This second nine-day period may be compared with the interval that takes place between the time of birth and the naming of the newborn on the so-called *dies lustricus*. This naming ceremony, performed on the ninth day for sons (but, for an unclear reason, on the eighth for daughters), concludes a period during which "the child was apparently not fully included among human beings, and therefore was exposed to all sorts of malign influences."[138] Just as the newly deceased requires nine days before being effectively separated from his lived past, in an apparent inversion the newborn male must pass through a nine-day liminal period after birth before being marked with a name by the community. It is only then that his social identity can be attached to his physical presence.[139]

To repeat my main points: Roman funerary ritual does indeed replicate a dual birth process. The first escorts the dead from the land of the living, and the second ushers the corpse into its new life. I would like now to return to the swimming pool of the chapter's epigraph, to the subject of breast-feeding. The claim of the Vergilian scholiast that women rending cheeks and beating breasts to produce blood and milk to nourish the corpse no longer seems as absurd, at least not on a symbolic level, since it coincides with other physical actions on the part of mourning women. I would like to close, then, by considering evidence outside death ritual that indicates how, in Italic society, feeding an adult at the breast was seen as a way of ensuring immortality.

[135] Van Gennep [1908] 1960.147, who cites Hertz [1907] 1960.

[136] Petron. 65.10; Apul. *met.* 9.31 (*nono die*); Porph. Hor. *epod.* 17.48 (*nona die qua sepultus est*); Don. Ter. *Phorm.* 40.1. This period normally lasts seven days in Hebrew scriptures (Stählin 1965.838, 842); in classical Athens, it apparently did not end until the thirtieth day (Wyse 1904.264–65, with 243–44; Garland 1985.38–41); in other parts of Greece the period varied: Sparta, e.g., prescribed 11 days (Lécrivain 2.2: 1381).

[137] See Samter RE 5.219–20, on Varro *ling.* 5.23; see, too, Cic. *leg.* 2.55, Fest. p. 148.

[138] H. J. Rose 1924.210 on Plut. *mor.* 288C-E, where Plutarch offers potential explanations for the numbers eight and nine. Other important testimonia include Macr. *Sat.* 1.16.36, Paul. Fest. p. 120.

[139] Köves-Zulauf 1990.221–22. I am indebted for these parallels to a suggestion made by Jennifer Carlson.

Milk as Nurture for an Adult

The medical writers offer clear indications of the symbolic associations of breast-feeding. Galen attests to a traditional treatment for ailing elderly people that recommends drinking human milk. The nourishment is most effective, he writes, if taken directly from the breast (ἐντιθέμενος τῷ στόματι γυναικεῖον τιτθόν).[140] The effectiveness of this treatment can easily be rationalized: mother's milk was considered easily digestible and of course it provides adequate nourishment for the newborn. Nevertheless, two details given by Galen invite reflection: first, the specification that this treatment is intended for the elderly—that is, those nearing the ends of their lives—and second, that, if possible, the milk be sucked directly from a woman's breast.

Images of breast-feeding held far more importance in Italy than in classical Greece.[141] The silence of this plentiful visual evidence invites us to be more speculative. I would now like to look at four representations of suckling from different parts of Italy and Sicily in light of both the medical tradition just mentioned and the Roman mourning practice of beating the breast (see fig. 14). This Sicilian sculpture, from the sixth century BCE, depicts in native limestone the figure of a female suckling two children at her breasts. Its findsite indicates that the piece originally acted as a funerary marker. Arguing from this provenance, Holloway has recently compared Pausanias's description of the Chest of Cypselus in order to identify the group as mother Night suckling her children Sleep and Death.[142] While acknowledging that the subject is appropriate for a funerary monument, he does not speculate over why this new context, different from its apparent Greek model, would appeal to a sixth-century Sicilian—why depict Death feeding at the breast?

Moving to the north of Italy we encounter a depiction that seems independent of Greek precedent. A well-known, if mysterious, Greek myth records how the goddess Hera once suckled the infant Herakles. Even more mysterious is the spin put on the myth by the Etruscan tradition. Here it was understood that Uni (the Etruscan equivalent of Hera) suckles Hercle (Herakles) not while he was a child, but after his death.[143] Accordingly, Hercle could be depicted on Etruscan mirrors as an adult (see fig. 15). The suckling appears to represent the final step in the symbolic "adoption" of Herakles by Hera re-

---

[140] Galen περὶ μαρασμοῦ 7.701 (Kühn), following Euryphon and Herodikos (Deonna 1954.156; see, too, Artem. 1.16, where milk, presumably mother's milk, is taken by sick adults; Ps. Quint. decl. 10.3).

[141] Bonfante 1997, esp. 174, 184–88.

[142] Holloway 1991.82–83, citing Paus. 5.18.1. The identification is accepted by M. Bell 1993.366 and Bonfante 1997.179; contra Wilson 1994.217–18.

[143] Deonna 1954.155, 356; he also provides parallels in numerous cultures for lactation as a symbol of resurrection (157–66); see, too, Eitrem 1915.101–2; Cumont 1949.33–34; Gricourt 1957. For illustrations, see LIMC 5.1: 238–39, 253 (S. Schwarz, s.v. "Herakles/Hercle").

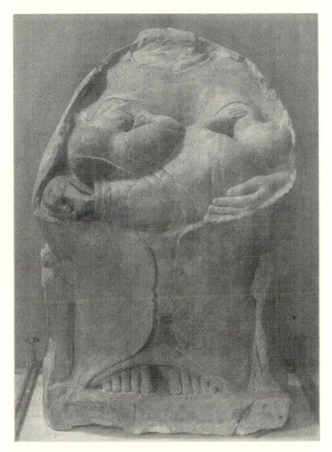

14. Mother-figure suckling twins (possibly Night suckling Sleep and Death). Limestone statue from Megara Hyblaia, Sicily. 6th–5th c. BCE. Museo Archeologico, Syracuse, Sicily, Italy (copyright Scala/Art Resource, NY).

corded in Greek sources.[144] After Herakles' death, it is only the nourishment of Hera's breast that guarantees his entry into Olympus as a deity, for it is through this milk that the human portion of Herakles obtains immortality. That this deathless quality of Hera's milk endured is supported by a seemingly later legend found in the *Geoponica*, a tenth-century-CE collection of much earlier agricultural lore. After telling how portions of Hera's milk scattered in the sky to produce the Milky Way, the author relates how some milk landed on earth to produce lilies, symbolic of death in antiquity because of their short

[144] At Diod. Sic. 4.39.2, Hera adopts Herakles by pretending to give birth to him; discussion in Deonna 1954.154–55; Wagenvoort 1956.136–38.

15. Etruscan mirror. Uni (Juno) suckling Ercle (Hercules). Museo Archeologico, Florence, Italy (after Gerhard et al. 1840-1897, vol. 5, pl. 60).

life spans.[145] Before leaving this mirror, I would like to list briefly other artifacts found in Etruscan funerary contexts that highlight further a probable relationship between breasts, lactation, and the notion of an afterlife for the deceased: the stylized breasts found at tomb entrances in the Banditaccia necropolis; a frieze of breasts depicted on a sixth-century-BCE cinerary urn from the same site; figurines of lactating women found in tombs throughout Etruria.[146] These scattered references further reinforce the fertile significance that Etruscans attached to the female breast.

These considerations of the associations of breast milk with death and immortality in Sicily and Etruria lead us to representations from Roman Pompeii. Figure 16 shows a wall painting that presents a theme borrowed from Greek models. The subject has come to be well known as a depiction of the girl Pero

[145] *Geoponica* 11.19; for lilies, see Austin 1977 on Verg. *Aen.* 6.883.
[146] Figurines: E. Richardson 1976.57–58 (with pl. XI) and, in general, Haynes 1971.14; cinerary urn from Banditaccia: Moretti 1975.5–7.

16. Wall painting of Micon and Pero from Pompeii (IX 2,5).
Museo Archeologico Nazionale, Naples, Italy (photo
Koppermann; Deutsches Archäologisches Institut
Rom, inst. neg. 66.1189).

suckling her father in prison in order to prevent him from starving to death.[147]
Tradition came to identify this story with the foundation of the temple of
Pietas in Rome's Forum Holitorium.[148] This way of representing filial devotion
embodied, apparently, some of the essence of Pietas. In a series of articles
published in the mid-1950s, Waldemar Deonna placed this legend in the context of adoption rituals, breast-feeding, and visual images such as the Etruscan
mirror of Uni nursing Hercle. This scene of Pero and Micon, he argues convincingly, originally depicted not a daughter with her dying father but a lactating woman ushering a dying man into a new world.[149] What is represented,
then, is not a man approaching death, but one being nourished into a new
life. Deonna does not mention the role of the breast in funerary lamentation
as I have been attempting to reconstruct it, but it is clear how our findings

[147] LIMC 7.1: 327–29 (G. Berger Doer, s.v. "Pero II").
[148] For the history of the connection, see Deonna 1954.364–71.
[149] Ibid., 361.

17. Marble relief from the "Fortunati" sarcophagus. Museo Nazionale, Rome, Italy (photo Koppermann; Deutsches Archäologisches Institut Rom, inst. neg. 65.1122).

depend upon complementary assumptions. In each case, female nurture is thought to offer immortality.

This quick tour of nursing images ends in Rome, with the most familiar image from that city: the she-wolf suckling the twin founders, Romulus and Remus. With over 220 visual examples extant, the depiction of the wolf rescuing Rome's foundling heroes far surpasses in quantity any other representation from Rome's mythical tradition; the next closest candidate is the Aeneas-Anchises group, of which only approximately 70 examples survive.[150] The image of the twins with the she-wolf has undeniable power as a symbol of Rome's permanence, a power clearly attested by its continued use to represent the modern city of Rome. And yet the popularity of the wolf and children as a sepulchral motif throughout the ancient Mediterranean indicates that they represented not simply the city itself, but the notion of the eternal aspect of Rome and its empire.[151] This immortalizing aspect of the group explains its placement on the sarcophagus illustrated in figure 17. On this relief the position of the suckling children under the lion protome on the left clearly contrasts the figure of three-headed Cerberus beneath the right-hand protome. The hell-hound of death balances the eternal life symbolized in the female wolf's actions.[152] To indicate further the expectation that the deceased will

[150] Schauenburg 1966.306, supplemented by Horsfall 1979.386–87; LIMC does not specify how many representations survive.

[151] Schauenburg 1966.304–9, who surveys other possibilities for their popularity in funerary art. The interpretation offered by Zanker 1988b.8–11 of the images of lactation on an Augustan altar is interesting but purely speculative.

[152] Schauenburg 1966.285–86, 304; Berczelly 1987.63, following Schauenburg, notes other, similar contrasts on the relief.

enjoy eternal life, the artist depicts him as one of the divine Muses, dressed in women's clothing.[153]

Schauenburg, in his persuasive survey of the funerary symbolism of the *lupa Romana*, also notes the popularity of the funerary motif of Telephus being suckled by a deer, and attributes this popularity to the occasional role that Telephus, like Romulus and Remus, occupies as an ancestor of the Roman people.[154] This surely could explain the choice of Telephus by a person commissioning a funerary monument, but our discussion suggests a deeper context within which the suckling Telephus would have particular appeal to a grieving Roman. Like the lupine wetnurse, who in rescuing Romulus and Remus offers them new life, the lactating deer extends to the corpse and the viewers of funerary art a promise of rebirth.[155]

CONCLUSION

During his travels through southern Italy in the early part of the twentieth century, Norman Douglas describes a rite he witnessed in a Roman Catholic church at Venosa, the birthplace of the Roman poet Horace. He was attracted by the unusual activity of a group of female pilgrims, who were gathered around a baptismal font that had been carved from an old Norman capital:

> Trembling with emotion, they perambulated the sacred stone, kissing every one of its corners; then they dipped their hands into its basin, and kissed them devoutly. An old hag, the mistress of the ceremonies, muttered: "tutti santi—tutti santi!" at each osculation. Next, they prostrated themselves on the floor and licked the cold stones, and after wallowing there awhile, rose up and began to kiss a small fissure in the masonry of the wall, the old woman whispering, "Santissimo!" . . . This anti-hygienic crack in the wall . . . attracted me so strongly that I begged a priest to explain to me its mystical signification. But he only said, with a touch of medieval contempt: "*Sono femine!*"[156]

Douglas seems satisfied with the priest's terse explanation, since he immediately turns to inquire about other items in the church that interest him. "They are women!" One can hear echoes in the priest's remark of the Roman authors who, two millennia earlier, attempted to attribute the activities of grieving women to an inherent emotional instability that requires no further scrutiny of details. I have attempted in this chapter to approach the ritual from the perspective of the participants. Perhaps these silent women do have something to say.

---

[153] Amedick 1993.146.
[154] Schauenburg 1966.294–95, 308. For Telephus and Rome, see Roscher 5.291–92.
[155] See, too, Dulière 1979.291, who notes that the newborn "n'est jamais qu'un mort en sursis."
[156] N. Douglas [1915] 1983.40.

In contrast to the ways in which gender-specific roles in mourning seem to function in other traditional societies, I hope I have shown how gender division in Roman funerary practice does not require us to regard women simply as scapegoats absorbing the pollution allegedly connected with death. Rather, the use of the body in mourning reinforces, through ritual, the roles appropriate to men and women in Roman society at large. Men maintain continuity in the community, while women regulate passage into and out of that community when it is disrupted by death. Women as gatekeepers during periods of transition may have a divine analog in an obscure goddess of archaic Rome, Genita Mana, who appears to have protected the life of residents within the household.[157] Her name clearly recalls the dual liminal function of human women, encompassing the notion of not only death (Mana; cf. Manes) but birth as well (Genita). This combination renders all the more interesting Pliny's note that the ancient Romans sacrificed to this goddess puppies not yet weaned of their mothers.[158] Birth, death, and nursing appear in combination yet again.

Perhaps, then, pseudo-Servius was not so far off. The breast Uni offers Hercle, the breast Pero offers Micon, the udder suckled by Romulus and Remus, and the breast the mourning woman at Rome offers to the corpse are part of the same gesture. Far from being intimidating, the association of birth, death, and nursing provides comfort. By placing ourselves in the position of a Roman woman, faced with the control of a human being at each terminus of its existence at birth and death, we can posit the inconceivable, a kind of mourning *not* accompanied by guilt and self-degradation.[159] The gestures of mourning women in ancient Rome—their blood, milk, and tears—celebrate the rejuvenating and life-giving powers of the female body.

---

[157] Wissowa 1912.240; see Guarducci 1946–1948.8 for Genita Mana's possible relation to the even more mysterious Parca Maurtia.

[158] Plin. *nat.* 29.58 (*catulos lactentes*).

[159] Pace Devereux 1982.168: "it is simply not conceivable that there should exist mourning *not* accompanied by a feeling of self-degradation and by manifestations of self-depreciation" (italics in original).

Chapter 4

POLITICAL MOVEMENT: WALKING AND IDEOLOGY IN REPUBLICAN ROME

DAUGHTER: Daddy, why do Frenchmen wave their arms so much?

FATHER: . . . What does it make you think when a Frenchman waves his arms?

DAUGHTER: I think it looks silly, Daddy. But I don't suppose it looks like that to another Frenchman. They cannot all look silly to each other. Because if they did, they would stop it, wouldn't they?

THE SHORT dialogue of Gregory Bateson from which I have taken this excerpt is entitled "Why do Frenchmen?"[1] In his title, Bateson intentionally omits a predicate, since the predicate is always shifting. At the same time, the question mark remains constant—"Why do Frenchmen?" As one reads the dialogue, the missing verbal idea moves from "wave their arms so much," to "act differently from us (that is, act differently from non-Frenchmen)." In part, of course, the French act differently because of various social and cultural factors in France, some of which could be traced historically, but of equal importance—and, I think, more interestingly—they act differently because we perceive them as acting that way. In Bateson's dialogue a question posed about a third party becomes an opportunity for self-reflection: why do *we* think arm-waving is funny? In other words, whenever we ask "Why do Frenchmen?"—or "Why does anybody?"—we are also asking "Why *don't* we?"

In the Roman Republic of the first century BCE, Cicero publicly voices similar questions concerning segments of his own society. Marcus Tullius Cicero was a prominent speaker and politician born outside Rome who became established as an important member of the urban elite, first by absorbing and then by perpetuating its most deeply held notions of the role of the citizen in the state. Essential to these notions is the need to restrict access to the elite. In this chapter I shall focus on a particular aspect of Cicero's polemic against his political opponents: his criticism of the way they walk. I do not,

---

[1] Bateson1972. 9–13; the quotation is from Bateson 1972.9–10.

however, want to learn why Cicero's opponents walk a certain way, so much as what investment Cicero has in showing that his opponents have a distinctive and distinguishing form of body movement. Or, to adapt the title of Bateson's essay, "Why do popular politicians?"

PHILOSOPHY IN ACTION

In chapter 1 I surveyed the ways in which bodily movements in Roman medicine and ritual depended on the notion that the human physique participates actively within its environment. As a consequence, physical movements, when properly orchestrated, are able to influence and manipulate the more-than-human world. In the present chapter I would like to demonstrate one way in which this notion manifests itself in the entirely human arena of Roman politics. Recent studies of bodily expression in antiquity have highlighted the importance the ancients attached to an individual's stride.[2] In the Roman Republic, as well, different forms of walking were used as a means of maintaining political and social boundaries. I am interested especially in why certain forms of movement had become standardized, and how the meanings of these movements were able to remain stable. This is what I mean by the "ideology" of this chapter's title: body movements have become systematized in such a way that some forms become perceived as natural and others as unnatural (contra naturam). The means available for judging the naturalness of bodily activity arise from the interplay between political posturing, audience expectations, scientific speculation, and the public spaces within which political debate occurred.

"Isn't it true that we consider many people worthy of our contempt when they seem, through a certain kind of movement or posture, to have scorned the law and limit of nature? (nonne odio multos dignos putamus, qui quodam motu aut statu videntur naturae legem et modum contempsisse?)"[3] This assertion, cast by the Latin particle nonne as a question with which the reader is expected to agree, appears near the end of Cicero's moral treatise On the Limits of Good and Evil. The context clarifies why Cicero must make this claim: he wishes to demonstrate that the workings of natural justice are discoverable and, for this to be so, nature must be decipherable in all its manifestations. The code for decipherment includes the marks nature fixes on the movement of its human participants. In the perfection that is Roman nature, the gods both witness and judge the actions of each individual within the community.[4] Fellow citi-

---

[2] Bremmer 1991; Gleason 1995.60–64. Church fathers: Adkin 1983. For John Wayne, see Wills 1996.

[3] Cic. fin. 5.47.

[4] Cic. leg. 2.16. Perfection of nature: for example, Cic. de orat. 3.178–79; nature as guide: Cic. Lael. 19, Cato 5.

zens have the ability to practice this kind of surveillance, as well. We read in Cicero's work *On the Nature of the Gods* that the properly discerning eye can recognize deviance in a human being's movement in the same way that it can judge an art object: the appraisal of how an artist employs color and shape and of how the individual embodies virtue and vice rests on similar assumptions.[5] In republican Rome, the reading of morality becomes an aesthetic practice, and one that can be learned. But like any aesthetic practice, the ability to make moral judgments endows authority only upon those with the time and opportunity to master its intricacies. Moral sensibilities become necessarily the sensibilities of the intellectual elite.

In this chapter, I shall borrow the French sociologist Pierre Bourdieu's notion of bodily *habitus*. Every social and economic group, Bourdieu has argued at length, can be characterized by a particular set of external characteristics he calls the *habitus*, as a function of which the political mythology particular to a given group is "*em-bodied*, turned into a permanent disposition, a durable way of standing, speaking, walking, and thereby of feeling and thinking."[6] Simply put, socioeconomic origins determine body language. According to Bourdieu's system, the various forms of the *habitus* affect and help define one another. In other words, in Cicero's day, the elite-based body of texts—both clearly prescriptive moralizing texts such as *On the Limits of Good and Evil* and public works of oratory, which play a less apparent but no less crucial role in political self-definition—all serve to enforce a particular aristocratic *habitus*. In response to this *habitus*, those persons who have been denied access to the elite create their own particular notions of behavior. From this perspective, bodily movements are not only the product of individual idiosyncrasies, but are an integral part of the way the individual interacts with the social world. All members literally embody the values of their *habitus*—the way you move your mouth or blow your nose or walk all become a function of background, both past and present.[7]

This theory of *habitus* is especially helpful in understanding political competition in the Roman world, for two reasons. First, it can allow access to the beliefs and manners of largely inaccessible members of Roman society—those not belonging to the traditional elite. In fact, an analysis of *habitus* may

---

[5] Cic. *nat. deor.* 2.145: *oculi in his artibus quarum iudicium est oculorum, in pictis, fictis, caelatisque formis, in corporum etiam motione atque gestu multa cernunt subtilius, colorum etiam et figurarum venustatem atque ordinem et, ut ita dicam, decentiam oculi iudicant, atque etiam alia maiora; nam et virtutes et vitia cognoscunt;* see, too, *off.* 1.128, *Lael.* 88. On modern linkings between aesthetics, ethics, and *habitus*, see generally Bourdieu 1984, esp. 44–50.

[6] Bourdieu 1990.69–70 (emphasis in original); 1984.170–75, passim, applies *habitus* to class structures in contemporary France.

[7] Bourdieu 1990.68 allows the possibility of changing one's *habitus* only "by a slow process of co-option and initiation which is equivalent to a second birth." Jenkins 1992.76–84 critiques Bourdieu's imprecision on this matter.

provide more insight than an explicit written work precisely because we are not asking what these people consciously think, but observing how beliefs have been embodied. *Habitus* expresses not what has been taught in the traditional sense, but what has been experienced: "It is because agents never know completely what they are doing that what they do has more sense than they know."[8] Second, Bourdieu's theories state in essence, but in a more objective and politically correct way, notions of social constructionism that are similar to those underlying the passage from Cicero I quoted earlier, about certain physical postures scorning the laws of nature. The properly discerning eye, concurs this respected twentieth-century critic of class structures, *can* judge the social status of a person by bodily movement: by being born into a certain *habitus*, each person becomes naturally inculcated as a representative, and a potential reproducer, of that *habitus*.

I do not wish to claim, however, that Romans continually monitored movements such as their walk. On the contrary, the very fact that physical movement is so often unconscious makes it a significant resource for gaining access to a given person's—or a given set of persons'—thoughts and beliefs, thoughts and beliefs that might otherwise be inaccessible. Our movements give ourselves away. In the particular case of Cicero, this hypothesis provides a nice tool of interpretation. We may not—and probably should not—always believe what Cicero says in a political speech about the nature of justice, but we have much less reason to doubt the accuracy of how he describes the physical movements of his enemies and allies. His audience, after all, was ever present, and the speaker held its attention with continual reminders to "look" at the evidence offered, as either physically present or accessible to the imagination. These frequent enjoinders to remain alert and use the eyes help explain why "Ciceronian oratory was . . . characterized by its constant allusions to 'things.' "[9] Oratory among the Romans, more than among the Greeks, appealed to the physical senses as much as to reason and emotion.[10] In a period when government was enacted most clearly in the exchange between orator and audience, the visual element of Roman oratory cannot be undervalued. Hence it is going too far to claim that for "Cicero this sort of dialogue with the crowd was a dangerous innovation which was all too like the uncontrolled license of Greek democracies."[11] While it is true that Cicero was no fan of what he perceived to be democracy, it does not necessarily follow that, as an orator, he neglected to take into account the power of his audience. It is instead through the very reliance on the concrete and the visible that the possible license of the crowd could be checked. In cases where Cicero offers

[8] Bourdieu 1990.69.
[9] Vasaly 1993.256.
[10] Pöschl 1975.215; A. Bell 1997.
[11] Millar 1995.112.

up physical movement for public scrutiny, his audience, presumably, could easily verify the validity of his descriptions. At the same time, however, I do not mean to claim that every description reveals a true and historically specific deviant act. Cicero is, of course, capable of exaggeration. But what cannot be doubted are the modes of representation that Cicero employs in describing ways of walking (and manner of dress), modes that must have had recognizable meaning to his contemporary Romans. As a result, when Cicero calls attention to an opponent's body language, I have decided to join his audience in taking notice, and in trying to make sense.

Underlying my investigation is the assumption that Cicero consistently applies his philosophical speculations to political practice. Even the casual reader of Ciceronian oratory, especially invective, is struck by the frequency with which opponents are characterized by descriptions that emphasize their sheer physicality. Cicero's oratory, I shall claim, attempts to represent physically the dominant political agendas of his period. Rather than involving simply ad hominem attacks, Roman invective against the gait is informed by a complex and yet coherent combination of physiognomics—the study of how physique indicates character—natural philosophy, and political competition. The urban elite, as the dominant force not only in the political sector of Roman society but in the cultural and educational sectors, as well, constructed an understanding of nature, a will to truth, by which they could maintain their own ascendancy.[12] When the senatorial-based party refers to itself as the *optimates*—that is, as literally "the best people"—they are not simply using transparent rhetoric. They are affirming their self-perceived and self-defined role as those who are by nature best suited to rule.

BODY MOVEMENT AND POLITICAL COMPETITION

In assessing the interrelationship between physical movement and political ideology, I shall be focusing both upon those politicians designated in extant texts as "popular" (*populares*) as well as upon other politicians perceived as presenting a threat to urban-based aristocratic politics in Rome. I shall try to explain, insofar as our sources permit, how these politicians walked. By this term *popularis*, I do not refer to a "political party" in the modern sense. Ancient historians now generally agree that these "popular" politicians were not so much defined by their membership since, like their opposition, the *optimates* or "best men," those labeled as *populares* came entirely from the Roman senate or senatorial class.[13] As is usual in the ancient world, attempts at political change—even of an apparently populist bent—originated from divisions

---

[12] For the will to truth, Foucault 1984.114.

[13] L. R. Taylor 1949.13 and n. 52; Meier 1965.572–83 can name only one *eques* who is called a *popularis* (L. Gellius Poplicola, at Cic. *Sest.* 110).

within the dominant classes, not as a result of protest from below.[14] In fact, these two groups, the *optimates* and the *populares*, were not even defined by a specific political program, but rather by their method: the *populares*, for example, took advantage of those aspects of the Roman political system that allowed them to bring about change through the people assembled as a whole, such as through public assemblies led by the tribunes of the plebs; the *optimates*, on the contrary, tended to act through the oligarchic senate.[15] The distinction between these groups, however, constantly blurs. Even the venue of the speaker could affect self-presentation, so that during his consulship Cicero could, when addressing the people, maintain he was a *popularis consul*.[16] One fact remains indisputable: *popularis* could provide an alluring label for Cicero, who uses it well over one hundred times in his orations to describe at times himself, but more often his most hated opponents. It is in what Cicero's use of this label evoked in the Roman audience that I am interested.

Perhaps the most fitting description for my purposes would be that the popular politicians were those individuals who presented themselves as not subscribing to the traditional values of the aristocracy at Rome. The historical record shows that this group had frequent successes in achieving its goals. In light of these successes, modern historians, most recently Fergus Millar, have used the abundant ancient testimonia describing the interaction between populace and speaker to argue that the Republic was structured much more as a democracy than has been previously acknowledged.[17] This may be true on a purely structural level, on what we might call a "constitutional" level, but on an ideological level things were different. An important feature distinguishes Roman politics from Athenian democracy: the fact that republican Rome was dominated by a firmly established oligarchy, one that has been claimed to wield "inherited, unchallenged authority."[18] And yet if the people as a whole had the potential to create change, why did elite ideology continue to dominate Roman politics? One fruitful approach to explaining this stability lies in examining the self-conscious exploitation of public display, as embodied in funeral processions, triumphs, and art.[19] Yet there simultaneously existed

[14] MacMullen 1966, esp. 242–43. Millar 1998 offers a model in which popular protest plays a more active role.

[15] L. R. Taylor 1949.12; Seager 1972; Gruen 1974, e.g. 27–28. Perelli 1982.5–21 offers a concise overview of scholarly debate on the issue.

[16] *Leg. agr.* 2.7–9; see, too, *Rab. perd.* 11. I follow the thesis of Perelli that *popularis* was meaningful as a label for a particular person at a particular time—an ambitious politician who advances his views by appealing to the voting potential of the disempowered citizenry (1982.5–21); compare North 1990b.18–19, Vasaly 1993.74, A. Bell 1997.3.

[17] Millar 1984, 1986, 1995, and 1998. Among the many responses to Millar, see Jehne 1995, Pina Polo 1996, and their bibliographies.

[18] North 1990b.15–17.

[19] For the role of display in promoting dominant values, see Gruen 1996 and the perceptive analysis of spectacle in Polybius by A. Bell 1997.3–5.

an equally effective way of maintaining ascendancy: in the assumptions and biases that were displayed less prominently by the very fact that they were encoded in the body. Regardless of how we may try to reconstruct actual factions and parties, public texts performed before the public eye constructed the popular politician as constituting a class of persons against whom any clear-thinking Roman must rebel. In other words, the elite as a body created a defense against the power that the Roman people held in theory.[20] I focus on nonverbal forms of representation because, as will become increasingly clear, Roman audiences were trained to decipher a speaker's politics without a word being spoken.

Jean-Michel David has focused on speaking styles as a way of showing what distinguishes the established orator in Rome from the fledgling provincials who are relatively new to big-city politics: their accent, pronunciation, sense of humor, and speaking gestures distinguish them as incompatible with the urban elite.[21] In turn, their opponents in Rome mark with a specific vocabulary these perceived threats to the dominant politics—their movements become labeled as "fierce" (*acer, vehemens*), their way of speaking as "rustic" (*rusticus*).[22] The belittling of fierceness and alacrity that we find in Rome has a parallel in fifth-century Athens, especially in the figure of the demagogue Cleon, whose violent movement, public shouting, way of dress, and frenetic stride marked his nontraditional approach to democratic politics.[23] This portrait is closely echoed in Plutarch's description of Gaius Gracchus, a figure whose innovative physical presence became the prototype for future politicians wishing to associate themselves with his style of antiestablishment politics: "intense and vehement, ... Gaius was the first Roman to walk around on the rostra and to pull the toga from his shoulders while speaking."[24] Cicero's own physical descriptions, then, inherit a tradition that aims not at specific individuals or specific programs, but at any perceived threats to the status quo. Moreover, the structures existing at Rome for the political advancement of young orators only served to validate the accuracy of these labels. To make a name for themselves, political outsiders commonly took on the role of prosecutors in the criminal indictment of established politicians.[25] This path to success, so common as to be almost traditional, could understandably lead to unpopularity

[20] Gruen 1991, esp. 252–54 discusses the importance of inquiring into the elite's "stimulus to unity rather than the mechanism of [its] fragmentation."

[21] David 1980 and 1983a; Ramage 1961 provides a collection of the evidence.

[22] *Acer* and *vehemens*: *Brut.* 130, 136, 186; *Clu.* 140. *Rusticus*: Ramage 1961.483–86. This behavior is to be distinguished from the use of *amplificatio*: Rhet. Her. 2.48–49; Cic. *inv.* 1.100–5, *S. Rosc.* 12; David 1979.153–62.

[23] Ps. Arist. *Ath. Pol.* 28.3, with Rhodes 1981.351–54; Plut. *Vit. Nic.* 8.3.

[24] Plut. *Vit. Ti. Gracch.* 2.2; David 1983b.

[25] David 1979 traces the political risks and rewards of this practice; see, too, David 1992.497–589.

among the powerful; as a result, rising newcomers ended up being objects of elite invective. In my subsequent remarks, then, I shall assent to the labels of the elite at Rome and refer to as "popular politicians" not persons representing a definable political platform or even necessarily a specific individual who has received the label *popularis*, but rather all those enemies whom the elite attack in their rhetoric for allegedly demagogic behavior.

MOVEMENT IN ORATORY AND PHILOSOPHY

A young orator at Rome would have heard something like the following at an early stage in his rhetorical training: "Every movement of the soul is endowed by nature with its own corresponding facial expression, voice quality, and gesture"; "gesture is used not merely to emphasize words, but to reveal thought—this includes the movement of the hands, the shoulders, the sides, as well as how one stands and walks."[26] In the early Empire, the rhetorician Quintilian was to continue this pedagogical tradition in his own treatise on the education of the orator. Among the fifty or so pages that he devotes to the various ways in which the orator should best position his head and fingers, Quintilian includes numerous references to how the gait conveys thought and intention, and how the speaker is justified in reproaching his opponent for the way he walks.[27] And yet stride reveals more than simply the presence or lack of refinement. Human beings, argues Cicero in his *On Duties*, are disposed by nature to disapprove morally of ways of sitting and standing that displease the eyes and ears. He includes among the postures especially to be avoided those of the effeminate and the rustic.[28] A letter by the philosopher Seneca further demonstrates that gait was believed to reveal not only temporary thought, but permanent dispositions of character. In attempting to teach his correspondent Lucilius how to distinguish between true and false praise, Seneca draws an analogy from daily life, an analogy that indicates common attempts to standardize body language: "Everything," he writes, "has its own indicator, if you pay attention, and even the smallest details offer an indication of a person's character. An effeminate man (*impudicus*) is revealed by his walk, from [the way] he brings his finger up to his head, and from his eye-movement. . . . For those qualities come into the open through signs."[29] The gait is an emerging indicator to watch for in oneself and to be wary of in others.

---

[26] See, for example, Cic. *de orat.* 3.216: *omnis . . . motus animi suum quendam a natura habet vultum et sonum et gestum* (for the triad of expression, voice, and gesture consult TLL 6.2: 1970.42–1971.45 [I. Kapp and G. Meyer]); *Brut.* 141 (Antonius's opinion); Val. Max. 8.10.1–2 (Hortensius); Sen. *epist.* 114.22.

[27] Quint. *inst.* 11.3.66, 124, 126, 150; *inst.* 1.2.31, 5.13.39.

[28] Cic. *off.* 1.128–29.

[29] Sen. *epist.* 52.12.

This conception of the body and its visible manifestations as a text to be read contributes also to the ambivalent relationship Roman orators had with theatrical actors. As is clear from epigraphic and other textual evidence, those actors at Rome who were citizens had limited civic rights, since their profession, predicated on public display and the need for profit, marked them as dishonorable.[30] Yet in spite of this lower status, recent studies justly remark on the orator Cicero's emphasis on theatricality, and accordingly the ancient rhetorical treatises continually stress how much a political speaker can gain from observing an actor.[31] In fact, Cicero and Demosthenes, the two ancient orators best known for their impeccable delivery, were both reputed to have trained with the best actors of their day. But these same treatises also include a caveat: imitate actors, but only up to a point.[32] What is signified by that point has been the topic of much recent discussion. Most obviously, the respectable orator could sacrifice his reputation from too close an association with the dishonorable character of the actor's profession. Too close a resemblance to acting could also endanger the masculine status of the speaker.[33] More importantly, the association will have had implications for the speaker's relation to truth. Treatises repeatedly stress how important it is that an orator's speech reflect true feelings; Cicero clearly draws this distinction between actor and public speaker in *On the Orator*, when he defines the medium of actors as "imitation" (*imitatio*) and that of the orator as "truth" (*veritas; de orat.* 3.215).[34] Hence the orator should cease from using the actor as a guide at that point at which the body stops imitating the movements of the soul and begins to display emotions that are no longer actually being felt internally. When Cicero finds himself in the potentially difficult position of speaking in defense of the comic actor Quintus Roscius, he steps over himself in apologizing for his client's chosen profession: "I swear to god! I speak with confidence: Roscius has in him more trustworthiness than artful skill, more truth than training. The Roman people judge him a better man than actor—his talent makes him as worthy of the stage as his restraint makes him worthy of the senate house."[35] In Roscius's case, humanity overshadows histrionics. Only through such an appeal can Cicero convince the jury of Roscius's believability.

[30] Iulian. *Dig.* 3.2.1, citing the praetor's edict (further, Ulp. *Dig.* 3.2.2.5); Gardner 1993.138–49; Edwards 1993.123–26 and Edwards 1997.

[31] See bibliography in Axer 1989, esp. 299–303, who offers a salutary refinement of previous views.

[32] A very select list: Rhet. Her. 3.26; Cic. *de orat.* 3.220, *Brut.* 203; Sen. *contr.* 3 praef. 3; Quint. *inst.* 1.11.3, 11.3.184; Mart. Cap. 5.543.

[33] Gleason 1995.105–7, 114–16; Richlin 1997.99–108. Edwards 1997, esp. 79–81.

[34] Select parallels: Phld. *Rh.* 1.195 (Sudhaus); Cic. *de orat.* 3.220, *Brut.* 87–88, *div.* 1.80; Quint. *inst.* 4.2.127; Gleason 1995.117, on Quint. *inst.* 1.11.9; Narducci 1997.77–96, who treats the apparently contradictory claim at Cic. *Tusc.* 4.55. Actors cannot blush: Sen. *epist.* 11.7; contrast Quint. *inst.* 6.2.36.

[35] Cic. *Q. Rosc.* 17. Cic. *de orat.* 1.132 preserves Roscius's own comments on propriety.

The careful distinction between actor and orator also explains the force behind a cryptic joke of Cicero. An opposing speaker had given a particularly serene performance in court, although he was referring to a time when Cicero's client had attempted to poison him. Cicero rebuked his opponent with the sarcastic question: "if you weren't faking it, would you be *acting* like that?" The pun on "acting" works in Latin as it does in English; in both languages the verb (*agere* / "to act") can describe the natural actions of the body as well as its self-conscious performance.[36] In this case, the speaker's bodily movement did not accurately reflect his expected internal anguish. The tirade did not simply involve an attempt at winning over the jury with his humor. Cicero recalls later how this remark helped dilute the believability of the charge of poisoning; the audience accepted the orator's contention that the body should not lie.[37] In his treatise *On the Orator*, Cicero has the great orator Antonius give the following praise to Lucius Crassus: "You are in the habit of representing such strength of spirit, such force, such grief, by using your eyes, expression, gesture—even with a single finger— . . . that you seem not only to ignite the judge, but to catch fire yourself."[38] And yet Crassus was known for his calm demeanor when speaking—his vehemence was projected instead through his language and the slight bodily indications noted by Antonius.[39] Not present was the physical excess that marked the actor. Crassus could convey emotions without appearing emotional, perform convincing actions without acting.[40] For the political speaker, then, gesture and idea must cohere. Marcus Scaurus, to cite another example, receives praise from Cicero for possessing such natural authority as an orator "that you'd think he wasn't pleading a case, but rendering testimony."[41] In light of these repeated assertions of how bodily demeanor contributes to persuasion, it comes as little surprise that the Romans were fond of repeating a story about Demosthenes, the finest orator of Athens; when asked what he thought were the three most important aspects of public speaking, Demosthenes replied, "Delivery, delivery, delivery."[42]

[36] *Brut.* 278: *tu istuc, M. Calidi, nisi fingeres, sic ageres?*; compare Val. Max. 8.10.3. Gotoff 1986.128 discusses a similar contrast in *On behalf of Caelius*; see, too, Cic. *S. Rosc.* 82, with Gotoff 1993.307–8.

[37] *Brut.* 278.

[38] Cic. *de orat.* 2.188. The "single finger" seems to be the index (Quint. *inst.* 11.3.94).

[39] Cic. *Brut.* 158: *non multa iactatio corporis, non inclinatio vocis, nulla inambulatio, non crebra supplosio pedis.*

[40] The illustrated manuscripts of Terence do not seem to illuminate the relationship between acting and rhetorical training. Weston 1903.37 and Aldrete 1999.54–67 attempt to connect these illustrations with the oratorical gestures in Quint. *inst.* 11.3; Maier-Eichhorn 1989.145–49 effectively casts doubt on such attempts.

[41] Cic. *Brut.* 111.

[42] Phld. *Rh.* 1.196 (Sudhaus); Cic. *Brut.* 142, *de orat.* 3.213; Val. Max. 8.10. ext. 1; Quint. *inst.* 11.3.6; Plut. *Vit. Dem.* 8.

MOVEMENT IN DAILY LIFE

This attention to fine points of movement was not confined to those trained in rhetoric and philosophy. As early as the third century BCE, the family of Claudia described on her epitaph not merely her skills as a conversationalist, but how her walk was appropriate to her station in life (*sermone lepido, tum autem incessu commodo*; CLE 52.7). I mentioned in the previous chapter how, in the public staging of funeral processions, the elite hired actors to impersonate deceased ancestors. Among the features of these ancestors that our sources single out as worthy of imitation is their particular way of walking.[43] The audience of Roman comedies was also expected to recognize correlations between movement and character—members of the dominant class move slowly upon the stage, whereas slaves, attendants, and workers were marked by stereotypically swift movements.[44] Further proof that the different codes for walking were widespread is found in the fact that transgressing them provided opportunities for mockery. In the *Poenulus* of Plautus, some pretentious legal advisors are made to justify their calmness by proclaiming that a moderate gait marks a freeborn person, whereas to run about in a hurry bespeaks the slave.[45] In fact, the "running slave" appears so often in Roman comedy as to render the expression almost tautological.[46] The literary tradition depicts the gods themselves as conscious of the ways human beings move. In Vergil's *Aeneid*, Cupid's impersonation of the young Ascanius involves mimicking his gait, whereas Iris's disguise as Beroe is penetrated in part because the goddess fails to walk appropriately.[47] Indeed, when hymns request the appearance of a deity, Greeks and Romans commonly paid special attention to the gait the divinity should adopt upon visiting the person praying.[48]

The type of walk adopted could also convey an individual's sexuality. Among Ovid's instructions in his *Art of Love* are details on the carriage that a woman should adopt to best attract a man.[49] In this area, a particularly telling anecdote comes from Petronius's romance, the *Satyricon*. The maid Chrysis remarks at one point in the story to the hero Encolpius: "I don't know how to predict the future from bird signs, and I don't usually bother with the zodiac, and yet I infer character from the face (*ex vultibus*), and when I see somebody

---

[43] Diod. Sic. 31.25.2: μιμητὰς ἔχοντες ἐκ παντὸς τοῦ βίου παρατετηρηκότας τήν τε πορείαν καὶ τὰς κατὰ μέρος ἰδιότητας τῆς ἐφάσεως (see, too, Polyb. 6.53.6: ὡς ὁμοιοτάτοις εἶναι δοκοῦσι κατά τε τὸ μέγεθος καὶ τὴν ἄλλην περικοπήν).

[44] Quint. *inst.* 11.3.112.

[45] *Poen.* 522–23: *liberos homines per urbem modico magis par est gradu / ire; servile esse duco festinantem currere*; see, too, Turp. *com.* 102.

[46] See esp. Ter. *Haut.* 37; Lindsay 1900.294–95.

[47] Verg. *Aen.* 1.690; 5.646–49 (Apul. *met.* 10.32 describes the walk of "Venus").

[48] Fraenkel 1957.204 n. 4.

[49] Ov. *ars* 3.298–310.

walking, I know what they're thinking."[50] This Petronius passage, I should
note, depicts the maid discussing the walk that characterizes a male prostitute.
This is not an irrelevant coincidence. It's not a big step to move from the walk
of the effeminate male to that of the popular politician of the late Republic. In
fact, I will argue that it is the same step.

INCESSUS IN CICERO

The word most commonly used in invective texts to describe a person's walk
is *incessus* (the corresponding verbal form *incedo*, on the contrary, occurs only
twice in Cicero outside of quotations). The words alone appear to be colorless,
meaning simply "to travel by foot," and they can designate any type of gait,
from a slow stride to speedy determination.[51] Like the maid in Petronius or
the watchful Seneca, however, the spectator of Roman oratory would have
had no trouble discerning the reasons why a public speaker such as Cicero
would choose to call attention to his opponent's gait. A passage from his
speech on behalf of Sestius exhibits Cicero's two principal uses of this practice.
Amid vicious invective against two of his favorite enemies, Piso and Gabinius,
Cicero exclaims to the jury:

> quorum, per deos immortales! si nondum scelera vulneraque inusta rei publicae
> vultis recordari, vultum atque incessum animis intuemini. (*Sest.* 17)

> By the immortal gods! if you're not ready yet to recall the crimes and wounds
> with which Piso and Gabinius have branded the state, then consider in your minds
> their expression (*vultus*) and their walk (*incessus*).

As I shall demonstrate below, Cicero refers here to two distinct types of stride:
in the case of Piso, to an affected stately gait; in the case of Gabinius, to an
effeminate stroll. These two types correspond to the dichotomy of the walk
offered by the extant surviving texts on physiognomy—those scientific texts
that are predicated on the notion that the universe is rational, consistent, and
decipherable.[52] On the one hand, writers describe the feigned gait (*incessus
affectatus*), by which individuals try to suppress their true nature; and on the
other, the "natural" walk (*naturalis*), which a spectator can use to read character. Piso's walk, in fact, is too impressive—"how monstrous was his walk, how
aggressive, how frightening to behold!"[53] His gait exceeded the moderation of
the normal magistrate, cultivating instead a showy appearance worthy of the
excesses of the trendy shopping districts of Capua, where his arrival is likened

---

[50] Petron. 126.3.
[51] Köstermann 1933; Horsfall 1971.
[52] Gleason 1995.29–37 provides a review of the physiognomical writings.
[53] *Sest.* 19: *quam taeter incedebat, quam truculentus, quam terribilis aspectu.*

to a *pompa*, a formal procession.[54] Since he does not have the gentle inclination of the head that the physiognomists ascribe to the *magnanimus*, he betrays himself by being too serious, too *gravis*.[55] Cicero advises in *On the Limits of Good and Evil* against affecting a walk that is too pompous, and the physiognomic treatises declare this practice to be especially dangerous, warning that those who feign a dignified walk are "easily uncovered as their true nature conquers them, and leaves them naked."[56]

The tribune Rullus also adopted an outward appearance, resembling Piso's in its intent to deceive. Cicero claims that one of the credentials that allowed Rullus to present the land bill of 63 BCE was his ability to project an exceptionally aggressive persona. Among the external features he adopts—worn clothing, shaggy beard and hair, a generally unkempt countenance—Cicero includes aspects of his physical demeanor. Rullus presents to the Roman people a new countenance, voice, and walk. Cicero suggests that Rullus adopted these elements of deportment to convey bodily the power of the office of tribune.[57] These attacks by Cicero would seem to provide rare instances in which seeming is not being, since his invective normally depends upon the ability to read morality from a person's appearance. And sure enough, Cicero spends the bulk of his invective speeches against Piso and Rullus exposing their hypocrisy and demonstrating that they are not, and never have been, what they seem. As a result, in both cases Cicero is careful to stress that the appearances of his opponents are far from natural. In fact, the word *truculentus*, commonly used to denote the behavior of beasts or of men who act like beasts, occurs only twice in Cicero's speeches: to describe the physical deportment of Rullus and Piso. Like the actor whose extreme showiness the training orator is warned to avoid, these men adopt walks that go over the top. Their motions are calculated to deceive the people. By appealing to gait, Cicero can prove this assertion through visual cues. In the case of Rullus he recalls the tribune's dissimilar appearance in the past; Piso is exposed by his overly solemn eyebrows and the revelation that he has assumed a false name.[58]

The exposure of Rullus and Piso depends upon showing the audience how to penetrate and read through appearances. More commonly the relationship between internal character and its external manifestation is more direct: Cicero claims that a walk directly reveals a depraved character. The popular poli-

[54] *Pis.* 24: *fuit pompa, fuit species, fuit incessus saltem Seplasia dignus et Capua*; for criticism of walking as if in a *pompa*, see Cic. *off.* 1.131.

[55] Physiogn. 76; see, too, Hor. *sat.* 2.3.310–11: *corpore maiorem rides Turbonis in armis / spiritum et incessum.*

[56] *Fin.* 2.77. Physiogn. 74; Gleason 1995.76–81.

[57] *Leg. agr.* 2.13: *truculentius se gerebat quam ceteri. iam designatus alio voltu, alio vocis sono, alio incessu esse meditabatur, vestitu obsoletiore, corpore inculto et horrido, capillatior quam ante barbaque maiore, ut oculis et aspectu denuntiare omnibus vim tribuniciam et minitari rei publicae videretur.*

[58] Rullus: *Leg. agr.* 2.13; Piso: *Pis.* 1 and frg. 8; see further Corbeill 1996.169–73.

tician in particular seemed to have his own distinct gait. In a digression on
the sensitivity of Roman crowds to contemporary political issues, Cicero discusses the fame of Saturninus and the Gracchi, three popular tribunes from
Roman history (the word Cicero uses to describe them is *populares*). The men
were always greeted wildly in public assemblies. The people, Cicero tells us,
"loved these men's name, speech, face, . . . and walk" (*Sest.* 105: *horum homines
nomen, orationem, vultum, incessum amabant*). Cicero calls attention to similar
features of the Antonii brothers in his *Thirteenth Philippic*: their mouths, faces,
breath, look, and manner of walking all indicate, in Cicero's words, that "if
they have a place in this city, there will be no room for the city itself" (13.4).
The walk again intrudes with teasing concision—its connotations presumably
clear to Cicero's audience. A section of *On Duties* in which Cicero warns his
son Marcus against an excessively slow walk permits us to reconstruct something of those connotations: deviation from a normal speed makes it more
difficult for a person to observe propriety.[59] Still, precision is wanting. Cicero
the orator seems unwilling to describe the walk in detail, and yet the context
shows he probably did not have the need. Even when not immediately visible
as Cicero delivered his attack, the opponents he describes are well-known
public figures. Even if the modern reader allows room for exaggeration, this
repeated emphasis on gait indicates that his audience must have recognized
something behind Cicero's references.

CINAEDI AND ELITE POLITICIANS

> May those who love us, love us.
> And those that don't love us, may God turn their hearts.
> And if He doesn't turn their hearts, may He turn their ankles,
> So we'll know them by their limping.
> —Gaelic blessing

The modern reader of Republican Roman texts that mention bodily movement needs to go further than the words that have come down to us. It is
possible, I believe, to recover from our extant texts the connotations of the
popular walk by carefully considering what type of invective is applied toward
whom, and by accepting Bourdieu's contention that the body languages of
different social and political classes are in a constant state of mutual determination: if the dominant class behaves in one way, it does so in a negative-
feedback relationship with nondominant groups. I begin from the abuse levied
against three men in particular, three men closely allied to what were usually
recognized as "popular" causes: Sextus Titius, Publius Clodius, and Aulus Ga-

---

[59] *Off.* 1.131.

binius. Gabinius, as I have already mentioned, was notorious for his effeminacy, and on one occasion Cicero calls him a "female dancer" (*saltatrix*; *Pis.* 18). Similarly, Clodius's impersonation of a woman during the Bona Dea scandal gave rise to accusations that he had the walk (*incessus*) and voice of a "Greek female lyre player" (*psaltria*; *In Clod.* 21). Titius, a tribune of the plebs, was so gentle in his bodily movements that a dance, the "Titius," was named in his honor (*Brut.* 225). Similar charges were levied against the great orator Hortensius, whose politics would seem to make him out of place in this company.[60] Perhaps it is relevant that the one attested attack on him occurred when defending an alleged ally of the Catilinarians, a particularly notorious group of *populares* who were thought to dance naked at predawn banquets.[61]

All this emphasis on dancing and graceful movement becomes suspicious in light of one of Quintilian's guarded remarks regarding the education of the public speaker. The rhetor, he says, is justified by precedent in allowing potential orators to study under instructors of bodily movement, who will teach proper positioning of the arms and hands, as well as the appropriate ways to stand and walk. During boyhood, however, the instruction must only be of limited duration and, once the boy reaches adolescence, it should be stopped altogether.[62] To show that he has given this matter sufficient consideration, Quintilian justifies the teaching of dance through such respectable precedents as Platonic philosophy, Spartan military training, and archaic Roman religious practice. The reason for Quintilian's uneasiness about dance instruction becomes clear from a complaint of Scipio Aemilianus uttered over two hundred years earlier: young Romans "are learning to sing, something our ancestors wanted to be considered disgraceful to the freeborn; they go, I say, to dancing school, freeborn girls and boys among the *cinaedi*."[63] Scipio plays here with the Greek loan-word *cinaedus*. As is commonly known, this word, a frequent term for referring to a dancer in early Latin, denoted in Greek culture the sexually penetrated male in a homoerotic relationship. By this point it should come as little surprise to learn that numerous texts—both political and nonpolitical—attest that the *cinaedus* revealed himself by his walk.[64] As was the case with studying under an actor, Quintilian seems to fear that students may learn too much.

---

[60] Gell. 1.5.2–3 (ORF 92.XVI offers historical testimonia); for Hortensius's histrionic delivery, see, too, Cic. *Brut.* 303, Val. Max. 8.10.2; Berry 1996.24–26.

[61] For the connotations, see Corbeill 1996.138–39.

[62] Quint. *inst.* 1.11.15–19, who particularizes the instruction as a type of dance: *neque enim gestum oratoris componi ad similitudinem saltationis volo*; 1.12.14.

[63] Macr. *Sat.* 3.14.7 = ORF 21.30.

[64] Walk of *cinaedi* or effeminate males: Varro *Men.* 301, with CIL 4.1825 and Cèbe (1987) 8.1324–25; Sen. *contr.* 2.1.6; Phaedr. 5.1.12–18; Sen. *epist.* 114.3; Petron. 119, l. 25; Juv. 2.17; Quint. *inst.* 5.9.14; Carm. *ad senat.* 13; Housman on Manil. 4.519. Compare Zeno SVF 1.82; Cic. *off.* 1.129. On the *cinaedus* in general, see Richlin 1993, Parker 1997, C. Williams 1999.160–224.

Turning to how the writers on physiognomy describe the *cinaedus*, one can discover striking correspondences between the movement of the sexually submissive male and the popular politician of the Republic. What seems to emerge is that *cinaedi* divide into two types: those that try too hard to hide their natures, and those for whom their "true" movements are observable. Among the former strides Rullus, distinguishing himself among his tribunician colleagues: he steps very slowly with a feigned aggressiveness. The latter group encompasses our dancing politicians: their arms and fingers gesticulate in a manner overexuberant for a person moving at a leisurely pace, and both the neck and the sides of the torso sway gently from side to side.[65]

In contrast, the elite politician—or the politician who wishes to appear allied with the elite—can also be described as he walks before his colleagues. Extant texts prescribe for the aristocrat a way of walking in direct contradistinction to the type I have been reconstructing for the popular politician. A full gait, according to the second-century-CE physiognomist Polemon, exhibits loyalty, efficacy, a noble mind, and the absence of anger.[66] Cicero requires the same type of stride for the proper orator, without alluding to physiognomic principles. He also adds features that directly oppose the physiognomist's vision of the *cinaedus*: keep the neck and fingers still and the trunk straight, bending it only as a man does; the right arm should remain close to the body, extended solely in times of impassioned delivery. In other words, "let nothing be superfluous" (*nihil ut supersit*).[67] As for speed, these empiricists advise the elite politician to be slow—*bradus* in Greek, *gravis*, not surprisingly, in Latin—but not too slow, for that marks a lack of effectiveness.[68] It was tricky to maintain the appropriate balance; hence Cicero's admiration of Crassus's ability to effect the difficult combination of being both dignified and elegant.[69] Criticism could also arise if the speaker was overly erect in the upper body—this overcompensation appears to be what betrayed the hypocrite Piso and was later to constitute part of Augustus's criticism of the way Tiberius carried

---

[65] Ps. Arist. *Phgn.* 808a 14–15: ἡ μὲν [βάδισις] περινεύοντος, ἡ δὲ κρατοῦντος τὴν ὀσφυν; Physiogn. 74: *et collum et vocem plerumque submittunt et pedes manusque relaxant*; . . . *plerumque etiam oscitantes detecti sunt*; 98 and 115 (numerous details); Polemon 50: *latera moventem articulosque agitantem.* Herter (1959) 4.635–36 offers evidence from other kinds of texts.

[66] Polemon 50; compare Ovid's *Tragoedia* (*am.* 3.1.11). For Greek precedents, see Bremmer 1991.16–20.

[67] Cic. *orat.* 59; see, too, *de orat.* 3.220; Sen. *epist.* 40.14, 66.5. Efron [1941] 1972.22 discusses how researchers of the Third Reich reached quite different conclusions about their Mediterranean neighbors, whose "mental energies are all turned rather outwards, in the Nordic inwards. . . . Mediterranean ferment stands opposed to Nordic restraint" (citing H. Günther, *Rassenkunde des deutschen Volkes* [Munich 1925]).

[68] Physiogn. 100, with André 1981 ad loc.; Clem. Al. *Paed.* 3.11.73. *Gravitas* as a moral and political designation: Achard 1981.392–99; Hellegouarc'h 1972.279–94; Wagenvoort 1947.104–19, who speculates over the word's semantic evolution.

[69] *Brut.* 158; see, too, *Brut.* 143.

himself.[70] Instead, the neck should lean slightly forward in a sign of determination while the shoulders gently move. In a word, remarks the pseudo-Aristotelian treatise on physiognomics, the dignified man walks like that "most male of animals," the lion.[71]

This reconstruction of the elite walk recalls one of the emperor Augustus's cryptic mottoes—"hurry up . . . slowly."[72] That the emperor was conscious of the public recognition of proper modes of walking is clear from a letter he wrote to his wife Livia, in which he worries about the walk of the young Claudius.[73] In fact, the motto "Hurry up . . . slowly" may find concrete exposition in the famous statue of Augustus from Prima Porta. One art historian has argued in detail that the position of the feet in the Polykleitan antecedent of this sculpture depicts a man commencing "very slow gait activity."[74] And yet the Roman artist has adapted his model, making the original statue more tense and concentrated. The result is that Augustus, although stopped in movement, presents an impression of potential motion different from that of the Greek model: "his next step is unimaginable, as is his prior one."[75] The ready determination of Augustus's pose, in other words, quite possibly finds its inspiration not only in artistic precedents, but in an elite ideology of the body.

Types of walk provide a model for how ideology permeated Roman society at all levels. Moralizing texts of Cicero's day such as I quoted in my opening remarks assert that nature desires internal character to be manifested externally. Judging a human being according to physical movement was not simply a social construction that went unexamined. Rather, this notion, a notion upon which the entire study of physiognomy was based, depends upon an understanding of what is essential—and not constructed—about being a human being. By simple observation, we recognize that proper care of the body undoubtedly affects clarity of thought and so, it follows, the soul must conversely affect the body. Beginning from this premise, a close empirical observation of nature—"science"—combined with a speculation on the origin of the world and its inhabitants—"philosophy"—becomes a powerful *political* tool, a way of separating us from them, a way of proving, from objective, external signs, who is naturally born to lead and who, misled, is simply dancing his way through politics.

---

[70] Physiogn. 75; compare Cic. *off.* 1.131. Tiberius: Suet. *Tib.* 68.3, Tac. *ann.* 1.10.7.

[71] Ps. Arist. *Phgn.* 809b 15–35 (summarized in Polemon 50). Winkes 1973.902–5 considers whether Roman artists attempted to express leonine characteristics in portraiture.

[72] Suet. *Aug.* 25.4 (σπεῦδε βραδέως); Gell. 10.11.5.

[73] Suet. *Claud.* 4.5. Pliny, by contrast, praises Trajan's stride for matching the vigor of his soul (*paneg.* 83.7).

[74] Tobin 1995.52–64.

[75] Kähler 1959.13 ("Anders als beim Doryphoros ist ihr nächster Schritt undenkbar, der vorige ist es ebenso").

But an important question remains; if there really did exist some kind of political etiquette of bodily aesthetics, and if it really were so all-pervasive as I
claim, then why would anyone even bother to try to violate it? In other words,
if there were some transitive equation between being a popular politician, an
effeminate male, and a social deviant, then what prevents someone like Gabinius from simply moving with more determination and holding his head and
flanks still? I would like to suggest three possible answers: they entail 1) access
to education; 2) the topography of political debate; and 3) willful self-definition on the part of the popular politicians themselves.

1. Education

I have already mentioned David's research on "popular eloquence" (*eloquentia
popularis*)—that is, the speaking style of political newcomers, people who may
have been important in their native communities but who, upon arrival in
the big city, became labeled because of their non-Roman style of pronunciation, use of vocabulary, and even sense of humor.[76] I would add that these
newcomers also probably had styles of deportment that distinguished them
from their counterparts in the urban elite. Numerous examples survive, as we
have seen, describing the ways in which rhetorical treatises from ancient
Rome instruct their pupils in proper body language. Other ancient references
make it clear that this kind of physical training would have been clarified and
reinforced through constant practice before a teacher.[77] In fact the *Rhetorica
ad Herennium*, an anonymous rhetorical treatise from the early first century
BCE containing the kind of instruction that Cicero and his elite contemporaries would have received, apologizes for even trying to discuss delivery in a
written form. When he reaches the point in his discussion where he must
begin to give details, the lesson abruptly ends: "the rest we'll leave for practice
drills" (*reliqua trademus exercitationi*).[78] The meaning of the visible becomes,
in effect, invisible to the reading audience.

So it seems likely that in the late Republic the means of learning proper
gesture rested with those who had access to an urban education. Urban education at this period would have entailed intimate association with members of
the elite, an education recently characterized as "wordless replication of the

---

[76] David 1980 and especially 1983a.

[77] Sen. *epist.* 94.5, 8.

[78] Rhet. Her. 3.27; see also 3.19: "No one has written carefully on delivery;" he either does not
know or respect the work of L. Plotius Gallus (Quint. *inst.* 11.3.143). Quintilian seems to have
been the first writer to describe oratorical gesture in any detail (Cousin [1935] 1.626–27); for
Theophrastus's lost work on delivery, see Fortenbaugh 1985.

elite *habitus*."[79] What is more, during this period rhetorical training would have been almost entirely in Greek, not Latin, thereby further restricting the class of students who could learn at these schools.[80] When Latin teaching was eventually introduced, it gained immediate popularity, as students flocked to lessons.[81] In fact, in the early first century, rhetoricians in Rome who tried, for the first time, to establish schools for the instruction in Latin of potential orators, were rebuked in an edict from the censors on the grounds that—to quote the words of the censors—"our ancestors have decided what they wanted their children to learn and what schools they should attend."[82] Cicero puts in the mouth of Crassus, one of the censors responsible for this edict, the additional opinion: "these new teachers could teach nothing—except daring."[83] Is this a distinctly Roman appeal to tradition?[84] Or do we have here a means of maintaining the ascendancy of the elite, who of course are the *real* descendants of "our ancestors?" It is an intriguing coincidence that Lucius Plotius Gallus, one of the rhetors at whom this edict seems to have been aimed, wrote in Latin a work on gesture—perhaps the first such work entrusted to writing.[85] Here as elsewhere, we are hampered from further conclusions by the fact that direct references to the edict are confined to elite sources. But to have had available a written text on gesture would of course risk raising questions about the validity of the elite model, by which items of decorum such as stance, carriage, and gesture are not "learned" but, in the words of Bourdieu, "are able to pass directly from practice to practice without moving through discourse and consciousness."[86] A Greek philosopher, writing on rhetoric at about the same period as Plotius Gallus and probably in Italy, echoes this sentiment of Bourdieu, giving clear voice to what I believe the censors couched in their language of tradition. Philodemus writes: "Instruction in delivery is a product of recent foolishness. . . . The writers on rhetoric are in fact making clear a basic truth that is hidden by politicians, namely that they are designing their delivery to appear dignified and noble and, most of all, to mislead their audience."[87]

[79] Gleason 1995.xxv conjectures that the proliferation of written handbooks during the second century CE corresponds to a broadening of education that allowed greater permeation into the cultural elite (which can no longer be identified with the political elite); see further 162–68.

[80] Cic. *Brut.* 310; cf. Quint. *inst.* 1.1.12; Corbeill 2001.

[81] Cic. apud Suet. *rhet.* 26.1; Rawson 1985.146–47 discusses teaching resources available in Latin.

[82] Suet. *rhet.* 25.2: *maiores nostri quae liberos suos discere et quos in ludos itare vellent instituerunt*, 26.1; Cic. *de orat.* 3.93–94; Gell. 15.11.2; Tac. *dial.* 35.1. For bibliography, see Gruen 1990.179–91; Kaster 1995.273–75, 292–94; Pina Polo 1996.65–93.

[83] *De orat.* 3.94.

[84] Gruen 1990.179–91 examines the paradox of Greek training becoming an integral part of Roman tradition. See further Corbeill 2001.

[85] Quint. *inst.* 11.3.143.

[86] Bourdieu 1990.74.

[87] Phld. *Rh.* 1.200–1 (Sudhaus); my translation borrows from Hubbell 1919–1920.301.

2. Topography

Archaeological studies of the past two decades indicate that beginning around 290 BCE the comitium at Rome consisted of a space measuring approximately 1000 square feet, situated between the speaker's platform at the Republican rostra and the senate house, the *Curia Hostilia*.[88] By this reconstruction, in the third century the Roman citizenry assembled as a whole would have been sandwiched in an open-air space between the speaker and the senate house. It is little wonder that literary sources regard it as a popular move when in 145 BCE the tribune Gaius Licinius Crassus transferred popular legislation from this limited area to the more spacious Forum.[89] In a similar, but likely separate, move, Gaius Gracchus first began the practice of addressing from the rostra the people assembled in the Forum—and not in the comitium. The man who, as noted earlier, fashioned a public *habitus* that became identifiable with his popular intentions, also refashioned spatial relations in the forum through a move Plutarch hails as another step toward "democracy" (*demokratia*).[90] Plutarch's enthusiasm about the change in venue entices us to agree with recent claims that the Roman Republic functioned more as a popular democracy than is normally recognized.[91] In this context, Millar has appositely observed that the comitium has much greater importance in the archaeological and literary record when compared with the meeting places of the Senate.[92] And it is in open spaces like the comitium and elsewhere in the Roman Forum, as opposed to within the roofed and walled curia, where the majority of the texts I have been examining were played out. But what had the two tribunes Crassus and Gracchus achieved other than provide a larger area for popular assemblies, which could number several hundred people in the comitium but approximately six thousand in the open forum?[93] The dynamic between speaker and audience has not changed, and in fact I will argue that the new orientation, resulting in a larger and more dispersed group of auditors, serves only to increase the distinction between senatorial-based and popular-based political appeals. Cicero himself points to one feature of the new dynamic. The arrangement by which the crowd faces the speaker, framed by the senate-house, creates a situation in which "the curia watches over and presses upon the speak-

---

[88] Coarelli (1992) 1.148–51, summarized by him in LTUR s.v. "comitium," argues that the space was circular; Carafa 1998.132–51 reexamines the evidence to show that the space was triangular (Mouritsen 2001.18–19 is skeptical about Carafa's conclusions).

[89] Cic. *Lael.* 96; Varro *rust.* 1.9.

[90] Plut. *Vit. C. Gracch.* 5.3; I follow Coarelli (1992) 2.157–58 in distinguishing between the actions of Crassus and Gracchus, contra L. R. Taylor 1966.23–25.

[91] Millar 1984, 1986, 1995, 1998; Thommen 1995.363.

[92] Millar 1989, esp. 141.

[93] Estimates from Thommen 1995.364.

er's platform, as an avenger of rashness and a regulator of civic duty."[94] Visually, the senatorial element of the government looms larger than ever before.

Archaeologists have reconstructed the comitium in Rome in part by comparison with other extant comitia in Italy and Sicily. I am not here concerned so much with their reasoning—although the identification of these provincial structures is not entirely certain—as much as with a singular and obvious way in which the meeting places outside the capital seem *not* to be parallel.[95] Simply put, outside of Rome no traces of a rostrum survive, and there are no clear indications that a raised speaker's platform parallel to the type found in Rome ever existed.[96] Moreover, and as a result, it seems likely that, as in Greek places of assembly during the Hellenistic period, everywhere in Italy but at Rome the speaker spoke *up* to the citizens assembled around him.[97] Detienne has neatly demonstrated how this arrangement, with speaker at center (ἐς μέσον), provides a physical analog to the value Greek society placed on democracy and equality of speech.[98] Contrast then the situation in Rome, where the elevated magistrate literally looks *down* upon (*despicere*) his listeners.[99] In both civil and criminal proceedings, the presiding magistrate sits on a raised platform, at a higher level than the participants in the case and the crowd of listeners.[100] A similar relationship governs the magistrate addressing the people ranged below, a situation that presupposes the unequal position between speaker and addressees.[101] While retaining the Greek architectural form, the Romans invert the relation between speaker and citizen.[102] Insodoing, the physical relationship mirrors the relationship of political status.[103] The symbolic value of this relationship was recognized by Cicero and, in fact, the level at which one stood while addressing the people at a public assembly could

[94] Cic. *Flacc.* 57: *speculatur atque obsidet rostra vindex temeritatis et moderatrix offici curia.* The passage offers a strikingly visual illustration of the principle enunciated at Cic. *leg.* 2.30. Bonnefond 1983 speculates on other indirect means, both temporal and spatial, by which the senate dominated the political process.

[95] Krause 1976.53–61 evaluates the evidence for comitia outside Rome.

[96] F. Brown et al. 1993.27–28 consider the possibility that the speaker at Cosa spoke from a raised position.

[97] See Camp 1996, who argues that the arrangement by which the ground slopes up away from the speaker begins only with the Hellenistic period, and was not a prominent feature of the Pnyx at any stage (contra Kourouniotes and Thompson 1932).

[98] Detienne 1965, whose focus is on archaic Greece.

[99] Pina Polo 1996.23–25. See Cic. *har. resp.* 33 for the pun (*tollam altius tectum, non ut ego te despiciam*).

[100] Greenidge 1901.133–34, 458–59.

[101] Gell. 18.7.7, where Gellius claims that one of the three meanings of *contio* is the platform to which the speaker ascends.

[102] Krause 1976, following the suggestions of Sjöqvist 1951.405–11, details Greek influence on Rome's comitium; Coarelli (1992) 1.146–51 follows Krause but differs on the date when this phase of the comitium may have been introduced in Rome.

[103] A. Bell 1997.2.

depend on one's political rank at the moment. Cicero implies it was not normal for a nonmagistrate to speak from the rostra during an assembly (and he could do so only at the invitation of the presiding magistrate) and that magistrates who had not called the assembly spoke from steps lower than the speaker's platform proper.[104] This hierarchy of speaking height literalizes the notion of "rank," which is normally rendered by the Latin word *gradus* ("step"). The contrast between Greek and Roman modes of civic communication becomes especially interesting since inside the senate-house there would have persisted the Greek-style relationship of speaker below, with the audience of peers ranged above on benches (*subsellia*).[105]

Yet the simple physical relationship between political speaker and listening populace does not tell a complete story. We still need to look at the question "Why do popular politicians?" I return to the motifs that recur in Cicero's attack on opponents he designates as popular politicians, where he employs a rhetoric centering on peculiarities of the body and of physical movement. It is no coincidence that these are the very attributes that would be visible on the rostra to the *populus* gathered in the forum. The orator associates the tribune Vatinius's foul political program with an equally foul external appearance.[106] In his speech *On Behalf of Sestius*, Cicero mocks the walk of Aulus Gabinius, the Gracchi, and Saturninus, marking their gait as distinct from that of a serious politician.[107] Even the amount of control the speaker had over his mouth had political connotations.[108] The popular ideology, it is clear, has become literally embodied in its proponents. It is surely no accident that the elite virtues of *gravitas* and *constantia* stand in direct opposition to the swaying walk and gaping mouth of Cicero's popular politicians. In the section of *On Duties* where Cicero is purportedly instructing his son on the proper carriage of the body, he warns against an excessively quick walk, since it prompts "quick breathing, a changed facial expression, a misshapen mouth—these features," he continues, "make perfectly clear a lack of *constantia*."[109] The equation of physical with moral stability also informs the historiographic tradition. Pro-Gracchan sources show Tiberius Gracchus firm and silent in the face of death, whereas hostile writers depict him during the same period scurrying all

---

[104] Botsford 1909.149, on the basis of Cic. *Att.* 2.24.3, *Vat.* 24. Pina Polo 1996.34–38, 178–82 notes that of the *privati* known to have addressed *contiones*, two-thirds consisted of former consuls (34).

[105] LTUR 1.333 (E. Tortorici).

[106] For example, *Vat.* 4, 10.

[107] *Sest.* 17 (Gabinius); 105 (Gracchi, Saturninus).

[108] Richlin 1992.99; Corbeill 1996.99–127.

[109] *Off.* 1.131: *anhelitus moventur, vultus mutantur, ora torquentur; ex quibus magna significatio fit non adesse constantiam*; at Cic. *de orat.* 1.184 an arrogant orator, ignorant of the laws, wanders with a crowd in the forum *prompto ore ac vultu*.

around the city.[110] An unrestrained speaker such as Gracchus could not, of course, be imagined as facing death in any other manner.

Artistic representations support this contrast between elite self-mastery and popular excitability. Brilliant has posited for Roman art what he calls an "appendage aesthetic:" rather than imitating classical Greek practice by using anatomical details of the human figure to render meaning to the viewer, Roman artists concentrated principally on those attributes that are attached to the torso, especially the head, arms, and dress. The appendage aesthetic presumably finds its origin in Roman daily experience. The gestures of public figures as rendered in art rely on "the developed sensitivity for gesticulate address" possessed by those familiar with daily oratory.[111] I have already suggested how such a reliance may have affected the stance of Augustus's statue from Prima Porta. The walk functions in a way analogous to the folds of the toga in sculpture—just as the literal and metaphorical *gravitas* ("heaviness") of the garment "dematerializes the body" and makes the once-living model into a political icon, so, too, that gait impresses most that draws the least attention to itself.[112] In a study of Roman portrait busts, Luca Giuliani has suggested that the Romans tried to convey political signs in portraiture as well—the elite, for example, wished their marble not only to bear a physical likeness, but also to express sternness and steadfastness (*gravitas, constantia*), two key concepts underlying the ideological program of the conservative *optimates*.[113] At the same time it is apparent that Roman sculptors of the elite tended to avoid sculptural techniques popular in Hellenistic times that represented movement, enthusiasm, and excited breathing.[114] Giuliani even conjectures that depictions of Pompeius strike us as strange because Magnus is, characteristically, trying to have it both ways: he is *popularis* from the eyebrows up, as embodied especially in the evocation of Alexander the Great's hairstyle, but stern optimate from the eyes down (fig. 18).[115] Pompeius's portrait provides a physical analog to the multifaceted general that Cicero praises in his speech *On the Manilian Law*: both the physical and the verbal representations stress how their subject display a unique (but not precarious) blend of military might and political reserve.[116] Unlike Brilliant, however, Giuliani balks at whether these artistic practices have a direct correlation with the real physical appearance of the persons so represented.

---

[110] Sordi 1978.306–7, 318. Compare how the sources depict Cicero's calm acceptance of death (Livy apud Sen. *suas.* 6.17; Plut. *Vit. Cic.* 48).

[111] Brilliant 1963.10 (quoted here), 26–37.

[112] On the limited gesticulation depicted on togate statues, see Ibid. 69.

[113] Giuliani 1986.214 and 322 n. 44.

[114] Ibid.239–45, with 215.

[115] Ibid.97–100, citing Cic. *fam.* 8.13 for comparison.

[116] Giuliani 1990.111–12.

18. Portrait of Pompey the Great (courtesy of Ny Carls-
berg Glyptotek, Copenhagen; cat. 597, I.N. 733).

I would like to suggest that the invective texts already cited from Cicero
allow us to glimpse this elusive physical reality. It is not only the way we
move, but the space within which we move that shapes personal ideology.
Elite politicians, speaking within the confines of the curia, easily maintain
constantia, or self-mastery. Cicero remarks from the rostra that consuls regularly considered it a "legal condition" (*lege et condicione*) to avoid addressing
the *populus* assembled as a whole.[117] He of course exaggerates motive—but the
people must have been able to judge the accuracy of his primary claim. Men
of consular rank should not grandstand. When speaking from the rostra, a
concern for restraint dominates: the rhetorical tradition stresses repeatedly
how the serious orator moves slowly, avoiding excessive gesticulation.[118] The
same reserve applies to the magistrate. In a passage from his *Florida*, Apuleius
remarks that the more important a person is, the more he should expect public

[117] *Leg. agr.* 2.6.
[118] Graf 1992.46–47.

scrutiny for his speech and demeanor. As an example of this predicament, Apuleius contrasts the public restraint of a proconsul, speaking quietly and infrequently from a seated position, with the public crier who stands, walks, and shouts contentiously. "Being low class provides plenty of excuses, having status plenty of difficulties."[119]

Vocabulary is also a function of public demeanor. It is a common phenomenon in Latin for words denoting ethical and aesthetic concepts to derive from concrete and tangible notions in the external world: *rectus* means physically "straight" as well as morally "upright;" behavior that is *perversus* has "turned away" from a posited straight course, and so on.[120] The same tendency toward the concrete prevails both in political terminology—the "magistrate" (*magistratus*) has "more" (*magis*)—and in public behavior—the "heaviness" (*gravitas*) and "coherence" (*constantia*) of the admirable citizen.[121] In a world of embodied political ethics such as this, it is natural to assume that sensitivity to bodily movement be at least subliminally active in daily interaction and that any disruption of physical realities could provoke a disruption in politics. Such concerns were still felt in the twentieth century: "During the debate on restoring the House of Commons after the war, Churchill feared that departure from the intimate spatial pattern of the House, where opponents face each other across a narrow aisle, would seriously alter the patterns of government."[122] "We shape our buildings," Churchill remarked famously on this occasion, "and afterwards our buildings shape us."

The popular politician, especially the tribune of the plebs, reached his constituency while speaking in the open spaces of the forum and in other wide-open areas such as the Circus Flaminius.[123] Even speeches in important political trials would have an audience that extended beyond the judges to the corona of interested citizens.[124] A reference in a speech of Cicero, where he describes "a packed forum and the temples filled to the brim" gives us an idea of how difficult it would have been for a speaker to make himself heard at these gatherings.[125] To reach the people gathered in such open spaces, exaggerated movement, expansive gesticulation, and open, shouting mouths were essential. In fact, recent studies of the role of charisma in mass persuasion suggest that sheer physical presence could compensate for not being heard; being

[119] Apul. *flor.* 9.1–12 (9.8: *tantum habet vilitas excusationis, dignitas difficultatis*).

[120] Corbeill 1996.34.

[121] Paul. Fest. p. 126; Wagenvoort 1947.104–27.

[122] Hall 1966.106–7.

[123] Cic. *Att.* 1.14.1–2, *p. red. in sen.* 17, Sest. 33; Liv. 27.21.1; L. R. Taylor 1966.20–21; Thommen 1995.367.

[124] Millar 1998.91.

[125] Cic. *Man.* 44 (the occasion is the voting on the *lex Gabinia*); see, too, Catil. 4.14, Tac. *dial.* 39.5.

audible, in other words, is not a necessary precondition to being persuasive.[126] In Rome, we are told, one popular tribune captivated the people not through his persuasive ability, but through, in Cicero's words, his "public appearance, his gestures, and even through his very clothing."[127] *Species, motus, amictus*— these qualities may in fact have been the only aspects of the speaker much of his audience was able to perceive. Representations of the emperor addressing the people show "an arrangement of the *populus* according to the status of its members."[128] There is no reason to think republican gatherings offered an appreciably different scenario; a clear parallel is offered by the hierarchical seating arrangements at public festivals, whereby senators sat close to the action, with those of lesser rank ascending behind in descending order of status. It is hardly surprising to read an imperial writer remark about how the "unwashed crowd" of the empire takes special pleasure in the speaker who claps, stamps his feet, and strikes his chest.[129] In a nearly inescapable double-bind, the politician becomes his demeanor, the demeanor denotes his politics.

The popular politician excited not just aesthetic revulsion. His very appearance was represented as combating truth-telling. In one of Cicero's direct confrontations with the popular tribune Rullus in 63 BCE, he spitefully remarks that, unlike the tribunes, he himself owes his popularity—the word he uses ironically is *popularis*—to "truth, not display" (*veritate, non ostentatione*).[130] In contrast, he remarks later in the same speech how the attacks of Rullus and his allies forced him to "stand firm (*consistere*) in the public assembly."[131] The subdued appearance of the consul Cicero provides direct access to truth. In his philosophical works, as well, Cicero warns against the extremes of showy *ostentatio*, since it involves the altering of an individual's "facial expressions, walk, and clothing" (*fin.* 2.77: *vultum incessum vestitum*), precisely those features of his appearance that Cicero accuses Rullus of manipulating upon taking office as tribune: "he planned to have another expression, another voice, another walk; with more worn-out clothing."[132] Display (*ostentatio*) also comes under criticism in Cicero's prose treatises as being insufficient for securing an individual's *gloria* and as inappropriate for a senator speaking in the curia. As an example of excessive display being ineffective, Cicero offers the two famous tribunes, Tiberius and Gaius Gracchus.[133] The continued contrast between

---

[126] Atkinson 1984.88.

[127] Cic. *Brut.* 224.

[128] Torelli 1992.90–91.

[129] Quint. *inst.* 2.12.10.

[130] Cic. *leg. agr.* 1.23; see, too, 2.15, *consul re non oratione popularis*, where *oratio* presumably refers to "way of speaking" (OLD 1) as opposed to simply "words," which would have been expressed by the common *re non verbo* (or similar; OLD s.v. *res* 6b). A similar distinction occurs at *Brut.* 116 (*simplex in agendo veritas, non molesta*), where again a comparison is made with acting.

[131] Cic. *leg. agr.* 1.25.

[132] *Leg. agr.* 2.13: *alio vultu alio vocis sono alio incessu esse meditabatur, vestitu obsoletiore.*

[133] *Off.* 2.43; *de orat.* 2.333.

ostentatio and *veritas* brings us back to Roman notions of acting, where gestures of the stage are contrasted with those of the orator, a contrast represented as being between *demonstratio* and *significatio*, between artful mimicry and the natural expression of the emotions.[134] Hence the elite politician could point to the mere physical presence of a popular opponent to demonstrate the visible violation of the elite virtues of *gravitas* and *constantia*, virtues not only endorsed in literary, rhetorical, and philosophical texts, but delineated in contemporary portraiture.

One final consideration needs to be confronted. If a popular and a senatorial speaker are both speaking in a public assembly, experience and common sense would seem to dictate that the elite speaker exhibit greater gestures in this setting than when speaking in more confined quarters. An observable fact argues against such an hypothesis. Cicero's references to walking and movement occur in all types of speeches—in juried trials, in the senate, as well as before the people. This indicates that each audience would be attuned to the same contrasts in carriage regardless of the venue. Furthermore, recent studies of the role of gesture in communication show that, when attention is drawn to excessive gesturing, the audience does indeed notice. Not only that, but drawing attention to gesture induces the hearer to find the speaker *less* persuasive because, in a sense, the body, and not the emotions, is perceived as doing the speaking.[135] Elite ideology succeeds in part by intruding the gestures of opponents on the listeners' attention. When not distracted by gesture, as would be the case in the elite construction of *gravitas*, attention focused on words. *Veritas, non ostentatio*.

3. The Self-Made Popularis, or "Sulla Made Me a Homosexual"

My third point considers the possibility that some popular politicians, by embracing the *habitus* that formed in response to their elite rivals, consciously advertised to the populace their political stance.[136] As has been recently argued, "the popular will of the Roman people found expression in the context, and only in the context, of divisions within the oligarchy."[137] The adoption of a popular persona, then, together with a popular agenda, could provide a member of the elite the opportunity to promote his own projects. The display of battle wounds, for example, seems to have been a component of popular rhetoric used by prominent politicians to contest elite claims to privi-

[134] Cic. *de orat.* 3.220.

[135] Rimé and Schiaratura 1991.272–76 (quotation is from 276).

[136] This section offers a new perspective on passages discussed in Corbeill 1996.194–97, and is inspired in part by Kennedy 1992.39, who discusses Maecenas's alleged effeminacy in similar terms.

[137] North 1990b.18.

lege of birth.[138] I use as my own test case Julius Caesar, who during his life-time was subjected to accusations of being an androgyne, a catamite, and a wearer of effeminate clothing. Rather than rejecting, as every ancient histo-rian does, the truth-content behind these charges, I would like to consider instead what these accusations may reveal about political competition and self-representation.

Charges of wearing nonmasculine dress appear frequently in the late Repub-lic in connection with two major political figures, Julius Caesar and Publius Clodius.[139] References to Clodius's activities occur only in connection with his violation of the rites of the Bona Dea in 62 BCE, during a religious celebration normally restricted to Roman matrons. On this occasion, Clodius's alleged adoption of female dress did not represent the adoption of an effeminate life-style, in spite of Cicero's frequent claims to the contrary. Instead, the clothing simply provided Clodius a means for escaping detection, for covering up what he was *not*.[140] Caesar's choice of dress, on the other hand, seems to represent a move not toward deception, but toward political self-advertisement.

When captured by pirates in the 70s BCE, Julius Caesar was careful to con-tinue wearing in their presence the toga, the typical mark of Roman citizen-ship, perhaps as a sign to his captors of his claims to sexual inviolability.[141] If we can trust our sources, Caesar had already displayed this awareness of the symbolic power of dress while a young man in Rome. The image he wished to project in the empire's capital was, however, quite different. During the rule of Sulla, a clear opponent of popular politics, the dictator warned his political allies to beware of the young man Caesar, whose style of wrapping the toga denoted an effeminate character.[142] Clothes, in this case, literally unmake the man. The threat that Sulla envisions from Caesar dressing up is not immediately clear, and one is quick to dismiss the attendant claim that Caesar's peculiar apparel almost drove Sulla to kill him.[143] Yet Suetonius, too, mentions Sulla's desire to eliminate the young Caesar: something, "either di-vine inspiration or personal inference," told him that the boy had "a lot of Mariuses in him" and that his rise to power would signal the end of the opti-

[138] Leigh 1995, esp. 202–7.

[139] Other examples of this charge from the Republic include Gell. 6.12.4–5 (P. Sulpicius Galus); Cic. *Verr.* 2.4.103, 5.31, 5.86 (Verres); *Catil.* 2.22 (Catiline and his followers); cf. Varro *Men.* 313. Manfredini 1985.257–71 surveys the stigma of cross-dressing from late-Republican invective to the codex of Theodosius.

[140] Cic. *in Clod.* 21; Geffcken 1973.82.

[141] Vell. 2.41.3; A. Bell 1997.15 n. 102.

[142] Suet. *Iul.* 45.3, Macr. *Sat.* 2.3.9. Clothing reveals effeminacy: Hor. *sat.* 1.2.25; Sen. *nat.* 7.31, *epist.* 114.21; Mart. 1.96. Sulla's stance has uncomfortable resonance with Nazi propagan-dists who claimed that bodily *habitus* determines choice of dress ("Der Stil der leiblichen Gestalt und Gebärde bestimmt den Stil der artrechten Kleidung," L. F. Clauss, quoted in Efron [1941] 1972.26 n. 7).

[143] Dio 43.43.4.

mate party.[144] Jokes of Cicero, furthermore, suggest that Julius Caesar's appearance had some connection with his eventual victory in the Roman civil war. As Cicero says, "I never would have thought that a man who scratches his head with one finger and has such exquisitely arranged hair could have ever overthrown the Roman state."[145] Cicero's alleged failure to read Caesar correctly constitutes his wry commentary on the political codes of external appearance. The figure of the effeminately adorned male represents, I suggest, a recognized social construction that Caesar has adopted for a specific reason: to align himself with modes of behavior contrary to those of the dominant political class. Contrary, that is, not only to the Sullas, but also to the Ciceros, who would have adopted the elite model for their own success.

I have already mentioned Pierre Bourdieu's theory of bodily *habitus*, whereby the different segments in a given society express values through specific forms of dress, language, and gesture. According to Bourdieu's theory, the various forms of the *habitus* affect and help define one another. One of Bourdieu's contemporary examples provides a parallel to what I am suggesting about Julius Caesar. In twentieth-century France, Bourdieu claims that members of the dominant social class have acquired effeminate characteristics that stand in contradistinction with the values of the working classes. The style of the elite, Bourdieu writes, "is seen as a repudiation of the virile values."[146] In the creation and maintenance of the values of the working classes, then, two isolable vectors are at work—one that labels from above, and one that labels from within.[147] Applying these notions of the *habitus* to the case of Julius Caesar, one can observe that the optimate class, through its public invective, has identified certain forms of behavior, speech, and action as contrary to its own *habitus* and has, as a further corollary, defined these characteristics as being contrary to the proper Roman way of life.[148] It is not surprising that in the creation of this dichotomy, divisions arise along lines of gender: since the elite adopts masculine-coded walk and dress, the popular politicians become aligned with feminine traits.[149] The popular politicians were forced

[144] Suet. *Iul.* 1.3: *satis constat Sullam . . . proclamasse, sive divinitus sive aliqua coniectura, . . . [Caesarem] quandoque optimatium partibus . . . exitio futurum; nam Caesari multos Marios inesse.*

[145] Plut. *Vit. Caes.* 4.9; see, too, Macr. *Sat.* 2.3.9, Dio 43.43.5. Corbeill 1996.164–65 discusses the head-scratching gesture. The disjuncture of effeminate appearance and masculine reality resembles Phaedrus's story of the *cinaedus* soldier who quite unexpectedly turns out to be a great warrior (Phaedr. app. 8). Gleason 1995.134 relates the story to Phaedrus's status as a freedman, speculating that "some males might deliberately opt out of the competition that governed public interaction among 'real' men."

[146] Bourdieu 1991.88.

[147] Hacking 1986.234 and, for a general discussion of societies as self-regulating systems, Bateson 1972.88–106 ("Morale and National Character").

[148] Bourdieu 1990.62; 1984.170–72.

[149] Bourdieu 1990.70–79 speculates on the origin of dividing gait along gender lines (for details, see 1990.271–83).

into their own particular *habitus* through both the power of the aristocratic ideology and through their own willingness to comply with the rhetoric of that ideology.

To return to Caesar's case. In addition to sporting a form of dress readily identifiable as feminine, Caesar flouted other traditional categories of sexual behavior. All these maneuvers should be attributed to the same identity, but it is a political, not a sexual, identity. In a public oration, the elder Curio referred to Caesar as "a man for all women, and a woman for all men;" Marcus Bibulus, Caesar's colleague in the consulship of 59 BCE, published official edicts in which Caesar's alleged sexual involvement with the Asian king Nicomedes yields for him the nickname "the queen of Bithynia"; this affair also produced for Caesar the descriptive epithet "innermost support of the royal bed."[150] The sources do not preserve Caesar's immediate reactions to this abuse; but if he had followed both the rhetorical handbooks and contemporary oratorical practice, he would have immediately denied these allegations with a quick and witty joke. One-upmanship was a skill to be pursued and mastered.[151] Another anecdote finds Caesar exposed to a similar type of abuse. His response on this occasion would have surprised his teachers of rhetoric. According to the historian Suetonius, after Caesar was granted the proconsulship of Transalpine Gaul, he boasted in a crowded senate house that he would force all his opponents to fellate him. "Whereupon," Suetonius continues, "somebody said abusively, 'That would be hard to do to a woman!' Caesar replied, in an allusive manner, 'In Syria, Semiramis had been a queen too, and the Amazons once possessed a great portion of Asia.' "[152] This refusal to deny the implications of an opponent's abuse is rare for rhetorical invective.[153] The fact that the charge here is effeminacy makes Caesar's retort all the more peculiar since, despite the numerous charges of effeminacy one finds in Roman texts, "no Roman author ever calls himself effeminate in surviving Latin literature."[154] By embracing the charges, Caesar focuses attention upon them in order to expose them to ridicule. In so doing, he positions himself in opposition to the dominant standards of appearance that this type of humorous abuse is designed to enforce. Other jokes of the future dictator reveal a desire to align himself in opposition to the normally acceptable representations of political conduct. As general, Caesar was accustomed to excuse the extravagance permitted his victorious soldiers by saying, "My soldiers can fight well even while

---

[150] Suet. *Iul.* 52.3; Suet. *Iul.* 49.

[151] See, e.g., Quint. *inst.* 6.3.72–74; Cic. *de orat.* 2.220.

[152] Suet. *Iul.* 22.2.

[153] Corbeill 1996.196 n. 38. Dio 43.20.4 describes Caesar after the civil war as pained by the charges concerning Nicomedes, which Suetonius contends was the only challenge to his *impudicitia* (*Iul.* 49.1). This behavior contrasts markedly with that at the senate meeting a decade earlier.

[154] Edwards 1993.66; see, too, Hortensius at Gell. 1.5.2–3 (discussed earlier in the chapter).

wearing perfume."[155] It is not necessary to assume, presumably, that the Romans fighting in Gaul actually did use the local *eau de cologne*. It is the political fact standing behind this playful fiction that Caesar is attempting to isolate.

Julius Caesar's public persona constituted an obvious target for humorous abuse.[156] Even if this invective has been preserved principally from postmortem attacks arising in the aftermath of his assassination (although the anecdote from Suetonius is likely to be historical), it is still necessary to explain why this particular kind of invective arose. I present as one possibility that this polemic finds its origins in the deliberate misrepresentation on the part of the elite of the ways in which popular politicians appealed directly to the assembled people—through self-consciously untraditional dress, gestures, and speaking styles. In the case of Julius Caesar, the three commonest areas in which abuse circulated all promote a potentially ambiguous sexuality. The opportunities that these features provided for the invective of his opponents could have been neither a secret nor a surprise to Caesar himself. In fact, Julius Caesar's intimate knowledge of "the game" is precisely what allows him to step outside and interrogate its rules.[157] We recall Quintilian's judgment: if Caesar had had the time to devote to study, his oratorical skills would have rivaled Cicero himself (*inst.* 10.1.114). The likeliest explanation, then, for Caesar's willingness to expose himself to ridicule lies in the representational tension that continually existed between senatorial and popular politics.[158] By not avoiding behavior specifically marked in his society as feminine, Caesar could be perceived as transgressing normal modes of male, aristocratic behavior. In violating the accepted relationship between appearance and reality, Caesar fashions himself as a proponent of political change.

Conclusion

The spectacle-oriented aspects of Roman culture have received much attention in recent scholarship. In the area of politics, however, to recognize spectacle simply means to recognize the existence of an audience, not necessarily to

---

[155] Suet. *Iul.* 67.1; it is interesting that the sole surviving fragment of Caesar's poetry mentions people anointing themselves with scent: *corpusque suavi telino unguimus* (Isid. *orig.* 4.12.7).

[156] I have not found a source that attacked him for effeminate gestures; on the contrary, Cic. *Brut.* 261 describes his oratorical style as *voce motu forma etiam magnificam et generosam quodam modo* (whatever *quodam modo* means; see, too, Suet. *Iul.* 55).

[157] Bourdieu 1990.66–67.

[158] Compare the similar findings of Gleason 1995.161–62, who believes that effeminate speakers in the second century CE adopted their persona since "there was something manly, after all, about taking risks—even the risk of being called effeminate. Then there may also have been a temptation to appropriate characteristics of 'the other' as a way of gaining power from outside the traditionally acceptable sources." She declines, however, to speculate why "this more androgynous style of self-presentation was so effective with audiences."

conclude that that audience constitutes a healthy democracy.[159] We can read about what the Romans saw, but it is much more difficult to determine how they were taught to see. It is likely, however, that a speaker's awareness of a large public will increase the performative aspects of those politicians who wish to direct their appeals primarily to that public. This is precisely the situation Cicero must exploit in his attempt to safeguard the interests of the elite.

So as we stand back from the rostra, one hundred or even one thousand heads back from the rostra, struggling to hear the speaker, who are we to believe, the calm and composed Cicero, his right arm elegantly harmonizing with his rhetorical points, or the excited, shouting popular politicians? "Why do popular politicians?" I have two answers, one Cicero's and one mine. The popular politician moves about so much because he is trying to reach me, cramped in a space arranged almost by accident and not designed for a proper political assembly—although purportedly an auditor, I am simultaneously aware of my own physical needs. Cicero's answer to the same question? The overt physicality of the popular speaker betrays his disconnectedness with *gravitas* and *constantia*, with stability and composure, with truth and reason.

And yet I do not intend to be offering a necessarily negative critique of the elite ideology that dominates our sources for ancient Rome. Roman society was able to justify some of its most deeply felt religious and social values by pointing out that such values stem from a proper understanding of nature. My primary aim in this chapter has been to narrate how the Romans pushed one specific form of bodily movement from what we would consider the learned realm (the way we walk). The Romans categorized these movements differently, as "natural" (nature has encoded in human beings that a certain kind of politician should walk a certain way). The Romans order the apparent arbitrariness of their own society by deifying nature and then by making its contemplation the greatest activity a human being can have.[160] With this model lost, aporia results. I would like, therefore, to close with an historical moment of particular uncertainty for Cicero, and for the elite ideology to whose construction and maintenance he had devoted a glorious oratorical career. During the political turmoil and shifting alliances that followed Julius Caesar's assassination on the Ides of March, Cicero learns while in his villa at Tusculum that a group of discharged soldiers has been attempting

---

[159] See Jehne 1995.7–8 and, in more detail, Flaig 1995, who argues that the popular assemblies acted not as a body making decisions, but as one marking consensus (*Konsensorgan*, as opposed to *Entscheidungsorgan*).

[160] Sen. *dial.* 12.8.4.

to stir up trouble in Rome. Cicero writes his friend Atticus to say that the potential for violence prevents him from returning to the capital, the site of his life's greatest glories. "Besides," he writes, " among people of *that sort*, what kind of facial expression should I adopt and how," he concludes, "how should I walk?"[161]

---

[161] Cic. Att. 15.5.3: *quis porro noster itus, reditus, vultus, incessus inter istos?*

Chapter 5

FACE FACTS:
FACIAL EXPRESSION AND THE
NEW POLITICAL ORDER
IN TACITUS

Reading facial expressions is an important art in Italy,
to be learned in childhood, perhaps more important for
survival than the art of reading.
—Barzini 1964.64

CICERO'S TREATMENT of the walk of his opponents has shifted our perception of how Romans used gesture. In the opening three chapters of this book, the significance of bodily movement resided predominantly in the ability to communicate with the nonvisible, more-than-human elements of the external world: in religious and medical practice, for example, the expert gesture ensured that the objectives of prayer and curative incantation were properly met, while in mourning ritual women worked their bodies to effect spiritual rebirth of the dead. Such a hopefully positivistic interpretation of the world, however, contains in its logic the seed of its own destruction. If properly orchestrated gestures could signal, and even produce, a harmony with nature, it is inevitable that society should begin constructing an opposing class of movement—the discordant, the deviant, the unnatural. Late-Republican politics, as described in chapter 4, showed one particular way in which the notion of the participatory body could be exploited. Elite politicians construct a body that moves in contradistinction to their own, and one that thereby signals a cathexis of moral and political deviance. In teaching the Roman audience to read such deviance correctly, the elite maintains ascendancy. The body, rather than working with its external environment, has become a text that allows access to the thoughts lying behind a gesture.

GESTURE AS METAPHOR

In this chapter I shall demonstrate further the inroads that can be made on the model of the naturally harmonious body. Our principal sources, identifying in typical fashion the moral with the political, correlate the dissolution of this model with the collapse of the Republican form of government at Rome. I shall move from the synchronic analyses of the previous chapters, with their emphasis on the body as a stable means of affecting the world and reflecting character, to a diachronic analysis that charts a developing instability in how much trust one may place in reading gestures. I shall trace the treatment of facial expressions from Cicero, writing in the Republic, to Tacitus, whose works bear witness to the rise and fall of both good and bad imperial leaders. In addition to allowing me to focus on change, facial expression introduces a type of gesture hitherto unexplored: the silent use of the body to express emotions. In the examples that follow it is the manipulation of the face and not spoken language that provides the primary means of communication with the external world.[1] And yet, as a replacement for language, these facial expressions are as susceptible as linguistic expression to ambiguity, multiple interpretations, and deception, and it is here that their threat to stability lies.

In my first chapter, I argued that the Romans depended in their religious and medical practice on the potential for the properly deployed human body to affect nature. This conception of a harmonious interaction between human beings and their world, well demonstrated in scholarly discussions of the "power of the word," extends as well to a perceived power of gesture. During such a golden age, when human language can be conceived as allowing access to objective truths in nature, any dissimulation in communication between individuals becomes unnatural and suspect—perhaps even impossible. Todorov has suggested that such a state of understanding existed for the Aztecs before the arrival of Cortés, a period when "signs automatically and necessarily proceed from the world they designate"; as a result of this relationship, Todorov claims, there existed "a certain incapacity of the Aztecs to dissimulate the truth."[2] The resultant willingness of the Aztecs to believe the promises of the conquistadors, he further argues, led to their destruction. Todorov's reconstruction offers a helpful model for analyzing the changing attitudes toward facial expression in Latin texts. In employing this parallel, however, I do not mean to suggest that the early Romans were as incapable of dissimulating as Todorov suggests was the case for the Aztecs. After all, the ability of the observant Romans to forestall dissimulation is well represented in their foundation legend of the temple of Jupiter Optimus Maximus referred to in chapter 1, when the Etruscan Olenus attempted through manipulation of word and gesture to appropriate for his own people the divine power of Rome's Capitoline hill and was countered by the alert response of Roman envoys (Olenus: "Is *this* what you are saying, Romans? *Here* will be the temple of Jupiter Optimus Maximus, *here* we have found a head?" Romans: "Not *here* of course but *at*

---

[1] For the history of this dichotomy and a survey of recent studies of human expression, see Ekman 1973 and 1998.

[2] Todorov 1984.89–90.

Rome we say the head was found").[3] As I noted earlier, however, this anecdote illustrates not the Roman skill at verbal trickery but in fact the opposite. The action of the envoys rests on the belief that both their verbal and physical language—the deictic words ("here," "this") and the pointing arms and fingers—are rooted in the world and derive their strength from a proper understanding of that rootedness. Facial expressions find their own significance in an analogous sense of rootedness.

The natural model of language survives in another attitude toward linguistic expression that the Romans shared with Todorov's Aztecs: a suspicion of metaphor.[4] Metaphor does of course exist in the earliest extant Latin texts. Indeed, it is difficult to conceive of any language capable of abstract expression to which the principle of metaphorical similarity is not central.[5] Cicero detected an example of the figure in the Twelve Tables, traditionally thought to have been composed in the fifth century BCE, where a weapon is described as "fleeing from" the hand (*si telum manu fugit*).[6] Despite such venerable instances, the Romans seem to have been especially sensitive to a metaphor's semantic status as a false statement. The power of this figure resides in its clear status as an untruth, an untruth that the hearer or reader must somehow manipulate and distort to create an approximation of truth.[7] The famous example of Aristotle will illustrate the point (*Rhet.* 3.4.1): if in describing Achilles a poet should write "he charged, a lion," sense can be made of this clear falsehood—Achilles is not a lion—only by exercising ingenuity to discover ways in which this lie could be true. Both the lion and Achilles, for example, share characteristics such as courage, strength, determination, and so forth. This kind of clear-cut use of metaphor is not as prevalent in early Latin literature as one might expect.

The comedies of Plautus represent our oldest full literary testimony from the Roman world. Even in the works of this comic playwright, whose language is characterized by exuberant expression and vigorous imagery, metaphor normally appears in a form where there is no room for confusion on the part of his audience. A particular species of folk metaphor preserved by the playwright takes the form *musca est meus pater: nil potest clam illum haberi* ("my father is a fly: you can't do anything without him around").[8] In the numerous Plautine examples of this type of metaphor, the figure takes the form of an enigmatic, almost riddling, expression (the metaphor proper), that is immediately followed by a paratactic explanatory phrase in asyndeton. The humor in these

---

[3] Plin. *nat.* 28.15.

[4] Todorov 1984.90.

[5] Two well-known demonstrations of this claim are Lakoff and Johnson 1980 and Lakoff 1987.

[6] Cic. *de orat.* 3.158 (= Lex XII tab. frg. 8.24 Warmington); the metaphor may be a calque from the law's Greek source (LSJ s.v. φεύγω II 2).

[7] On the semantic status of most metaphors as lies, see Davidson 1978.41–47.

[8] Plaut. *Merc.* 361; full discussion in Fraenkel 1960.35–46.

early uses of metaphor rests, I suggest, in the way the metaphor, the lie, is immediately transformed into a truth; in other words, the absurd identification (the father is not in this case literally a fly) is made possible and therefore even more absurd by explaining its relevance. The attraction to the Roman crowd in this particular form of metaphorical expression is attested not only by its frequency, but by the fact that the formula appears only once in inverted form, with explanation followed by metaphorical identification ("the wine is out to get my feet: it's a tricky wrestler").[9] To a modern audience there would not be a clear preference for either order of expression. By placing the metaphor first, Plautus wishes to highlight its unexpectedness. In later Roman antiquity, this form of folk metaphor is no longer in common use, with the second, explanatory element either replaced by hypotactic explanations ("my father is a fly *because* . . .") or dropping out altogether.[10] As in so many other aspects of Plautine theater in which illusion is created only to be shattered in metatheatrical game-playing, this favored and native form of verbal manipulation finds its impetus in the desire to confound the audience's faith in truthful appearance.[11]

This suspicion of metaphor's relation to truth survives even in the most polished treatise on public speaking from the Republican period, Cicero's *On the Orator*. The orator Crassus opens a discussion of the ornate speaking style by isolating three ways in which speech can be adorned by single words. He includes in this category two contrasting items. First, he lists "authoritative and fixed words, those practically born, as it were, together with the things themselves [sc. that they denote]" (*propria sunt et certa quasi vocabula rerum paene una nata cum rebus ipsis; de orat.* 3.149). This first category seems to allude to a theory of natural language such as that of Nigidius Figulus, discussed in chapter 1.[12] Cicero's second category of rhetorical adornment includes metaphor, a figure of speech whose use Crassus justifies by saying that metaphor allows the speaker to compensate for the poverty of vocabulary in the first category (*quem* [*modum transferendi verbi*] *necessitas genuit inopia coacta et angustiis; de orat.* 3.155). When he comes to discuss metaphor in more detail, Crassus advises caution in the use of the figure, recommending that the speaker qualify his usage with a phrase such as *ut ita dicam* ("so to speak").[13] These qualifying phrases serve to warn the listener that the expression the speaker uses is not to be taken literally. Cicero as orator tends to follow this advice in his own oratorical practice. The apparent exceptions, those cases where no apology is made for metaphorical expressions, fall into clearly deline-

[9] Plaut. *Pseud.* 1251: [*vinum*] *pedes captat primum, luctator dolosust*; Fraenkel 1960.38.

[10] Fraenkel 1960.41 (on the misunderstanding of the expression by Donatus and Sacerdos), 44.

[11] For recent scholarship into Plautine metatheater, see especially Slater 2000 and Moore 1998.

[12] See Rudd 1989 ad Hor. *ars* 234–35.

[13] Cic. *de orat.* 3.165; see, too, *orat.* 79–81. On the *tenuis orator*, Rhet. Her. 4.45.

ated areas: images drawn from natural phenomena, of which the metaphor of
the ship of state troubled by storms constitutes the majority of examples, or
in self-consciously grand works such as his speech *On Behalf of Sestius*. Even
in these elevated contexts, however, the metaphors tend to be thematized,
deriving from actual events described in the speech, with the result that the
metaphorical usage verges on the allegorical (e.g., Clodius and his followers
are figured as firebrands and so the threatened destruction of the city is imagined as a conflagration).[14] An examination of Republican texts demonstrates
that Cicero's aversion is shared by other Republican writers of formal prose,
who either never employ a live metaphor (Caesar, Sallust) or tolerate the
figure only with difficulty, using it primarily in well-established contexts or
when following Greek models.[15] Even in poetic texts of the period, the use of
metaphor is commonly confined to folk models, with the full use of creative
metaphor not flowering until the Augustan age.[16] I do not wish to speculate
here on the reasons why metaphor grew more acceptable with time, but surely
the growing sophistication—and Hellenization—of Roman literature plays a
critical role. Instead I shall suggest ways in which the face, a one-time reposi-
tory of information regarding its bearer's essence, becomes represented as the
bodily analog of metaphor, joining this rhetorical figure in its retreat from the
direct representation of truth.

The Politics of the Face

The death of the princeps Augustus in 14 CE created a fundamental and un-
precedented political problem: who is to replace the dead leader and, more
importantly, what precisely is being replaced? With Tiberius begins the need to
define a new power structure, the post-Augustan principate, a process vividly
described by the historian Tacitus in the opening chapters of his *Annals*. As
the historian presents it, the dynamic consolidation of the new political order
resembles a game, one in which the opposing sides—senate and princeps—
are continually writing and rewriting the rules. Scholars have discussed thor-
oughly the historical facts and historiographical biases that could explain why
Tacitus's narrative of the succession highlights the senate's confusion and Tiberius's dissimulation.[17] I hope to contribute to this discussion by looking at a

[14] Ciceronian practice: Morawski 1910, LHS 780–81 (with bibliography); Fantham 1971.125–
36 (esp. 136: "metaphors correspond in their field to the literal actions described in their context").

[15] LHS 779–81 with detailed bibliography.

[16] LHS 781; see Fantham 1971.3–81 for a discussion of Plautus, Terence, and Cicero's correspondence; she does not, however, consistently distinguish metaphor from other forms of figurative language.

[17] See bibliography in Woodman 1998, 40 n. 2, to which add Corbeill 1989 and Hurlet
1997.156–62.

dominant feature of Tacitus's narrative that would seem divorced from political events. By examining how the historian's emphasis on facial expressions punctuates the narrated relationship between senate and princeps, I intend to demonstrate how the perception of a collapsing metaphysical order contributes to Tacitus's account. Tacitus isolates the reign of Tiberius as the starting point for the separation of the Roman emperor from the rest of the Roman elite. Facial expression, commonly invoked in oratory from the Republic in order to indicate character and intention, has evolved by the time of Tiberius into a shifting signifier, a reflection of the aporia that accompanied the formation of the principate.[18] The uncertainty of how to act manifests itself in the faces of the political participants: the elite hide their faces so as not to betray their own thoughts while they simultaneously baffle themselves in their attempts to interpret the expressions of the new leader.

What I propose, then, is another way of looking at spectacle in the Empire, a subject that has lately been receiving much scholarly attention. The games, the theater, the military triumph, and declamation all attest to the Roman love of being seen.[19] I discussed in the previous chapter a Republican aspect of spectacle; Roman oratory, performed before an attentive public, depends on the visual element for its persuasive power, as the orator continually enjoins his hearers to "look." Outside the public realm, even texts that were intended primarily for a reading audience attempt to recreate a narrative that appeals to the reader's use of the eyes. The frequent employment of *ekphrasis* in poetic texts offers one clear example of this tendency; less direct are the many invitations that poets such as Vergil give to their audiences to "see" the action, a device that attempts to make his epic a face-to-face narrative.[20] Working within this tradition, Tacitus sees the power of the new principate as lying in its subversion of the expectations of the seemingly ubiquitous Roman onlooker. Tiberius refuses to become a spectacle; instead he makes himself a spectator. I shall conclude this chapter by arguing that, ultimately, the tension within Tacitus's narrative between senatorial uncertainty and imperial deception results in the transformation of Tiberius into the ultimate viewer—an all-seeing deity. The symbiosis between human beings and more-than-human nature dissolves in the face of the all-too-human Tiberius.

---

[18] Bloomer 1997.154–95 discusses in detail other aspects of Tacitus's Tiberius that differ from the idealized image of Republican oratory. He concludes that "control of appearance no longer guards the self in the age of Tiberius" (166); I wish to trace what happened to that self.

[19] Recent bibliography is immense. Most studies emphasize the overt theatricality of imperial society: through gruesome public spectacles Romans externalize the anxieties accompanying one-man rule (Barton 1993); or that politics is itself a spectacle wherein emperor and citizen interchange as actor and spectator (Bartsch 1994, esp. 1–35; Dupont 1985). This chapter aims to locate the source of this fearful confusion.

[20] Ricottilli 2000.44–54; Cicero, in translating a short passage from the *Iliad*, twice adds the verb *vidimus* ("we saw"), to which Homer's text has no equivalent (Cic. *div.* 2.63).

Eye-Movement in Roman Antiquity

An understanding of the imperial gaze will be enhanced by looking at Roman conceptions of the eye and the act of seeing. In his survey of the ways in which the various body parts contributed to the functioning of the body as a whole, Pliny points to the superiority of the eyes as an indicator of the various emotions—pity, hatred, happiness—and states that the soul in fact "lives" in the eyes.[21] Roman texts from poetry to rhetoric to philosophy concur with this notion, commonly held in antiquity, that the eyes are the mirror of the soul.[22] As a result of this belief, specific signs in the eyes were able to indicate to a viewer the complete range of a person's internal activities, whether actively engaged in thinking, steadfast in opinion, or mentally unbalanced.

An actively thinking mind expressed itself in a corresponding activity of the eyes. In the final scene of Vergil's *Aeneid*, as Aeneas's foe Turnus begs the hero to spare his life, Vergil describes Aeneas as increasingly hesitant about the proper course of action (12.940: *iam iamque magis cunctantem*). The uncertainty of whether to kill Turnus or spare him is reflected in Aeneas's external physical appearance. Yet his gaze, rather than being in an analogous state of hesitation, betrays the active state of the mind, as the hero is described as "rolling his eyes" in thought (12.938: *volvens oculos*). In an earlier episode of the epic Vergil uses the same phrase to describe the king Latinus. Upon learning that Aeneas has arrived in Italy from the war at Troy, the king's eyes move as he reasons that this must be the foreign man prophesied to wed his daughter Lavinia (7.251: *intentos volvens oculos*). Here the commentator Servius provides a helpful gloss on the phrase: "*volvens oculos*: this is the gesture of a person who is thinking (*cogitantis est gestus*)."[23] Tiberius Claudius Donatus, another commentator on the epic, is more emphatic about the identity of this gesture: eye-movement of course reflects thought, since it would be against nature (*contra naturam*) for the eyes to remain fixed when the mind is in a state of activity.[24] This common identification of mobile eyes with active thought also appears explicitly in Sallust when Bocchus, contemplating the betrayal of Jugurtha, is described as "shifty in his expression and eyes in the same way as he was shifty in his spirit."[25]

---

[21] Plin. *nat.* 11.145: *neque ulla ex parte [sunt] maiora animi indicia cunctis animalibus sed homini maxime. . . . profecto in oculis animus habitat.*

[22] Cic. *de orat.* 3.221; Quint. *inst.* 11.3.75; for a full list of passages from Greece and Rome, see Wilpert and Zenker (1950) 1.960–61.

[23] Serv. *Aen.* 7.251. On this gesture, see Anderson 1971.58–65 and Ricottilli 1992, who offers a full analysis of this passage and Dido's analogous gesture at *Aen.* 1.561.

[24] Claud. Don. *Aen.* 7.251: *quasi toto cogitationis spatio inmobiles oculi teneri potuissent, quod est contra naturam.*

[25] Sall. *Iug.* 113.3: *dicitur secum ipse multum agitavisse, voltu et oculis pariter atque animo varius* (this passage is cited as a parallel by Serv. *Aen.* 7.251).

When the mind has come to a decision, the eyes accordingly stop moving. Consequently, to have a fixed gaze means to express resolve, and in many cases this physical fixedness reflects a mind unlikely to consider further alternatives. Literary descriptions of the immobile stare are many, from the gaze of Aeneas when he finally refuses to listen further to Dido's pleas to remain behind in Carthage (Verg. Aen. 4.331–32: *inmota tenebat / lumina*), to the look of the metamorphosed bear Callisto as she resigns herself to death at the hands of her human son Arcas (Ov. met. 2.502: *immotos . . . oculos*), to the emperor Tiberius, who greets the entreaties of a former associate, now accused of treason, with an unchanging expression (Tac. ann. 2.29: *immoto . . . vultu*). Each of these descriptions provides the viewer—and reader—with a succinct portrait of the character's mental state. In contrast to this fixed gaze, eyes that express an unsettled spirit either twist in unnatural directions or "burn" in ways visible to onlookers. This uncontrolled eye-movement, which finds its justification in medical treatises as symptomatic of abnormal mental states, can be appealed to in Ciceronian oratory to indicate the crazed state of his opponents: Verres' eyes "burn" in madness as he enters the forum of Messina; Catiline's "twist" in planning for Rome's potential destruction.[26]

Aspectus in Republican Tradition

Consideration of the ways in which mental states could be read in the eyes gives further nuance to the frequent claims that Roman Republican politics took place in a face-to-face society. Seeing and being seen determined reputations, and the vocabulary of observation—nouns such as *aspectus, os, vultus,* and verbs such as *video*—dominates not only in Roman oratory, but in other republican texts that detail social and political etiquette. Quintus Cicero's *Commentariolum petitionis,* an essay epistle written to his brother during Marcus's candidacy for consulship, draws a vivid picture of the kinds of facial interaction deemed necessary for a successful electoral campaign. As one recent study of this text demonstrates, success in the election depended upon "one's 'worthiness,' conceived of essentially in personal and moral terms."[27] Part of that worthiness consisted of accessibility, both physical and spiritual. Quintus emphasizes that the candidate's door should always be open; not only to his house but to his soul:

---

[26] Medical treatises and madness in tragedy: Dodds (1960) ad Eur. Bacch. 1122–23; Page (1967) ad Eur. Med. 1174–75. "Burning" and twisting eyes: Cic. Verr. 2.5.161: [Verres] *ipse inflammatus scelere et furore in forum venit; ardebant oculi,* 2.4.148; Catil. 2.2: *retorquet oculos profecto saepe ad hanc urbem;* TLL 9.2: 449.63–67 (G. Kuhlmann).

[27] Morstein-Marx 1998.267, who provides bibliography on the disputed authorship of the treatise at 260–61.

[est] cura ... ut aditus ad te diurni nocturnique pateant, neque solum foribus aedium tuarum, sed etiam vultu ac fronte, quae est animi ianua; quae [si] significat voluntatem abditam esse ac retrusam, parvi refert patere ostium. (Q. Cic. *pet.* 44)

Care should be taken that there be access to you day and night, not only through the entrance of your house but also through your facial expression (*vultu ac fronte*), which is the door to your soul. If your expression reveals that your will is hidden away, it makes little difference that your home is open.

In an earlier section, the author stresses that the candidate's facial expressions should take various forms according to the needs of the person addressed (42). In the passage just cited, however, the general rule underlying political canvassing is clear. In the electoral freedom of the late Republic, the face was thought to provide all voters with access to a candidate's interior. Openness of demeanor matched openness of the home at the *salutatio*. Dissimulation is easily detected, and not condoned.

When Cicero himself comes to warn against dissimulation in his philosophical treatises, he warns against adopting a walk or a facial expression (*vultus*) that, like clothing, can be put on or taken off as occasion warrants. The truly praiseworthy and honorable expression of opinion, he decides, is that which can be expressed "before the senate, the people—every gathering and council" (*fin.* 2.77). The proviso is that what would be shameful to say should also be shameful to think (*ne id non pudeat sentire quod pudeat dicere*). Again, interior and exterior are envisioned as matching. Quintus's practical advice to the electoral candidate finds justification in his brother's analysis of *pudor*, the sense of shame that governs personal interaction in the Republic and whose violation is also easily readable on the face.[28] For an individual to violate this sense causes the violation of one's status as a free-born citizen (Cic. *Lael.* 65). *Pudor* ensures that there does not occur a dissonance between what one says, feels, and outwardly expresses.

Although politics in classical Athens also surely depended on these kinds of face-to-face relations, it is remarkable that there is an "almost complete absence of description of facial expression or gesture in the Attic orators."[29] Ciceronian oratory, by contrast, contains constant textual cues to the need for visual vigilance; included especially are references to the visual appearance of the speaker, of the jurors or solo judge, and of the defendant. I would like now to treat each group in turn.

The person speaking in defense must offer an imposing presence in order to persuade successfully. In listing features that will lend authority to a person's persuasive abilities, Quintilian includes possessions that any Roman would value: wealth, influence, authority, and self-worth (*pecunia, gratia, auctoritas,*

---

[28] *Pudor*: Kaster 1997; on the blush: Barton 1999.
[29] Evans 1969.41.

dignitas). Quintilian caps this list of essential attributes with the speaker's "very appearance (*aspectus*)—even without speaking—through which judgment is rendered either by recalling each person's benefactions, or by a pitiful look, or through the beauty of one's aspect."[30] He draws his example from the Republic, recalling the moment when Antonius tore open his client's clothing to reveal the scars that had been received defending Rome. The act, Quintilian says, secured the defendant's acquittal not by relying on speech, but by "attacking the eyes of the Roman people" (*oculis populi Romani vim attulit*). In similar fashion, Cicero recalls how Marius escaped a guilty verdict in part on the strength of how he appeared in the eyes of the jury.[31] Cicero's remark in his *Brutus* seems apt in these contexts; a keen critic, he writes, can judge a real orator "with a passing glance" (200: *uno aspectu et praeteriens*). The *ethos* of the speaker, described in such detail by Aristotle, comes to include in Rome the arena of the visible.

A Roman orator also frequently calls attention to the "look" of the judging spectators, be they jurors, senators, or a single judge. In these instances the physical appearance of the face—marked often by *os*, *vultus*, or *aspectus*—is represented as chastening a defendant. Perhaps the most familiar example occurs in a long period at the beginning of the *First Oration against Catiline*, where Cicero speaks of how nothing deterred Catiline from his plans to over-whelm the city: neither city garrisons, nor a concern for the people and senate could stop him. The climax of this list is boldly expressed: "weren't you de-terred at all," Cicero asks Catiline directly, "by the faces and expressions (*ora vultusque*) of the senators here?"[32] In this, one of many examples of a familiar trope, the accused person's awareness of the reaction of others, a reaction he sees in their faces, should force him to reconsider the consequences of his own actions.[33] The Latin noun *spectator*, as Barton observes, encompasses the meanings "inspector, judge, and connoisseur."[34] Catiline, although observing, fails to judge the situation appropriately, a circumstance that only allows Cic-ero to incriminate further his unfitness for society.

Roman invective offers a third way in which the face is referenced: the face of the accused can stand as a readable set of signs pointing to guilt. The author of *Rhetorica ad Herennium* gives an example of this trope in his discussion of

---

[30] Quint. *inst.* 2.15.6: *verum et pecunia persuadet et gratia et auctoritas dicentis et dignitas, postremo aspectus etiam ipse sine voce, quo vel recordatio meritorum cuiusque vel facies aliqua miserabilis vel formae pulchritudo sententiam dictat.*

[31] Cic. *Balb.* 49 (*praesens . . . aspectus*); compare *har. resp.* 22.

[32] Cic. *Catil.* 1.1: *nihilne te nocturnum praesidium Palati, nihil urbis vigiliae, nihil timor populi, nihil concursus bonorum omnium, nihil hic munitissimus habendi senatus locus, nihil horum ora vultusque moverunt?*; compare *Catil.* 1.17.

[33] Other oratorical examples of an audience's expression reprehending a criminal (a partial list): *de orat.* 2.226 (L. Crassus); *Verr.* 2.1.1: *nemo . . . ora iudicum aspicere aut os suum populo Romano ostendere auderet; Verr.* 2.1.19: *qui non aspectu consessuque vestro commoveretur; Sull.* 74; *Deiot.* 5.

[34] Barton 2001.60.

notatio, a figure wherein the orator details the physical characteristics of an opponent as a way of pointing up his natural guilt: "consider first of all, judges, how he looks at us (*quo vultu nos intueatur*)."[35] Quintilian explains most clearly why the rhetorical tradition places such emphasis on facial expression: in an orator's delivery, he teaches, "the facial expression dominates most of all. . . . Through it we obtain the best understanding; often it replaces all speech."[36] Indeed, one peculiar example from Ciceronian oratory shows the face not only "speaking" about present circumstances but even recollecting past action. In the orations against Verres, Cicero emphatically enjoins the jury to look into the face of a malefactor to read his previous offences: "Observe, judges, the expression and look of the man, and from the brazen aspect he retains in this desperate situation recall (*recordamini*) those gusts of rage that you would imagine to have occurred in Sicily."[37] Tacitus, too, in his own rhetorical work—the *Dialogus*—uses "face" (*facies*) as a metaphor for "true nature" and so recalls the Republican ideal whereby faces could be trusted just as nature can be.[38] This recurrent emphasis on facial expression seems to stem from notions recurrent throughout antiquity—especially in Roman versions of Stoicism—that the face mirrors the soul. These rhetorical uses found further affirmation in the common assertion that located Rome's power in her understanding of how nature works. The necessity to interpret facial expressions emerges as a corollary to Roman mastery of both the natural and political worlds; other peoples may be superior to the Romans in number, shrewdness, and the arts, Cicero asserts, "but we have surpassed all nations in religious piety and in the knowledge that we have *perceived* how everything is ruled and governed by divine spirits."[39] The certainty concerning Rome's place in the divine order of things rests on the Romans' ability to "perceive" (*perspeximus*). On a smaller scale, the significance of the face can be put less abstractly: one judges a reaction in daily life according to facial expression; therefore within Roman culture, or within any isolated culture, there must be universality of interpretation for this type of communication to be successful. An irresistible conclusion, then, is to suppose facial expressions to be innate.[40]

---

[35] Rhet. Her. 4.63: *iudices, . . . primum nunc videte quo vultu nos intueatur.* Further examples of the guilty face—*os, vultus, aspectus,* and so forth—include (a partial list): *de orat.* 2.148; *Verr.* 2.3.22, 2.4.66; *Sull.* 74; *Clu.* 29, 54, 111; *Flacc.* 10; *Phil.* 11.7, 13.4. Compare the use in the *miseratio* (Quint. *inst.* 6.1.26; Cic. *Verr.* 2.5.128).

[36] Quint. *inst.* 11.3.72: *dominatur autem maxime vultus. . . . hoc plurima intellegimus, hic est saepe pro omnibus verbis;* see also *Brut.* 238, 265; *Font.* 28.

[37] Cic. *Verr.* 2.3.22 (Apronius): *aspicite, iudices, vultum hominis et aspectum, et ex ea contumacia quam hic in perditis rebus retinet illos eius spiritus Sicilienses quos fuisse putetis recordamini.*

[38] Tac. *dial.* 34.5 (in speaking of rhetorical training during the Republic): *ita nec praeceptor deerat . . . qui faciem eloquentiae, non imaginem praestaret.*

[39] Cic. *har. resp.* 19; Fowler 1911.357–79, esp. 365–72; Brunt 1989.182–84.

[40] Darwin drew the same inference; see Ekman 1973.169–74, who demonstrates that the inference is not a necessary one.

The Decline of Rhetoric as the Decline
of Physical Representation

I discussed in chapter 1 the curative properties derived from the principle of analogy. The Romans believed cures could be effected by exploiting the physical resemblance between an object in nature and the way in which a disease manifested itself on the body. The power of analogy was considered so strong that Romans could even consciously manufacture resemblances by giving similar names to disease and cure. In this section I wish to examine how an object in nature was perceived to possess an inherent resemblance not to other objects but to itself. This apparent tautology—how can something *not* resemble itself?—provides further support for the claim that, by nature, external appearance and internal character should coincide.

Cicero offers in his work *On the Laws* a particularly fascinating account of how nature shapes human character. As part of his demonstration that human beings are born to act in accordance with natural justice, he offers the following observation:

> Nihil est enim unum uni tam simile, tam par, quam omnes inter nosmet ipsos sumus. Quodsi depravatio consuetudinum, si opinionum vanitas non inbecillitatem animorum torqueret et flecteret, quocumque coepisset, sui nemo ipse tam similis esset quam omnes essent omnium. (Cic. *leg.* 1.29)[41]

> For no one thing is so similar and equal to another as we all are to ourselves. But if deviant practices and empty opinions were not twisting and bending in willful directions the weakness of our spirits, no one would be so like himself (*sui . . . similis*) as all people would be like everyone else.

This tortuous sentence presents one's "similarity to oneself" as a natural condition from which base actions and weak minds continually force us to deviate. An analysis of the range of uses of the phrase *similis sui* and related formulations will become relevant to how facial expressions are used in Roman society to judge character. Self-similarity and transparent facial expressions both represent the first chapter in a narrative of moral degeneration.

When occurring in texts heavily indebted to Greek predecessors, formulations of the type *similis sui* do not translate a specific Greek phrase. In philosophical contexts, the Latin expression describes a constant and unchanging state that inheres in nature and its components: the phrase can characterize one of the essences of which the universe is composed, the orbits of heavenly bodies, geographical features, and the universe itself.[42] By analogy with this

---

[41] I read *essent* with most editors; it is difficult to make sense of the manuscript reading *sunt*.

[42] *Essentia*: Cic. *Tim.* 21, *semper unius modi suique similis* (= Plat. *Tim.* 35A1–2: τῆς ἀμερίστου καὶ ἀεὶ κατὰ ταὐτὰ ἐχούσης οὐσίας), Apul. *mund.* 1.6; orbits: Cic. *Tim.* 34, *idem et semper sui similis orbis* (= Plat. *Tim.* 39D6: τῷ τοῦ ταὐτοῦ καὶ ὁμοίως ἰόντος . . . κύκλῳ); geography: Mela

well-ordered universe, the expression also describes the properly running state.[43] In contexts that are more in keeping with the natural human beings imagined in *On the Laws*, this state of self-consistency also characterizes the unadulterated human soul.[44] Each of these examples depicts entities reflecting back upon themselves their own similarity. In grammatical terms, the verbal notion of resemblance contained in the adjective *similis* takes the same concept as both its subject and object, the latter here expressed in the objective genitive *sui*.

When the term is applied to a specific individual, the phrase *similis sui* becomes less fixed, bifurcating semantically as the term "nature"/*natura* does in both Latin and English, where "nature" can describe a person's idiosyncratic and particular behavior ("it's in his nature") as well as "Nature," the fixed and unchanging principles that govern the natural world.[45] Similarly, some contexts indicate that the phrase *(dis)similis sui* can mean the equivalent of the English expression "that's so (un)like him," that is, an individual's behavior is judged depending upon how it accords with past observation.[46] In the *Brutus*, for example, Cicero attributes the decline in Hortensius's reputation as an orator to his increasingly careless lifestyle; when Hortensius perceived that he no longer had a potential equal in the courts he seemed to become, in Cicero's words, *sui dissimilior* (*Brut.* 320). The assessment "less like himself" indicates that Hortensius has deviated from the behavior that an observer would have expected on the basis of his past oratorical career.

More frequently, however, extant examples of the phrase *similis sui* reflect a notion of immutable character corresponding to that found in *On the Laws*, where the resemblance noted is between current behavior and an assumed preexisting pattern. This type of correspondence is supported by a recent survey of the Latin words for "face" and "facial expression" (*os, vultus, facies,* etc.), which concludes that each word was construed in antiquity as referring etymologically to characteristics "intrinsic to the subject"—the *os* "speaks" (*oro*) one's inner thoughts, the *vultus* expresses one's wishes (*volo*) and so forth.[47] A survey of *similis sui* allows us to view these findings in a diachronic frame. It is, in fact, late republican texts that present the clearest examples of the phrase used to describe inherent characteristics, a circumstance that does

---

1.116, 2.7, 3.24 (rivers), and 2.87 (land); *mundus*: Cic. *Tim.* 6, *semper idem <et> sui simile* (= Plat. *Tim.* 29A1: τὸ κατὰ ταὐτὰ καὶ ὡσαύτως ἔχον) and cf. Lucr. 5.830.

[43] Apul. *mund.* 19 (= Ps. Arist. *Mun.* 396B5–6: ὁμοίαν ἐξ ἀνομοίων . . . διάθεσιν).

[44] Cic. *Cato* 78, *Tusc.* 1.43.

[45] Corbeill 1996.14–16.

[46] Further examples (representative only): Cic. *Verr.* 2.5.55; *dissimilis*: Apul. *met.* 3.13; Juv. 10.192.

[47] Bettini 1996: "l'identità somatica, a Roma, non sembra tanto dipendere dall' 'essere visti' dagli altri, ma da caratteristiche in qualche modo intrinsiche al soggetto" (194).

not, I shall argue, simply reflect the paucity of evidence.[48] A passage in Cicero's speech *On Behalf of Cluentius* attests to the presupposition that one's behavior should follow a predictable pattern. After accusing Oppianicus of tampering with his father-in-law's will, Cicero launches into a typical *praeteritio*, one for which he is certain that the jurors can supply the missing vices:

> multa praetereo consulto; etenim vereor ne haec ipsa nimium multa esse videantur. vos tamen similem sui eum fuisse in ceteris quoque vitae partibus existimare debetis. (*Clu.* 41)

> I pass over many items on purpose, since I'm afraid that this might all seem to be too much. And yet you ought to judge that he was like himself (*similem sui*) in the remaining aspects of his life as well.

The phrasing here would seem to provide the foundation for the trope repeated in rhetorical treatises of the period: if a person can be shown guilty of one crime he may be accused of any.[49] The converse, not unexpectedly, also holds true. On two occasions in Cicero's oratorical corpus, the phrase *dissimilis sui* is used to argue that it is impossible—the grammatical construction in each case is a contrary-to-fact condition—for an honest man to act contrary to his morally upright character.[50]

The notion of the value of self-resemblance adds complexity to a famous scene in the underworld of Vergil's *Aeneid*. After Anchises has described to his son the future accomplishments of the elder Marcellus, Aeneas points out the shade of a younger man beside the hero, whose stature and placement lead Aeneas to believe that the young man is one of Marcellus's descendants. He remarks to Anchises on the shade's impressive and yet ambiguous approach:

> "qui strepitus circa comitum, *quantum instar in ipso,*
> sed nox atra caput tristi circumvolat umbra." (Verg. *Aen.* 6.865-866)

> "What a bustle of his comrades surround him, *how great an equivalence is in him,*
> and yet dark night flies around his head with a sad shadow." (italics added)

The interpretation of the phrase *quantum instar in ipso* is much disputed. The word *instar*, like most terms of moral evaluation in Latin, seems to have originated in the realm of the concrete to describe equivalence in weight or mass, perhaps reflecting an etymology from *instare* ("to stand in"), a verb that designates the state of two equal weights "standing in" balance.[51] In the Vergil

---

[48] I ignore, of course, the numerous occurrences of the phrase that are not truly reflexive, for instance, where another person or thing (children, paintings) is said to be a "good resemblance." For example, Apul. *met.* 10.32 (Venus promises Paris a woman *sui . . . consimilem*); Tac. *hist.* 1.38.

[49] *Inv.* 2.33; cf. 2.50 and Rhet. Her. 2.5.

[50] Cic. *Verr.* 2.4.16, *Phil.* 9.6.

[51] Wölfflin, with etymology at 1885.596–97, 1887.357, and Nettleship 1889.489; contrast Puhvel 1958.290–92, who traces its origins to Indo-European.

passage, it would be reasonable to assume that the young Marcellus is being compared to something or someone but—in contrast to all other instances of the word *instar* in Classical Latin, including its four other occurrences in the *Aeneid*—there is no accompanying noun in the genitive case that makes explicit the person or thing with which the young Marcellus is being compared.[52] This unusual circumstance has provided commentators with three possibilities for interpreting the phrase. The first is to understand the elder Marcellus as the implicit point of comparison ("How like Marcellus he is!"). Such a comparison, however, is hardly clear from the immediate context; one may also object that *instar* is used nowhere else to describe the similarity of human beings.[53] The second possibility sees the point of comparison in the lesser shades surrounding him: "he, singly, balances them all."[54] And yet by this reading the concluding phrase *in ipso* has no clear significance. A third, and the most commonly accepted, interpretation understands *instar* as a unique example of the word used absolutely, with no point of comparison supplied or implied ("What a majestic appearance!").[55] A number of considerations oppose this interpretation, as well. First, such an absolute use is nowhere else recorded among the extant uses of *instar*, so that this interpretation would find Vergil being willfully obscure.[56] Second, by this interpretation the concluding *in ipso* once again becomes otiose. Third, since Aeneas has just remarked on the shade's impressive external appearance (6.861: *egregium forma iuvenem*), it would be suitable and expected for Aeneas to remark here on something less tangible. Considering the implications of *similis sui* discussed above, I would suggest that a similar notion of "self-resemblance" is being noted in the young Marcellus's shade. By this interpretation, *in ipso* can be construed as taking the place of the expected genitive *sui*. Aeneas sees in the very appearance and stride of the young man the qualities that would have been familiar to Vergil's readers and Marcellus's contemporaries—"What a great state of self-balance he possesses!"

Keeping to one's true self—or, as with Marcellus, anticipating that self—becomes a matter of pride, provided that that true self is a worthy goal toward which to aspire. In 49 BCE, during the opening months of civil war, Julius Caesar writes a short note to Cicero in which he reacts calmly to the news

---

[52] Verg. *Aen.* 2.15, 3.637, 7.707, 12.923. TLL 7.1: 1968.64–66 (K. Alt and A. Szantyr) lists only Christian authors as omitting the genitive (or replacing it with a quasi-possessive adjective such as *divinum*), and Colum. 12.28.1, where the accusative is used.

[53] So, apparently, Servius ad loc. who simply notes "similitudo," with the Glossaries (see TLL 7.1: 1968.54–58 [K. Alt and A. Szantyr]); Henschel 1952; Williams 1972.515 ("possibly").

[54] Alt 1959, followed by Austin 1977.268 (quoted in the text).

[55] Claud. Don. *Aen.* 6.865 (*corporis forma*); Wölfflin 1885.585 ("Welch' stattliche Erscheinung!" or "Was für ein exemplar!"), followed by Norden 1903.333–34 ("quantum in eo inest ponderis atque amplitudinis").

[56] Alt 1959.161.

that some of the opponents he had recently pardoned are now threatening once more to take up arms against him. Caesar characterizes this ungrateful response as an indication of how an individual acts in accordance with predetermined character: the defections do not bother him, he claims, "since I prefer nothing more than that I be like myself and they like themselves" (*nihil enim malo quam et me mei similem esse et illos sui*; Caes. apud Cic. *Att.* 9.16.2). Caesar's use of the idiom *similis sui* not only displays clear contempt for his opponents' inborn character and satisfaction with his own, but further implies that that behavior should have been predictable.[57] Not surprisingly, the topos of unvaried character comes to find a comfortable home in Roman oratory.[58]

As the Republic declines, the equation of external appearance and internal character becomes problematized, as actors are shown to be increasingly capable of forging the pose of *similis sui*, of dis-simulating. Sallust famously traces the origin of this breakdown to Rome's emergence as the greatest Mediterranean power following the destruction of Carthage. With no real foreign threat left to check the growth of Roman extravagance, Sallust notes the negative influence of ambition (*ambitio*), "which has driven many people to have a good appearance (*voltum*) rather than a good character."[59] Greed and luxury cause the interior and exterior to separate. The problem seems to have grown particularly acute in the time of the Empire. Indeed, except for the instance from Suetonius with which I shall close this section, the only post-Republican example I have found of the phrase *similis sui* in describing a person's character occurs in the *Golden Ass* of Apuleius, where a woman who has poisoned her husband (and plans to poison her daughter) is "completely like herself, hiding the face of fidelity, but putting forward its appearance" (*met.* 10.27: *usquequaque sui similis, fidei supprimens faciem, praetendens imaginem*). Apuleius's use of "face" (*faciem*) is no mere metaphor; the nature of one's *fides* is properly sought in outward visage, but the woman is able to disguise it.[60] The irony intended by Apuleius becomes clear: the only person attaining the Republican ideal of self-resemblance is an innate master of dissemblance.[61]

I began this section with Cicero's explanation that complete self-resemblance is no longer possible because "deviant practices and empty opinions"

[57] D. Brutus's description of Labeo Segulius as *homo simillimus sui* seems similarly opprobrious (apud Cic. *fam.* 11.20.1); compare *Att.* 13.25.3, where the phrase *sui similem* refers ironically to the inherent skepticism of the Academy.

[58] See Riggsby (forthcoming) on fixed character, with bibiliography on its place in Roman culture generally.

[59] Sall. *Catil.* 10.5: *ambitio multos mortalis . . . subegit . . . magis . . . voltum quam ingenium bonum habere.*

[60] For *fides* readable in the face, see, too, Propertius's lament to Cynthia: "does no *fides* shout in my face?" (1.18.18: *non ulla meo clamat in ore fides?*).

[61] Compare Verres, who dissimulates in feigning *honest* behavior: *fuit tum sui dissimilis*; *Verr.* 2.2.48.

twist human beings from an imagined ideal state. One of Seneca's letters to
Lucilius charts the final stage in this deevolution. After quoting approvingly
Horace's assessment of Tigellius's inconsistent character (*sat.* 1.3.11-17), Sen-
eca remarks:

> homines multi tales sunt qualem hunc describit Horatius Flaccus, numquam eun-
> dem, ne similem quidem sibi; adeo in diversum aberrat. multos dixi? prope est ut
> omnes sint. (*epist.* 120.21)

> Many people are just as Horace describes this man here; never the same, not even
> resembling himself (*similem . . . sibi*). So much is he scattered in all directions.
> Did I say "many" people? Almost everyone is [this way].

Seneca uses our familiar phrase again, as he laments how human beings have
failed to live in accordance with some sort of prepatterned disposition. The
now familiar idea is, however, expressed with an unfamiliar construction: in
a significant variation from the examples encountered so far, *similis* governs
the dative *sibi* rather than the genitive *sui*.[62] When the adjective *similis* is used
to describe two distinct people or things, the substitution of the dative for
the genitive becomes common beginning with Livy, who appears to use both
grammatical cases with no distinction in meaning.[63] Before Livy, however,
Latin usage preserves a clear contrast between the two cases: "the genitive
is used by Cicero and older authors when it is a matter of an all-around,
comprehensive resemblance . . . , while the dative is used only for partial or
approximate resemblance."[64] Outside this passage from Seneca's letters, I have
found no example in Classical Latin of the dative construction *similis sibi* used
reflexively to describe a person's inner character.[65] I would like to suggest that
Seneca preserves in these remarks to Lucilius the use of the dative recognized
in earlier authors. Self-resemblance has declined to such a degree that not
only has self-identification become impossible (as would have been conveyed
by the genitive *similis sui*), but even any *similarity* between people and their
true selves has been lost (the connotations of the dative phrase, *similis sibi*).
The loss of clarity observed in the evolution of the construction of *similis*

---

[62] Seneca later speaks of an individual's own spirit (*animus*) being *impar sibi* (120.22, presumably after Hor. *sat.* 1.3.19).

[63] KS 1.450

[64] KS 1.449: "Der Genetiv wird von Cicero und den älteren Autoren gebraucht, wenn es sich
um eine allgemeine, umfassende Ähnlichkeit handelt (= Abbild, Ebenbild), hingegen der Dativ
bei nur teilweiser oder annähernder Ähnlichkeit;" LHS 78 seem to recognize the same distinction, writing that the genitive follows the substantized notion of *similis* ("entstanden durch Sub-
stantivierung") whereas the dative is used when the underlying verbal concept of the adjective
is more strongly felt ("entsprechend dem zugrundeliegenden Verbalbegriff").

[65] My source is the PHI disk. The reflexive phrase *similis sibi* is used, however, to describe
inanimate objects with durable and permanent features: a sphere (Manil. 1.213), the universe
(Manil. 2.704), and recurring feet in verse (Hor. *ars* 254, Quint. *inst.* 9.4.60, Ter. Maur. 1492).

represents, then, not simply another instance of grammatical boundaries loosening as Latin literature enters its so-called Silver Age. The change, rather, is driven by a new conception of how human beings have begun to lose their ability to identify with the more-than-human world. The development from *similis sui* to *similis sibi* provides an instance of meaning determining grammar.

I had mentioned that one imperial exception remains of the personal, reflexive use of *similis sui*. The speaker is the subject of the remainder of this chapter. The emperor Tiberius uses the phrase to describe himself.

ASPECTUS AS APPEARANCE

How does one see through the person who, like Apuleius's female poisoner, is not truly *similis sui* but only engaged in the act of dissimulating? The passages just discussed indicate that the dissemblance can be revealed in external appearance, including the face. It then surprises when Tiberius, whom the Roman biographical tradition consistently portrays as offering a willfully deceptive look, provides the following defense for refusing excessive honors upon succeeding Augustus:

> ait similem se semper sui futurum nec umquam mutaturum mores suos, quam diu sanae mentis fuisset. (Suet. *Tib.* 67.3)

> He said he would always be like himself (*similem . . . sui*) and would never change his character for as long as he remained sane.

As an orator who was, to a fault, picky in his speaking style, Tiberius must have chosen the phrase deliberately.[66] I do not wish here to attempt to historicize his promise by considering whether Tiberius dissembles in denying his ability to dissemble or whether hindsight has prevented later readers from recognizing in these kinds of statements a sincere desire to redefine the post-Augustan principate.[67] For when we turn to the depiction of Tiberius in Tacitus's *Annals*, the trust in the equation of physical and spiritual is gone. We no longer see faces, but only pretext, appearance, and dissimulation. *Species, imago, dissimulatio*—all are terms that recur when prominent politicians appear, and they are used to describe these people's attempts to alter self-resemblance.[68] The notion reflected in Tiberius's adoption of the phrase *similis sui* contradicts Tacitus's description of Tiberius on his deathbed. As the emperor loses the strength to

---

[66] Suet. *Tib.* 70.1: *adfectatione et morositate nimia obscurabat stilum*; on Tiberius's speaking style in general, see N. P. Miller 1968; Bloomer 1997, esp. 158–61.

[67] Woodman 1998 offers the most recent attempt to interpret favorably Tiberius's famous hesitation.

[68] On Tacitus's use of *species* and other such words, see Cousin 1951, esp. 235–39, Walker 1952.240–41, Martin 1981.284; among the many recent discussions of Tiberius's deceptive appearance, see Bloomer 1997.154–95, O'Gorman 2000.81–89.

control his body, his skill at dissimulation nevertheless remains (6.50.1: *iam Tiberium corpus, iam vires, nondum dissimulatio deserebat*). Tacitus wishes to demonstrate that the dead emperor did not uphold the very virtues he trumpeted upon entering the principate. Tiberius, he claims in this passage, matured so effectively as a master of dissimulation that the practice became a more stable part of his self than his own corporeality.[69] In a move away from the ways I have been describing the actions of Roman bodies throughout this book, the detachment of the physical from the self prevents the body from accurately displaying interior morality to the observer. At this point I would like to shift attention from Tiberius's possible intentions, which are ultimately unknowable, to the ways in which—and the reasons why—Tacitus puts so much emphasis on why he had to interpret the emperor's intentions as deceptive.

At the heart of Tacitus's historiography lies the hope that he can distinguish between truth and appearance; indeed, the principate of Tiberius, with its examples of judicial persecution that pale next to the tribulations of the Republican period, demands that Tacitus apply psychological analysis to get at the motivations of his protagonists. This analysis proposes a new way of looking, one that contrasts explicitly with the Republican model of truth in appearance. As Tacitus himself observes in one of his rare excursuses on historical method, the historian of the Republic simply had to know the nature of the mob and learn the minds of the elite in order to understand the workings of history and be considered a perceptive analyst of the period:

> olim plebe valida, vel cum patres pollerent, noscenda vulgi natura et quibus modis temperanter haberetur, senatusque et optimatium ingenia qui maxime perdidicerant, callidi temporum et sapientes credebantur. (Tac. *ann.* 4.33.2)

> At one time, when the common people were strong or when the senate reigned, one had to learn the nature (*natura*) of the crowd and how to handle it discreetly, and those who had clearly perceived the inherent dispositions (*ingenia*) of the senate and elite were considered shrewd observers of the times.

Note Tacitus's vocabulary in describing the qualities that the Republican historians must assess: the crowd's "nature" (*natura*) and the "inherent dispositions" (*ingenia*) of the elite. In this seemingly golden age of historiography, an analysis of the innate qualities of the people and their rulers yields an understanding of their actions and motivations. Contrast the situation under an empire or, more accurately, under an emperor, where circumstances force the historian to seek underlying causes. The new strategy that Tacitus must employ entails a new kind of looking. Tacitus introduced this excursus by remarking that "it would not be without profit to scrutinize (*introspicere*) those things that had seemed trivial at first sight" (*non . . . sine usu fuerit introspicere illa primo aspectu*

---

[69] I follow the arguments of Woodman 1989 that Tacitus does not claim for Tiberius at *Annals* 6.51 a constant character throughout his reign.

levia: ann. 4.32.2). A study of the verb *introspicere* has revealed that Tacitus's use of the word in this passage shows him inventing a new kind of Roman historiography that must "uncover what lies beyond the limits of the known."[70] Tacitus clearly believes, and the analysis of his new application of the verb *introspicere* both here and elsewhere underscores this belief, that the erection of the limits between what can and cannot be known is a symptom of Rome's advanced state of decline. Among the Germans of his *Germania*, for example, the equation of physical and spiritual still exists. In describing their state, Tacitus employs the phrase whose uses we have just surveyed: by being free from intermarriage with other tribes, the Germans remained a people having a similarity only to themselves (*sui similem gentem*).[71] The ideal state of Cicero's *On the Laws* can be glimpsed in these tribes to the north.

By contrast, the opening of the seventh chapter of Book 1 of the *Annals* contains the following description of the aristocracy under Tiberius: "the more respectable the person, the more deceptive and eager he was. They arranged their expressions (*vultu . . . composito*) so as not to seem too happy at Augustus's death or too upset at the new beginning, combining tears with joy, lamentation with flattery."[72] Tacitus believes he can account for this newly emerging lack of trust in appearances. Tiberius, he claims, has deliberately manipulated the equation of external form and internal intention to distinguish his supporters in the senate from his foes. The historian states authoritatively at *Annals* 1.7 a fact that he said was learned only later—that is, after Tiberius's position in power had become firm. The new princeps, he writes, "was storing away the words and expressions (*vultus*) of the elite, distorting [these expressions] to make them incriminating."[73] We learn later that Tiberius even has his aides note the *vultus* of his opponents when he is not present; after Drusus had been imprisoned, the emperor ordered that reports be made of his every facial expression (6.24.2). The Republican model of truth in appearance has been subverted; the faces of the elite have become texts that are deliberately misinterpreted by Tiberius, a perverse reader.[74]

Modern readers of these passages will most likely assume that Tacitus's characterization of events relies on literary imagination, taking place as they do a century before he describes them in his text. Tacitus understandably reconstructs from hindsight, one could claim, a senate that stands bewildered in the

[70] Lana 1989.6 ("a scoprire ciò che sta oltre i limiti del noto"); O'Gorman 2000.78–105 begins from this same premise to argue that "the difficulties of reading [Tiberius] are a dramatisation of the difficulties of reading the *Annals*" (78).

[71] Tac. *Germ.* 4.1: *ipse eorum opinionibus accedo, qui Germaniae populos nullis aliarum nationum conubiis infectos propriam et sinceram et tantum sui similem gentem existisse arbitrantur.*

[72] Tac. *ann.* 1.7.1: *quanto quis inlustrior, tanto magis falsi ac festinantes vultuque composito, ne laeti excessu principis neu tristiores primordio, lacrimas gaudium, questus adulationem miscebant*; compare the senate's reaction to Otho at Tac. *hist.* 1.85.

[73] Tac. *ann.* 1.7.7: *verba vultus in crimen detorquens recondebat.*

[74] Cousin 1951.236 nn. 13–18 catalogues Tacitus's description of the *vultus* used in dissimulation.

face of an untested autocrat. Yet there are cogent reasons to believe that the historian is not merely exercising his prerogative as a literary stylist when embellishing his account, as he often does, with details of the expressions and demeanor of his characters.[75] A particularly telling indication of his use of contemporary sources occurs in the description of the prosecution of Lepida in 20 CE, five years into Tiberius's reign. Tacitus describes the difficulties faced by observers in determining Tiberius's feelings: "not easily could someone discern (*dispexerit*) the emperor's mind during that trial, so much did he alternate and confuse signs of anger and clemency."[76] The tense of the potential subjunctive *dispexerit*, denoting action at the present time, indicates that the failure to make sense resides not among the contemporaries of Tiberius, but among those of Tacitus himself, who is likely using written narratives of the trial to determine for himself the meaning of the emperor's shifting expressions.[77] Tacitus follows the fascination of his sources in carefully recording Tiberius's unpredictable demeanor. On another occasion, Tiberius and Livia avoid being seen in public during the period of mourning that follows the death of Germanicus. This seemingly understandable unwillingness to display grief publicly is construed differently by Tacitus, who offers as one explanation for their behavior a desire that people not spot hypocrisy in their grieving faces.[78] Tiberius, then, is represented as the paradigm object for this new historiography, as one who works to obstruct "the limits of the known."

It may be possible to go further in reconstructing the historical Tiberius at whom the senators gaze in confusion and from whom they averted their own eyes. An interesting correspondence exists between the features of the emperor as described in Tacitus and other depictions of Tiberius's physique that survive from antiquity. The historian Velleius Paterculus, a contemporary of the emperor, mentions that, even before succeeding Augustus, Tiberius "had displayed [the qualities of an] emperor in the way he looked" (2.94.2: *visu . . . praetulerat principem*). My translation "the way he looked" tries to capture the full sense of Velleius's *visus*, a word meaning both the act of seeing and the object seen, "gaze" and "appearance" (compare English "sight"). This choice of noun to typify Tiberius's grandeur is suggestive.[79] In describing the physical

---

[75] See Talbert 1984.331–32 for a list of relevant passages.

[76] Tac. *ann.* 3.22.3: *haud facile quis dispexerit illa in cognitione mentem principis, adeo vertit ac miscuit irae et clementiae signa*; compare Tiberius at Piso's trial ([Piso] *Tiberium sine miseratione, sine ira, obstinatum clausumque vidit*; 3.15.2).

[77] On the aoristic perfect of the potential subjunctive used with present significance, see LHS 333–34.

[78] Tac. *ann.* 3.3.1: *ne omnium oculis vultum eorum scrutantibus falsi intellegerentur*. For the tradition of Tiberius's hypocrisy outside Tacitus, see Suet. *Tib.* 24.1, 65.1; Dio 57.1.1, 57.1.3.

[79] As it is suggestive to Velleius's commentator, whose note on the passage ranges from Tiberius's physical demeanor to his unusual eyesight (Woodman 1977.97–99). The claim of Bettini 1996.178 that *visus* never means "appearance" ("viso") in Classical Latin is incorrect.

19. Portrait of Tiberius. Museo civico, Jesi, Italy (photo
Rossa; Deutsches Archäologisches Institut Rom,
inst. neg. 75.1062).

appearance of the emperor, Suetonius notes Tiberius as having "very large
eyes," a feature confirmed by extant visual representations (*Tib.* 68.2; see
fig. 19). Portraits such as these are likely to represent a feature of the living
emperor since in these otherwise "smooth and idealized" works, "the oversized
eyes gave the heads a striking imbalance."[80] An equally characteristic feature
of the surviving portraits of the emperor is the mouth. Its disproportionately
small size, together with an overhanging upper lip, allow art historians to

---

[80] Kleiner 1992.124. Bartman 1999.107–8 suggests that the large eyes in Tiberian portraiture
may be among the iconographical elements inherited from his mother, Livia.

identify even fragmentary faces as depictions of Tiberius.[81] The combination of over-large eyes and small, sealed mouth captures well the description of Tacitus's Tiberius as he observes and records the expressions of others while offering in his own face features that resist being easily read.

Besides characterizing official portraiture, Tiberius's gaze also uniquely captured the popular imagination. The elder Pliny, born and raised to adolescence in the same emperor's reign, digresses in his remarks on the function of the human eye to register notable traits of each of the Julio-Claudian rulers: Claudius's eyes were commonly bloodshot, for example, while Nero's nearsightedness often caused him to squint. Among these mundane observations Pliny records a remarkable feature of Tiberius: "people say that Tiberius Caesar, alone of human beings, had a constitution such that, when awakened at night, he could see everything just as if it were daylight, until gradually darkness prevented him."[82] A common physiological explanation for eyesight in antiquity hypothesized that an internal fire streamed out through the pupils;[83] if such a scientific explanation lies behind this popular tradition about Tiberius, it would appear that contemporaries viewed the emperor's glare as an aberration of nature, as a clue to his uncomfortable fit with the rest of humanity. Even his stepfather Augustus recognized how Tiberius's physical features were both displeasing and intimidating in the face of Roman normative concepts. Suetonius tells us how Augustus "frequently tried to excuse, before the senate and the people, all [Tiberius's odd features of physique and demeanor] by saying 'the faults are of nature, not of his spirit, "(naturae vitia . . . esse, non animi)."[84] The dichotomy Augustus wishes to stress here between nature and internal character is, as we have seen, one that Cicero would not have chosen to make in the Republic, since the view of morality he asserted publicly rested upon the very equation of nature and spirit. And the behavior of Tacitus's senate shows that Augustus's defense offered them little consolation.

These two peculiarities characterizing the non-Tacitean Tiberius—reticent mouth and gleaming eyes—match the unreadability and the penetrating gaze we find in the historian. But do these features really represent something unique in the historian's view of power? Vasily Rudich has examined the Neronian senate which, like the senate under Tiberius, is represented as continually

[81] Fittschen and Zanker (1985) 1.16, on Museo Capitolino, Magazin. inv. 3029 (= Tafel 15, nr. 14). Polacco 1955 offers a synthetic overview of Tiberius's portraiture as derived from literature, coins, and sculpture.

[82] Plin. nat. 11.143: ferunt Tiberio Caesari, nec alii genitorum mortalium, fuisse naturam ut expergefactus noctu paulisper haut alio modo quam luce clara contueretur omnia paulatim tenebris sese obducentibus; see, too, Suet. Tib. 68.2: cum praegrandibus oculis et qui, quod mirum esset, noctu etiam et in tenebris viderent, sed ad breve et cum primum e somno patuissent; deinde rursum hebescebant.

[83] Seligmann 1929–1930.680.

[84] Suet. Tib. 68.3: quae omnia . . . excusare temptavit saepe apud senatum ac populum professus naturae vitia esse, non animi."

stumbling in a lack of certainty about the emperor's will. Rudich posits that
this uncertainty is a reflection of what he calls the "dissident mind"—that is,
the best means for a senator to survive Nero entailed concealing one set of
feelings and displaying another.[85] Rudich's explanation accounts well for individual motivation, as each senator attempts to secure his own safety. Yet Tacitus figures the origins of this change in senate-emperor relations as involving
more than individual psychology. Instead, a radical shift has occurred in the
relationship between ruler and ruled. Tiberius has himself become a god.

At this point I would like to return to the beginning of the chapter and the
analogy between the Roman suspicion of the trope of the metaphor and the
unwillingness to detach external appearance from internal morality, a conception that is most strongly embodied in the phrase *similis sui*. The ways in which
I posit the identification of linguistic practice with the physical world finds
analogies in Todorov's analysis of the uncertainty attendant upon the indigenous Americans of Mexico as they try to make sense of their first contacts
with European culture.[86] According to this analysis, the ability to communicate between the indigenous peoples and the Spaniards is flawed by their
differing means of using language. The Mexicans communicate with and
through the world, the Spaniards with and through men, a system in which
hypocrisy has developed as a means of deception. For example, when Cortés
requests gold, offering as a pretext that he needs it to cure a sickness, the
Mexicans, for whom gold has no symbolic or economic value, have difficulty
understanding the request.[87] The reason for this misunderstanding, Todorov
concludes, resides in the fact that the Mexican has the "capacity to feel in
harmony with the world, to belong to a preestablished order," in contrast with
the Europeans, whose detachment from the natural world—as exemplified in
this case by the symbolic valorization of gold—produces "the illusion that all
communication is interhuman communication."[88] I of course do not wish to
portray Tiberius as an early counterpart to Cortés, introducing into Roman
politics a worldview aimed at overturning the existing power structure. And
yet I sense in Todorov's account a deep parallel with that of Tacitus. When
interhuman communication becomes detached from a system where human
beings seek to make sense of the world, dissimulation becomes a useful tool.
I wish to suggest that it is this kind of momentous intrusion—figured as divine
disruption—that informs Tacitus's portrayal of this first emperor.

Tiberius's figural deification is clearly expressed in an echo from his predecessor Sallust with which Tacitus opens Book 4 of the *Annals*. The passage

---

[85] Rudich 1993.xxii–xxiii.
[86] Todorov 1984.53–123 ("The Reasons for the Victory"); this paragraph especially depends
on 93–97.
[87] Ibid.96.
[88] Ibid.97.

from Sallust occurs in the *Bellum Catilinae* during the historian's famous explo-ration into the causes of Rome's moral decline, where he locates the ultimate origin for the city's moral breakdown in the new lifestyle available to Romans following the destruction of Carthage. With Rome's primary opponent re-moved, he writes, "fortune began to rage and to mix up everything" (*saevire fortuna ac miscere omnia coepit*).[89] Tacitus's echo is as clear as the modifications he makes to his source are telling: *repente turbare fortuna coepit, saevire ipse [Tiberius] aut saevientibus vires praebere* ("suddenly fortune began to stir up, to rage began he himself [i.e., Tiberius] or to supply opportunities to those rag-ing").[90] In 23 CE, the ninth year of Tiberius's reign, Tacitus tells us that the emperor's affairs have reached both an acme and a point of decline, just as Rome had for Sallust two hundred years earlier. Yet note the striking change Tacitus makes in Sallust's formulation. In both authors, *fortuna* is a source of trouble—it "rages" (*saevire*) in Sallust and "stirs up" (*turbare*) in Tacitus. Tac-itus, however, then repeats Sallust's *saevire*, but changes its grammatical sub-ject; *ipse*—Tiberius—now rages in place of fortune and becomes the source of the rage of others (*saevientibus vires praebere*). The effect is striking in its abrupt clarity. By unexpectedly transferring agency from Sallust's impersonal *fortuna* to the emperor Tiberius, Tacitus attributes to him, in the words of recent commentators on this passage, "the characteristics of a perverse and powerful deity."[91] Tacitus here continues the conceit of deifying the still-living Tiberius that he adopted in Book 1 when describing the senate meeting held to discuss Tiberius's succession to Augustus: divine honors to the dead Augustus are juxtaposed with "prayers" to the living Tiberius (*preces*; Tac. *ann.* 1.10.8–1.11.1); the distraught senators plead with a new trinity—the gods, the newly deified Augustus, and the knees of the mortal Tiberius (1.11.3: *ad deos ad effigiem Augusti ad genua ipsius manus tendere*).

In describing this meeting in Book 1 Tacitus is intent on portraying not so much the senators fawning in insincere adulation as their new state, one completely different from republican notions in "its abject subservience to, and complete dependence on, the *princeps*."[92] The verb *miscere* ("to mix up"), which Tacitus had dropped in *Annals* 4.1 when imitating Sallust, has already appeared in this earlier context, at the very moment when Tiberius is able to succeed Augustus. The senators and *equites* are depicted as confused over how to greet the death of Augustus: "they were mixing (*miscebant*) tears, joy, lam-entation, flattery."[93] In describing this feigned adulation, Tacitus shows how perceptions have altered regarding the premises that informed the use of facial

[89] Sall. *Catil.* 10.1.
[90] Tac. *ann.* 4.1.
[91] Martin and Woodman 1989 ad loc.
[92] Woodman 1998.49.
[93] Tac. *ann.* 1.7.1: *lacrimas gaudium questus adulationem miscebant* (see, too, 3.67, where a man under trial composes a letter to Tiberius in which *invidiam et preces miscuerat*); the verb is used of

expression in Republican oratory. It is no longer possible to infer internal motivation from facial expression, since the philosophical equation that identifies reason (*ratio*), natural law (*natura*), and god (*deus*) has acquired a new member: the *princeps* Tiberius.[94] With the *princeps* now standing as a god who not only controls, but in fact replaces, *fortuna*, trust in external appearance becomes lost. Tiberius himself emerges as the ultimate and unsurpassable master of dissimulation.

Conclusion: Tiberius and the New World Order

After Tiberius, it is only the very worst emperors to whom Tacitus attributes the mastery of dissimulation: Nero and Domitian. Domitian is especially dangerous—he had the ability to read the slightest sigh or blush, while to a viewer his face provided an inscrutable text.[95] "The extreme of autonomy and self-mastery was the deliberate blush," and it was this skill that the emperor notoriously had perfected.[96] And yet it is with Nero's reign that Tacitus most clearly reveals the consequences of this autonomy. When Nero feels compelled to flee the site of his mother's murder, he is driven out by the "serious look" of the natural features of the place. In recording this event, Tacitus explicitly shows the discontinuity between the human self and the physical world: "the face of places cannot be changed like the expressions of human beings" (Tac. *ann.* 14.10.3: *non, ut hominum vultus, ita locorum facies mutantur, observabaturque maris illius et litorum gravis aspectus*). When sensations are felt purely, nature reacts fully, as in the way it reflects the massacre of Varus's legions. When Germanicus tours the site of this defeat in the first book of the *Annals*, he examines together with the readers a lost past. The episode provides not simply a vivid example of the limits of empire for Rome's military; at the same time it parallels the loss felt as a result of Tiberius's ability at dissimulation. What literary critics are trained to label as an example of the "pathetic fallacy" is hardly fallacious for Tacitus. The loss of the correspondence between the emotions of nature and the tragedies of humanity is what truly gives rise to pathos.

Nietzsche perceived a contrast between Rome's first two emperors: Augustus the master actor versus Tiberius, the "most tormented of all self-tormentors . . . genuine and no actor." Recent scholarly interpretations of Tiberius's reign have continued in the direction toward which Nietzsche gestures in

---

the dissimulating Tiberius also at 3.22 (*miscuit irae et clementiae signa*) and is used to typify a large portion of his reign at 6.51 (*inter bona malaque mixtus incolumi matre*).

[94] Sen. *benef.* 4.8.3 offers a clear enunciation of this principle, which is not exclusively Stoic; for a general discussion, see Beagon 1992.26–54.

[95] Tac. *Agr.* 45.2 and 42.2; Plin. *paneg.* 48.4.

[96] Barton 1999.222; cf. 224: "the voluntary blush was a mask disguising the collapse or rejection of the balancing systems of shame."

their attempts to rescue Tiberius from the role of calculated tyrant. Such resuscitation, whatever its historical value, surely opposes Tacitus's view of everything that Tiberius's accession entailed. In continuing his conceit of Augustus-actor and Tiberius-nonactor, Nietzsche imagines an appropriate contrast between the dying words of these two men. Augustus famously called together his friends while on his deathbed and bid them applaud him for playing well the comedy of life (Suet. *Aug.* 99.1: *mimum vitae commode transegisse*). In contrast, Nietzsche imagines that Tiberius would have inverted the role of actor and audience, proclaiming "what a spectator dies with me!"[97] It is the dual role of Tiberius, his ability to present not only a facial riddle but to penetrate through the attempts of others to deceive him, that Tacitus finds the saddest and most telling departure from Republican tradition.

Since the 1960s, social scientists have increasingly studied the interpersonal dynamics that have come to be classified generally as nonverbal communication. As this area of research has matured, its focus has expanded from pragmatic consideration of the ways in which two individuals interact in social situations to the importance such communication has for keeping society together.[98] Both spoken language and body language are necessary for social stability: in Bateson's words, "It seems that the discourse of nonverbal communication is precisely concerned with matters of relationship—love, hate, respect, fear, dependency, etc.—between self and vis-à-vis or between self and environment and that the nature of human society is such that falsification of this discourse rapidly becomes pathogenic."[99] Tacitus's detection of this type of pathogen in the reign of Tiberius forces him to envision a new intention for the enterprise of historical writing. With the transvaluation of values, Tacitus no longer shares with Cicero the necessity to teach his readers how to read; instead, attention now focuses on how to survive.[100] Yet the ever slippery nature of external appearance baffles Tacitus's attempts to read into history any stable meanings. This historiographic aporia is informed by the breakdown of a fixed system for understanding our relationship with the more-than-human, a system to which the Romans had traditionally turned for moral explanation and for the maintenance of a stable social and political order. Tacitus's emphasis on facial expression in describing the reign of Tiberius is not, therefore, simply a cynical view of the effect power politics has on its players. A successfully deceptive face signals a loss of innocence, and even

[97] Nietzsche 1974.105, playing on Nero's lament "What an artist dies with me!" (Suet. *Nero* 49.1: *qualis artifex pereo!*).

[98] See, for example, the overview in Argyle 1988, esp. 290–304.

[99] Bateson 1972.412–13.

[100] See, for example, his famous remarks on the lives of Manius Lepidus (*ann.* 4.20) and Agricola (*Agr.* 42.5).

raises doubts about the existence of divine providence, of *Fortuna*. For Tacitus, the accession of the emperor Tiberius and the introduction of a new political order have prompted the rise of a new cosmic order, a new perception of the increasingly inscrutable relationship between truth and the body. How can Tacitus help *not* being pessimistic? If he were to do otherwise, he would only be deceiving himself.

BIBLIOGRAPHY

Abram, D. *The Spell of the Sensuous: Perception and Language in a More-than-Human World* (New York 1996).

Achard, G. *Pratique rhétorique et idéologie politique dans les discours "optimates" de Cicéron* (Leiden 1981). Mnemosyne Supplementum 68.

——. *La communication à Rome* (Paris 1994).

Ackerman, G. *The Life and Work of Jean-Léon Gérôme* (London 1986).

Adkin, N. "The Teaching of the Fathers concerning Footwear and Gait," *Latomus* 42 (1983) 885–86.

Ahl, F. *Metaformations* (Ithaca 1985).

——. "*Ars est caelare artem* (Art in Puns and Anagrams Engraved)," in J. Culler ed., *On Puns* (Oxford 1988) 17–43.

Ahlberg, G. *Prothesis and Ekphora in Greek Geometric Art* (Göteborg 1971) 2 vols. Studies in Mediterranean Archaeology 32.

Aldrete, G. *Gestures and Acclamations in Ancient Rome* (Baltimore 1999).

Alexiou, M. *The Ritual Lament in Greek Tradition* (Cambridge 1974).

Allen, F. "On 'os columnatum' (Plaut. M.G. 211) and Ancient Instruments of Confinement," *Harvard Studies in Classical Philology* 7 (1896) 37–64.

Alt, K. "*Instar* (Verg. Aen. 6.865)," *Museum Helveticum* 16 (1959) 159–62.

Amedick, R. *Die Sarkophage mit Darstellungen aus dem Menschenleben. Vierter Teil: Vita privata* (Berlin 1991).

——. "Zur Ikonographie der Sarkophagen mit Darstellungen aus der *Vita Privata* und dem *Curriculum Vitae* eines Kindes," in G. Koch ed., *Grabeskunst der römischen Kaiserzeit* (Mainz 1993) 143–53.

Anderson, W. S. "Two Passages from Book Twelve of the *Aeneid*," *California Studies in Classical Antiquity* 4 (1971) 49–65.

André, J. *Traité de physiognomonie par un anonyme latin* (Paris 1981).

Appel, G. *De Romanorum precationibus* (Gießen 1909). Religionsgeschichtliche Versuche und Vorarbeiten 7: 2.

Argyle, M. *Bodily Communication* (Madison, Conn. 1988).

Atkinson, J. M. *Our Masters' Voices: The Language and Body Language of Politics* (London and New York 1984).

Aubert, J.-J. "Threatened Wombs: Aspects of Ancient Uterine Magic," *Greek, Roman and Byzantine Studies* 30 (1989) 421–49.

Aurigemma, S. *I mosaici di Zliten* (Rome 1926).

Austin, R. G. *P. Vergili Maronis Aeneidos Liber Sextus* (Oxford 1977).

Aubriot, D. *Prière et conceptions religieuses en Grèce ancienne jusqu' à la fin du Ve siécle av. J.-C.* (Lyon 1992).

Axer, J. "Tribunal-Stage-Arena: Modelling of the Communication Situation in M. Tullius Cicero's Judicial Speeches," *Rhetorica* 7 (1989) 299–311.

Bächtold-Stäubli, H., ed. *Handwörterbuch des Deutschen Aberglaubens* (Berlin and Leipzig 1927–1942) 10 vols.

Baltrusch, E. *"Regimen morum": Die Reglementierung des Privatlebens der Senatoren und Ritter in der römischen Republik und frühen Kaiserzeit* (Munich 1989). Vestigia 41.

Barasch, M. *Gestures of Despair in Medieval and Early Renaissance Art* (New York 1976).

Bartman, E. *Portraits of Livia. Imaging the Imperial Woman in Augustan Rome* (Cambridge 1999).

Barton, C. *The Sorrows of the Ancient Romans. The Gladiator and the Monster* (Princeton 1993).

———. "The Roman Blush: The Delicate Matter of Self-Control," in J. I. Porter ed., *Constructions of the Classical Body* (Ann Arbor 1999) 212–34.

———. *Roman Honor. The Fire in the Bones* (Berkeley and Los Angeles 2001).

Bartsch, S. *Actors in the Audience. Theatricality and Doublespeak from Nero to Hadrian* (Cambridge, Mass. 1994).

Barzini, L. *The Italians* (London 1964).

Bateson, G. *Steps to an Ecology of Mind* (New York 1972).

———. "This Normative Natural History Called Epistemology," in R. Donaldson ed., *Sacred Unity: Further Steps to an Ecology of Mind* (New York 1991) 215–24; orig. published as "Afterword" in J. Brockman ed., *About Bateson: Essays on Gregory Bateson* (New York 1977) 235–47.

Beagon, M. *Roman Nature. The Thought of Pliny the Elder* (Oxford 1992).

Beard, M. "The Function of the Written Word in Roman Religion," in J. H. Humphrey ed., *Literacy in the Roman World* (Ann Arbor 1991). *Journal of Roman Archaeology*, suppl. 3.

Belayche, N. "La neuvaine funéraire à Rome ou 'la mort impossible,' " in F. Hinard 1995 ed., 155–69.

Bell, A. "Cicero and the Spectacle of Power," *Journal of Roman Studies* 87 (1997) 1–22.

Bell, M. Rev. of Holloway 1991, *American Journal of Archaeology* 97 (1993) 366.

Berczelly, L. "The Soul after Death: A New Interpretation of the Fortunati Sarcophagus," *Acta ad archaeologiam et artium historiam pertinentia* 6 (1987) 59–90.

Berry, D. H. *Cicero: pro Sulla oratio* (Cambridge 1996). Cambridge classical texts and commentaries 30.

Bettini, M. " 'Guardarsi in faccia' a Roma. Le parole dell' apparenza fisica nella cultura latina," *Parolechiave* 10/11 (1996) 175–95.

Betz, H. D. "Fragments from a Catabasis Ritual in a Greek Magical Papyrus," *History of Religions* 19 (1980) 287–95.

Binford, L. "Mortuary practices: their study and their potential," in J. A. Brown ed., *Approaches to the social dimension of mortuary practices. Memoirs of the Society of American Archaeology* 25 (1971) 6–28. Special issue of *American Antiquity*, 36: 3 pt. 2.

Bloch, M., and J. Parry eds. *Death and the Regeneration of Life* (Cambridge 1982).

Bloomer, M. *Latinity and Literary Society at Rome* (Philadelphia 1997).

Bonfante, L. "Nursing Mothers in Classical Art," in A. Koloski-Ostrow and C. Lyons eds., *Naked Truths: Women, Sexuality, and Gender in Classical Art and Archaeology* (London and New York 1997) 174–96.

Bonnefond, M. "Espace, temps et idéologie: Le sénat dans la cité romaine républicaine," *Dialoghi di archeologia*, 3ᵈ ser., 1, no. 1 (1983) 37–44.

Bonner, C. "Note on the Paris Magical Papyrus," *Classical Philology* 25 (1930) 180–83.

Botsford, G. *The Roman Assemblies from their Origin to the End of the Republic* (New York 1909).

Bourdieu, P. "La maison kabyle ou le monde renversé," in J. Pouillon and P. Maranda eds., *Échanges et communications. Mélanges offerts à Claude Lévi-Strauss à l'occasion de son 60ᵉ anniversaire* (Paris and The Hague 1970) 739–58.

———. *Distinction: A Social Critique of the Judgement of Taste*, trans. R. Nice (Cambridge, Mass. 1984).

———. *The Logic of Practice*, trans. R. Nice (Stanford 1990).

———. "The Economy of Linguistic Exchanges," in J. B. Thompson ed., *Language and Symbolic Power*, trans. G. Raymond and M. Adamson (Cambridge, Mass. 1991) 37–89.

Bourdieu, P., and M. de Saint-Martin. "Scholastic excellence and the values of the educational system," in J. Eggleston ed., *Contemporary Research in the Sociology of Education* (London 1974) 338–71 (trans. J. C. Whitehouse). Originally published as "L'excellence scolaire et les valeurs du système d'enseignement français," *Annales* 1 (Jan./Feb. 1970) 146–75.

Bourguet, P. du. *Early Christian Painting*, trans. S. Taylor (New York 1966).

Boyancé, P. "La main de Fides," in M. Renard and R. Schilling eds., *Hommages à Jean Bayet* (Brussels 1964) 101–13. Collection Latomus 70. Repr. in Boyancé 1972.121–33.

———. *Études sur la religion romaine* (Rome 1972). Collection de l'École Française de Rome 11.

Brandt, E. *Gruß und Gebet. Eine Studie zu Gebärden in der minoisch-mykenischen und frühgriechischen Kunst* (Waldsassen 1965).

Breccia, E. *Catalogue général des antiquités égyptiennes du Musée d'Alexandrie. Iscrizioni greche e Latine* (Cairo 1911).

Brelich, A. *Aspetti della morte nelle iscrizioni sepolcrali dell'impero romano* (Budapest 1937). Dissertationes Pannonicae Musei Nationalis Hungarici, ser. 1, fasc. 7.

Bremmer, J. "Walking, Standing, and Sitting in Ancient Greek Culture," in Bremmer and Roodenburg eds., 15–35.

Bremmer, J., and H. Roodenburg eds. *A Cultural History of Gesture* (Ithaca 1991).

Brilliant, R. *Gesture and Rank in Roman Art. The Use of Gestures to Denote Status in Roman Sculpture and Coinage* (New Haven 1963). Memoirs of the Connecticut Academy of Arts and Sciences 14.

Brown, F., E. Richardson, and L. Richardson, Jr. *Cosa III: The Buildings of the Forum* (University Park, Penn. 1993). Memoirs of the American Academy in Rome 37.

Brown, R. *Words and Things* (Glencoe, Ill. 1958).

Brunt, P. A. "Philosophy and Religion in the Late Republic," in M. Griffin and J. Barnes eds., *Philosophia Togata* (Oxford 1989) 176–98.

Buck, C. A. *Dictionary of Selected Synonyms in the Principal Indo-European Languages* (Chicago 1949).

Burkert, W. *Homo necans. The Anthropology of Ancient Greek Sacrificial Ritual and Myth*, trans. P. Bing (Berkeley 1983).

———. *The Orientalizing Revolution*, trans. W. Burkert and M. E. Pinder (Cambridge, Mass. 1992).

Camp, J., Jr. "The Form of Pnyx III," in B. Forsén and G. Stanton eds., *The Pnyx in the History of Athens* (Helsinki 1996) 41–46. Papers and Monographs of the Finnish Institute at Athens 2.

Camporeale, G. "Le scene etrusche di 'protesi,' " *Mitteilungen des Deutschen Archäologischen Instituts, Römische Abteilung* 66 (1959) 31–44.

Carafa, P. *Il comizio di Roma dalle origini all'età di augusto* (Rome 1998). Bullettino della Commissione Archeologica Comunale di Roma, supplementi 5.

Caspar, J. *Roman Religion as Seen in Pliny's "Natural History"* (Chicago 1934).

Cèbe, J.-P. *Varron, Satires Ménipées* (Rome 1987) vol. 8. Collection de l'École Française de Rome 9.

Coarelli, F. *Il foro Romano* (Rome 1992) 2d ed., 2 vols.

Collart, J. *Varron, grammarien latin* (Paris 1954). Publications de la Faculté des Lettres de l'Université de Strasbourg 121.

Conte, G. *Genres and Readers*, trans. G. Most (Baltimore and London 1994).

Corbeill, A. "Augustus' *libellus*," in C. Deroux ed., *Studies in Latin Literature and Roman History* 5 (Brussels 1989) 267–78. Collection Latomus 206.

———. *Controlling Laughter: Political Humor in the Late Roman Republic* (Princeton 1996).

———. "Education in the Roman Republic: Creating Traditions," in Y. L. Too ed., *Education in Greek and Roman Antiquity* (Leiden 2001) 261–87.

Courtney, E. *A Commentary on the Satires of Juvenal* (London 1980).

Cousin, J. *Études sur Quintilien* (Paris 1935).

———. "Rhétorique et psychologie chez Tacite. Un aspect de la 'deinôsis,' " *Revue des études latines* 29 (1951) 228–47.

Crawford, M. *Roman Republican Coinage* (Cambridge 1974) 2 vols.

———. *Roman Statutes* (London 1996) 2 vols. Bulletin of the Institute of Classical Studies, suppl. 64.

Cumont, F. "Il sole vindice dei delitti ed il simbolo delle mani alzate," *Atti della Pontificia Accademia romana di Archeologia, Memorie* 1, ser. 3 (1923) 65–80.

———. *Lux perpetua* (Paris 1949).

Cuq, É. "Funus. Rome," in Daremberg and Saglio eds., 2.2: 1386–1409.

D'Agostino, B. "Società dei vivi, comunità dei morti: un rapporto difficile," in A. Sestieri et al. eds., *Archeologia e antropologia. Contributi di preistoria e archeologia classica* (Rome 1987) 47–58.

Daly, L., and W. Suchier. *Altercatio Hadriani Augusti et Epicteti Philosophi* (Urbana 1939). Illinois Studies in Language and Literature 24.

Daremberg, C., and E. Saglio eds., *Dictionnaire des antiquités grecques et romaines* (Paris 1877–1919) 4 vols.

Darwin, C. *The Expression of the Emotions in Man and Animals*, 3d ed., edited and with afterword by P. Ekman (New York 1998).

David, J.-M. "Promotion civique et droit à la parole. L. Licinius Crassus, les accusateurs et les rhéteurs latins," *Mélanges d'archéologie et d'histoire de l'École Française de Rome, Antiquité* 91 (1979) 135–81.

———. "*Eloquentia popularis* et conduites symboliques des orateurs de la fin de la République: problèmes d'efficacité," *Quaderni di storia* 12 (1980) 171–211.

————. "Les orateurs des municipes à Rome: intégration, réticences et snobismes," in *Les "bourgeoisies" municipales italiennes aux IIe et Ier siècles av. J.-C.* (Paris and Naples 1983a) 309–23.

————. "L'action oratoire de C. Gracchus: l'image d'un modèle," in C. Nicolet ed., *Demokratia et Aristokratia* (Paris 1983b) 103–16. Publications de la Sorbonne, Series Histoire ancienne et médiévale 10.

————. *Le patronat judiciaire au dernier siècle de la République romaine* (Rome 1992). Bibliothèque des Écoles Françaises d'Athènes et de Rome 277.

Davidson, D. "What Metaphors Mean," *Critical Inquiry* 5 (1978) 31–47.

Davies, P. "Trajan's Column and the Art of Commemoration," *American Journal of Archaeology* 101 (1997) 41–65.

De Jorio, A. *La mimica degli antichi investigata nel gestire napoletano* (Naples 1832). Ed. and trans. by A. Kendon, *Gesture in Naples and Gesture in Classical Antiquity* (Bloomington, Ind. 2000).

Denniston, J. *Euripides: Electra* (Oxford 1968).

Deonna, W. "Le genou, siège de force et de vie et sa protection magique," *Revue archéologique* 13 (1939) 224–35.

————. "La légende de Pero et de Micon et l'allaitement symbolique," *Latomus* 13 (1954) 140–66, 356–75. Repr. in W. Deonna, *Deux études de symbolisme religieux* (Brussels 1955). Collection Latomus 18.

————. "Les thèmes symboliques de la légende de Pero et de Micon," *Latomus* 15 (1956) 489–511.

Detienne, M. "En Grèce archaïque: Géométrie, Politique et Société," *Annales* 20 (1965) 425–41.

Deubner, L. Rev. of S. Eitrem ed., *Papyri Osloenses. Fasc. I: Magical Papyri* (Oslo 1925), in *Gnomon* 2 (1926) 406–12.

————. "Götterzwang," *Jahrbuch des Deutschen Archäologischen Instituts* 58 (1943) 88–92.

Devereux, G. "Mourning and Self-degradation," in V. Lanternari, M. Massenzio, and D. Sabbatucci eds., *Scritti in memoria di Angelo Brelich* (Bari 1982) 163–69. Religioni e Civiltà 3.

Dewar, M. *Panegyricus de sexto consulatu Honorii Augusti* (Oxford 1996).

Dieterich, A. "Der Ritus der verhüllten Hände," *Kleine Schriften* (Leipzig and Breslau 1911) 440–48.

————. *Mutter Erde. Ein Versuch über Volksreligion*, 3d ed. edited by E. Fehrle (Leipzig 1925).

Dodds, E. R. *Euripides: Bacchae* (Oxford 1960).

Dölger, F. "Vorbeter und Zeremoniar. Zu *monitor* und *praeire*," *Antike und Christentum* (Münster 1930) 2.241–51.

Domaszewski, A. von. *Die Fahnen im römischen Heere* (Vienna 1885). Abhandlungen des archäologisch-epigraphischen Seminares der Universität Wien 5.

Dorigny, S. "Sipho" in Daremberg and Saglio eds., 4: 2.1347–52.

Douglas, M. *Purity and Danger* (New York 1960).

Douglas, N. *Old Calabria* (London 1983 [1915]).

Drechsler, P. *Sitte, Brauch und Volksglaube in Schlesien* (Leipzig 1906) 2 vols.

Ducos, M. *L'influence grecque sur la loi des Douze Tables* (Paris 1978).

Dulière, C. *Lupa Romana. Recherches d'iconographie et essai d'interprétation* (Brussels 1979). Institut historique Belge de Rome, Études de philologie, d'archéologie et d'histoire anciennes 18.

Dumézil, G. *Archaic Roman Religion*, trans. P. Krapp (Chicago 1970) 2 vols.

Dunbabin, K. *The Mosaics of Roman North Africa* (Oxford 1978).

Dunbabin, K., and M. Dickie. "*Invida rumpantur pectora*. The Iconography of Phthonos/ Invidia in Graeco-Roman Art," *Jahrbuch für Antike und Christentum* 26 (1983) 7– 37, with plates 1–8.

Dupont, F. *L'Acteur-roi, ou Le théâtre dans la Rome antique* (Paris 1985).

Durkheim, E. *The Elementary Forms of the Religious Life*, trans. J. Ward Swain (New York 1965).

Echtermeyer, T. *Proben aus einer Abhandlung über Namen und symbolische Bedeutung der Finger bei den Griechen und Römern*. Programm der Lateinischen Hauptschule zur Halle (Halle 1835).

Edelstein, L. *Ancient Medicine: Selected Papers of Ludwig Edelstein* (Baltimore 1967).

Edwards, C. *The Politics of Immorality in Ancient Rome* (Cambridge 1993).

———. "Unspeakable Professions: Public Performance and Prostitution in Ancient Rome," in Hallett and Skinner eds., 66–95.

Efron, D. *Gesture, Race and Culture* (The Hague and Paris 1972 [1941]). Approaches to Semiotics 9.

Eitrem, S. *Opferritus und Voropfer der Griechen und Römer* (Kristiania 1915). Videns-kapsselskapets Skrifter, II. Hist.-filos. Klasse 1.

———. "Die Gestensprache: Abwehr oder Kontakt," in *Geras Antoniou Keramopoullou* (Athens 1953) 598–608. Hetaireia Makedonikon Spoudon Epistemonikai Pragma-teiai, Seira philologike kai theologike 9.

Ekman, P. "Cross-Cultural Studies of Facial Expression," in P. Ekman ed., *Darwin and Facial Expression: A Century of Research in Review* (New York 1973) 169–222.

———. "Introduction to the Third Edition," in P. Ekman ed., *Charles Darwin: The Expression of the Emotions in Man and Animals* (Oxford 1998) xxi–xxxvi.

Ernout, A., A. Meillet, and J. André. *Dictionnaire étymologique de la langue latine* (Paris 1985).

Evans, E. *Physiognomics in the Ancient World* (Philadelphia 1969). Transactions of the American Philosophical Society 59.5.

Evans-Pritchard, E. *Witchcraft, Oracles and Magic among the Azande* (Oxford 1937).

Fantham, E. *Comparative Studies in Republican Latin Imagery* (Toronto 1971).

———. "Quintilian on Performance: Traditional and Personal Elements in *Institutio* 11.3," *Phoenix* 36 (1982) 243–63.

Finch, C. "The Bern Riddles in Codex Vat. Reg. Lat. 1553," *Transactions and Proceedings of the American Philological Association* 92 (1961) 145–55.

Fischer, H. "Heilgebärden," *Antaios* 2 (1960) 318–47.

Fittschen, K., and P. Zanker. *Katalog der römischen Porträts in den Capitolinischen Museen und den anderen kommunalen Sammlungen der Stadt Rom*, vol. 1 *Kaiser- und Prinzenbild-nisse* (Mainz am R. 1985).

Flaig, E. "Entscheidung und Konsens. Zu den Feldern der politischen Kommunikation zwischen Aristokratie und Plebs," in M. Jehne ed., 77–127.

Flower, H. *Ancestor Masks and Aristocratic Power in Roman Culture* (Oxford 1996).

Fögen, T. "Ancient Theorizing on Nonverbal Communication," in R. Brend, A. Melby, and A. Lommel eds., *LACUS Forum XXVII: Speaking and Comprehending* (Fullerton, Cal. 2001) 203–16.

Forcellini, A. *Totius latinitatis lexicon*, rev. by J. Bailey (London 1828) 2 vols.

Fortenbaugh, W. "Theophrastus on Delivery," in W. Fortenbaugh et al. eds., *Theophrastus of Eresus: On His Life and Work* (New Brunswick, N. J. 1985) 269–88. Rutgers University Studies in Classical Humanities 2.

Foucault, M. "The Order of Discourse," in M. Shapiro ed., *Language and Politics* (Oxford 1984) 108–38.

Fowler, W. Warde. *The Religious Experience of the Roman People* (London 1911).

Fraenkel, E. *Elementi Plautini in Plauto*, trans. F. Munari with addenda by author (Florence 1960). Originally published as *Plautinisches im Plautus* (Berlin 1922).

———. *Horace* (Oxford 1957).

Franchi, L. "Rilievo con pompa funebre e rilievo con gladiatori al Museo dell'Aquila," *Studi Miscellanei* 10 (1966) 23–32.

Frazer, J. G. *Pausanias's Description of Greece* (London 1898) 6 vols.

———. *The Golden Bough: A Study in Magic and Religion. Part 1: The Magic Art and the Evolution of Kings*, 3d ed. (London 1911) 2 vols.

———. *Folk-Lore in the Old Testament* (London 1918) 3 vols.

———. *The "Fasti" of Ovid* (London 1929) 5 vols.

Friedländer, L. *Roman Life and Manners under the Early Empire*, trans. A. B. Gough (London 1928) 4 vols.

Frier, B. Rev. of Williams 1999, *Bryn Mawr Classical Review* 1999.11.05.

Gardner, J. *Being a Roman Citizen* (New York and London 1993).

Garland, R. *The Greek Way of Death* (Ithaca 1985).

Gaster, T. "Foreword," in T. Gaster ed., *The New Golden Bough* (New York 1959) xv–xx.

Geertz, C. "Common Sense as a Cultural System," in *Local Knowledge. Further Essays in Interpretive Anthropology* (New York 1983) 73–93.

Geffcken, K. *Comedy in the "pro Caelio"* (Leiden 1973). Mnemosyne Supplementum 30.

Gelzer, M. *Caesar: Politician and Statesman*, trans. P. Needham (Cambridge, Mass. 1968).

Gennep, A. van. *The Rites of Passage*, trans. M. Vizedom and G. Caffee (Chicago 1960 [1908]).

Gerhard, E., A. Klügmann, and G. Körte. *Etruskische Spiegel* (Berlin 1840–1897) 5 vols.

Germer-Durand, E., F. Germer-Durand, and A. Allmer eds. *Inscriptions antiques de Nîmes* (Toulouse 1893).

Giuliani, L. *Bildnis und Botschaft. Hermeneutische Untersuchungen zur Bildniskunst der römischen Republik* (Frankfurt am M. 1986).

———. "Zur spätrepublikanischen Bildniskunst. Wege und Abwege der Interpretation antiker Porträts," *Antike und Abendland* 36 (1990) 103–15.

Gleason, M. *Making Men: Sophists and Self-Presentation in Ancient Rome* (Princeton 1995).

Glorie, Fr., ed. *Tatuini opera omnia. Variae collectiones aenigmatum Merovingicae aetatis* (Turnhout 1968). Corpus Christianorum, Series Latina 133A.

Goetz, G., ed. *Corpus glossariorum latinorum* (Leipzig 1888–1923) 7 vols.

Golvin, J.-C., and C. Landes. *Amphitheatres & Gladiateurs* (Paris 1990).

Gordon, R. L. "The Real and the Imaginary: Production and Religion in the Graeco-Roman World," *Art History* 2 (1979) 5–34.

Gotoff, H. "Cicero's Analysis of the Prosecution Speeches in the *pro Caelio*: An Exercise in Practical Criticism," *Classical Philology* 81 (1986) 122–32.

———. "Oratory: The Art of Illusion," *Harvard Studies in Classical Philology* 95 (1993) 289–313.

Graf, F. "Gestures and Conventions: The Gestures of Roman Actors and Orators," in Bremmer and Roodenburg eds., 36–58.

Graham, J. "A Handful of Italian," *Gourmet* (May 1969) 24–26.

Gratwick, A. *Plautus: Menaechmi* (Cambridge 1993).

Greenidge, A. *The Legal Procedure of Cicero's Time* (Oxford 1901).

Gricourt, J. "À propos de l'allaitement symbolique: le domaine irlandais," *Hommages à Waldemar Deonna* (Brussels 1957) 249–57. Collection Latomus 28.

Grimm, J. *Deutsche Mythologie*, 4th ed. (Berlin 1875) 3 vols.

Grimm, J. and W. *Deutsches Wörterbuch* (Leipzig 1860) 12 vols.

Groß, K. "Finger," *Reallexikon für Antike und Christentum* 7 (1968) 909–46.

Gruen, E. *The Last Generation of the Roman Republic* (Berkeley 1974).

———. *Studies in Greek Culture and Roman Public Policy* (Leiden 1990).

———. "The Exercise of Power in the Roman Republic," in A. Molho, K. Raaflaub, and J. Emlen eds., *City-states in Classical and Medieval Italy* (Ann Arbor 1991) 251–67.

———. "The Roman Oligarchy: Image and Perception," in J. Linderski ed., *"Imperium sine fine:" T. Robert S. Broughton and the Roman Republic* (Stuttgart 1996) 215–34. Historia Einzelschriften 105.

Guarducci, M. "Tre cippi latini arcaici con iscrizioni," *Bullettino della commissione archeologica comunale di Roma* 72 (1946–1948) 3–11.

Gunderson, E. *Staging Masculinity: The Rhetoric of Performance in the Roman World* (Ann Arbor 2000).

Hacking, I. "Making Up People," in T. Heller, M. Sosna, and D. Wellbery eds., *Reconstructing Individualism. Autonomy, Individuality, and the Self in Western Thought* (Stanford 1986) 222–36.

Hall, E. *The Hidden Dimension* (Garden City, N.Y. 1966).

Hallett, J., and M. Skinner eds. *Roman Sexualities* (Princeton 1997).

Haynes, S. *Etruscan Sculpture* (London 1971).

Heckenbach, J. *De nuditate sacra sacrisque vinculis* (Gießen 1911). Religionsgeschichtliche Versuche und Vorarbeiten 9: 3.

Heim, R. "Incantamenta magica graeca latina," *Jahrbücher für klassische Philologie* suppl. 19 (1893) 463–576.

Hellegouarc'h, J. *Le vocabulaire latin des relations et des partis politiques sous la République* (Paris 1972) 2d ed.

Heller, J. "Nenia 'παίγνιον,' " *Transactions and Proceedings of the American Philological Association* 74 (1943) 215–68.

Henschel, E. "Quantum instar in ipso," *Gymnasium* 59 (1952) 78.

Henzen, W., as reported in "Adunanze," *Bullettino dell' instituto di corrispondenza archeologica* (1853) 130.

Herescu, N. "Au dossier des *decem menses*," *Revue de philologie* 72 (1946) 12–21.

———. "*Les decem menses* et les calculs chronologiques des romains," *Revue des études latines* 33 (1955) 152–65.

Héron de Villefosse, A. "Lampe romaine avec légende explicative," *Monuments et mémoires. Fondation Eugène Piot* 2 (1895) 95–98.

Herter, H. "Effeminatus," *Reallexikon für Antike und Christentum* 4 (Stuttgart 1959) 620–50.

Hertz, R. *Death and the Right Hand*, trans. R. and C. Needham (Glencoe, Ill. 1960). First essay originally published as "Contribution à une étude sur la représentation collective de la mort," *Année Sociologique* 10 (1907) 48–137.

Hinard, F., ed. *La mort, les morts et l'au delà dans le monde romaine* (Caen 1987).

———, ed. *La mort au quotidien dans le monde romain* (Paris 1995).

Hölkeskamp, K. "*Oratoris maxima scaena*: Reden vor dem Volk in der politischen Kultur der Republik," in M. Jehne ed., 11–49.

Holliday, P. "Roman Triumphal Painting: Its Function, Development, and Reception," *Art Bulletin* 79 (1997) 130–47.

Holloway, R. *The Archaeology of Ancient Sicily* (London and New York 1991).

Holst-Warhaft, G. *Dangerous Voices: Women's Laments and Greek Literature* (London and New York 1992).

Hönle, A., and A. Henze. *Römische Amphitheater und Stadien* (Freiburg 1981).

Horsfall, N. "*Incedere* and *incessus*," *Glotta* 49 (1971) 145–47.

———. "Some Problems in the Aeneas Legend," *Classical Quarterly* 29 (1979) 372–90.

———. *Virgil, "Aeneid" 7. A commentary* (Leiden 2000). Mnemosyne supplement 198.

Hubbell, H. "The *Rhetorica* of Philodemus," *Transactions of the Connecticut Academy of Arts and Sciences* 23 (1919/1920) 243–382.

Humphreys, S. *The Family, Women and Death. Comparative Studies* (London 1983).

Hurlet, F. *Les collègues du prince sous Auguste et Tibère* (Rome 1997). Collection de l'École Française de Rome 227.

Jakobson, R., and L. Waugh. "The Spell of Speech Sounds," in *The Sound Shape of Language*, 2d ed. (Berlin 1987) 181–234.

Jehne, M. ed. *Demokratie in Rom? Die Rolle des Volkes in der Politik der römischen Republik* (Stuttgart 1995). Historia Einzelschriften 96.

Jenkins, R. *Pierre Bourdieu* (London and New York 1992).

Jensen, W. *The Sculptures from the Tomb of the Haterii* (Ph.D. diss. Michigan 1978).

Jesperson, O. *Language—Its Nature, Development, and Origins* (New York 1922).

Johnson, E. "Grieving for the Dead, Grieving for the Living: Funeral Laments of Hakka Women," in Watson and Rawski eds., 153–63.

Kähler, H. *Die Augustusstatue von Prima Porta* (Köln 1959).

Kampen, N. *Image and Status: Roman Working Women in Ostia* (Berlin 1981).

Kaster, R. C. *Suetonius Tranquillus: "De Grammaticis et Rhetoribus"* (Oxford 1995).

———. "The Shame of the Romans," *Transactions and Proceedings of the American Philological Association* 127 (1997) 1–19.

Kendon, A. "The Study of Gesture: Some Observations on Its History," *Semiotic Inquiry* 2 (1982) 45–62.

———. "Did Gesture have the Happiness to Escape the Curse at the Confusion of Babel?," in A. Wolfgang ed., *Nonverbal Behavior. Perspectives, Applications, Intercultural Insights* (Lewiston, N. Y. 1984) 75–114.

Kennedy, D. *The Arts of Love* (Cambridge 1992).

Kierdorf, W. *"Laudatio funebris." Interpretationen und Untersuchungen zur Entwicklung der römischen Leichenrede* (Meisenheim 1980). Beiträge zur klassischen Philologie 106.

Killeen, J. "Plautus *Miles Gloriosus* 211," *Classical Philology* 68 (1973) 53–54.

Kleiner, D. *Roman Sculpture* (New Haven 1992).

Klíma, J. "Finger," in K. Ranke et al. eds., *Enzyklopädie des Märchens* (Berlin and New York 1975-) 4.1140–46.

Koch, C. *Gestirnverehrung im alten Italien. Sol Indiges und der Kreis der Di Indigetes* (Frankfurt am Main 1933). Frankfurter Studien zur Religion und Kultur der Antike 3.

Köstermann, E. "*Incedere* und *incessere*," *Glotta* 21 (1933) 56–62.

Kourouniotes, K., and H. A. Thompson. "The Pnyx in Athens," *Hesperia* 1 (1932) 90–217.

Köves-Zulauf, T. *Reden und Schweigen: Römische Religion bei Plinius Maior* (Munich 1972). Studia et testimonia antiqua 12.

———. *Römische Geburtsriten* (Munich 1990). Zetemata 87.

Krause, C. "Zur baulichen Gestalt des republikanischen Comitiums," *Mitteilungen des Deutschen Archäologischen Instituts, Römische Abteilung* 83 (1976) 31–69.

Kühn, K. G. *Claudii Galeni Opera Omnia* (Leipzig 1821–1833) 20 vols.

Kurtz, D., and J. Boardman. *Greek Burial Customs* (London 1971).

Lafaye, G. "Gladiator, " in Daremberg and Saglio eds., 2.2: 1563–99.

Lakoff, G. *Women, Fire, and Dangerous Things: What Categories Reveal about the Mind* (Chicago 1987).

Lakoff, G., and M. Johnson. *Metaphors We Live By* (Chicago 1980).

Lana, I. "*Introspicere* in Tacito," *Orpheus* n. s. 10 (1989) 26–57.

Lateiner, D. "Nonverbal Behaviors in Ovid's Poetry, Primarily *Metamorphoses* 14," *Classical Journal* 91 (1996) 225–53.

Latte, K. *Römische Religionsgeschichte* (Munich 1960). Handbuch der Altertumswissenschaft 5: 4.

Laughton, E. "Cato's Charm for Dislocations," *Classical Review* 52 (1938) 52–54.

Lécrivain, C. "Funus. Grèce," in Daremberg and Saglio eds., 2.2: 1367–81.

———. "*Manus*," in Daremberg and Saglio eds., 3.1586–87.

Leigh, M. "Wounding and Popular Rhetoric at Rome," *Bulletin of the Institute of Classical Studies* 40 (1995) 195–212.

Lenaghan, J. *A Commentary on Cicero's Oration "De Haruspicum Responso"* (The Hague 1969). Studies in Classical Literature 5.

Lévy-Bruhl, L. *How Natives Think*, trans. L. Clare (New York 1925).

Linderski, J. "Cicero and Roman Divination," *Parola del Passato* 202 (1982) 12–38.

Lindsay, W. *The "Captivi" of Plautus* (London 1900).

Lindstrom, L. "Doctor, Lawyer, Wise-man, Priest: Big-men and Knowledge in Melanesia," *Man* 19 (1984) 291–309.

Lizzi, R. "Il sesso e i morti," in F. Hinard ed. (1995) 49–68.

Lloyd, G.E.R. *Polarity and Analogy: Two types of argumentation in early Greek thought* (Cambridge 1966).

Löfstedt, E. *Syntactica. Studien und Beiträge zur historischen Syntax des Lateins* (Lund 1933 and 1942). 2 vols., 2d ed. of vol. 1.

L'Orange, H. P. *Studies on the Iconography of Cosmic Kingship in the Ancient World* (Oslo 1953). Instituttet for Sammenlignende Kulturforskning, Serie A, Forelesninger 23.

MacMullen, R. *Enemies of the Roman Order. Treason, Unrest, and Alienation in the Empire* (Cambridge, Mass. 1966).

Maier-Eichhorn, U. *Die Gestikulation in Quintilians Rhetorik* (Frankfurt am M. 1989). Europäische Hochschulschriften; Reihe 15, Klassische Sprachen und Literaturen 41.

Maltby, R. *A Lexicon of Ancient Latin Etymologies* (Leeds 1991).

Manfredini, A. "*Qui commutant cum feminis vestem,*" *Revue Internationale des Droits de l'Antiquité* 32 (1985) 257–71.

Marquardt, J. *Das Privatleben der Römer*, 2d ed. edited by A. Mau (Leipzig 1886). 2 vols.

Martin, E. "Gender and Ideological Differences in Representations of Life and Death," in Watson and Rawski eds., 164–79.

Martin, R. H. *Tacitus* (London 1981).

Martin, R. H., and A. J. Woodman. *Tacitus: Annals Book IV* (Cambridge 1989).

Maurin, J. "*Funus* et rites de separation," *Annali dell'istituto universitario orientale; sezione di archeologia e storia antica* 6 (1984) 191–208.

McCartney, E. "Verbal Homeopathy and the Etymological Story," *American Journal of Philology* 48 (1927) 326–43.

McDonald, W. *The Political Meeting Places of the Greeks* (Baltimore 1943).

McLuhan, M., and Q. Fiore. *The Medium is the Massage* (New York 1967).

McNeill, D. *Hand and Mind: What Gestures Reveal about Thought* (Chicago 1992).

McNiven, T. *Gestures in Attic Vase Painting: Use and Meaning, 550–40 B.C.* (Ph.D. diss. Michigan 1982).

Meier, C. "Populares," RE suppl. 10 (1965) 549–615.

Meschke, K. "Gebärde," in Bächtold-Stäubli ed., 3.328–37.

Metcalf, P., and R. Huntington. *Celebrations of Death. The Anthropology of Mortuary Ritual* (Cambridge 1991) 2d ed.

Millar, F. "The Political Character of the Classical Roman Republic, 200–151 B.C.," *Journal of Roman Studies* 74 (1984) 1–19.

———. "Politics, Persuasion and the People before the Social War (150–90 B.C.)," *Journal of Roman Studies* 76 (1986) 1–11.

———. "Political Power in Mid-Republican Rome: Curia or Comitium?," *Journal of Roman Studies* 79 (1989) 138–50.

———. "Popular Politics at Rome in the Late Republic," in I. Malkin and Z. W. Rubinsohn eds., *Leaders and Masses in the Roman World: Studies in Honor of Zvi Yavetz* (Leiden 1995) 91–114.

———. *The Crowd in Rome in the Late Republic* (Ann Arbor 1998). Jerome Lectures 22.

Miller, N. P. "Tiberius Speaks," *American Journal of Philology* 89 (1968) 1–19.

Miller, S. *Arete: Greek Sports from Ancient Sources*, 2d ed. (Berkeley 1991).

Mohrmann, C. *Études sur le latin des Chrétiens* (Rome 1958–1965) 3 vols.

Monceaux, P. "Funus. Étrurie," in Daremberg and Saglio eds., 2.2: 1382–86.

Montaigne, M. de. *Oeuvres complètes*, R. Barral and P. Michel eds. (Paris 1967).

Moore, T. *The Theater of Plautus: Playing to the Audience* (Austin 1998).

Morawski, G. "De metaphoris Tullianis observationes," *Eos* 16 (1910) 1–5.

Moretti, M. *Nuove scoperte e acquisizioni nell'Etruria meridionale* (Rome 1975).

Morris, D., et al. *Gestures, their Origins and Distribution* (New York 1979).

Morris, I. *Death-ritual and Social Structure in Classical Antiquity* (Cambridge 1992).

Morstein-Marx, R. "Publicity, Popularity and Patronage in the *Commentariolum Petitionis*," *Classical Antiquity* 17 (1998) 259–88.

Mouritsen, H. *"Plebs" and Politics in the Late Roman Republic* (Cambridge 2001).

Müller, F. *The So-called Peleus and Thetis Sarcophagus in the Villa Albani* (Amsterdam 1994). Iconological Studies in Roman Art 1.

Munari, B. *Il dizionario dei gesti italiani* (Rome 1994).

Narducci, E. *Cicerone e l'eloquenza romana. Retorica e progetto culturale* (Roma and Bari 1997). Quadrante Laterza 86.

Néraudau, J.-P. "La loi, la coutume et le chagrin. Réflexions sur la mort des enfants," in Hinard ed., 1987. 195–208.

Nettleship, H. *Contributions to Latin Lexicography* (Oxford 1889).

Neumann, G. *Gesten und Gebärden in der griechischen Kunst* (Berlin 1965).

Nicolson, F. "The Saliva Superstition in Classical Literature," *Harvard Studies in Classical Philology* 8 (1897) 23–40.

Niederer, A. "Beschämung, Lob und Schadenfreude. Hand- und Fingergebärden mit bestimmter Bedeutung," *Schweizer Archiv für Volkskunde* 85 (1989) 201–17.

Niedermann, M. "Sprachliche Bemerkungen zu Marcellus Empiricus *de medicamentis*," in *Festgabe Hugo Blümner* (Zurich 1914) 328–39.

Nietzsche, F. *The Gay Science*, trans. W. Kaufmann (New York 1974).

Nock, A. D. "Sarcophagi and Symbolism," in Z. Stewart ed., *Arthur Darby Nock* (Oxford 1972) 2.606–41; repr. from *American Journal of Archaeology* 50 (1946) 140–70.

Norden, E. *P. Vergilius Maro, Aeneis Buch VI* (Leipzig 1903).

North, J. "Diviners and Divination at Rome," in M. Beard and J. North eds., *Pagan Priests* (Ithaca 1990a) 49–71.

———. "Democratic Politics in Republican Rome," *Past & Present* 126 (1990b) 3–21.

Nußbaum, O. "Geleit," *Reallexikon für Antike und Christentum* 9 (Stuttgart 1976) 908–1049.

Ogilvie, R. M. *The Romans and their Gods* (London 1969).

O'Gorman, E. *Irony and Misreading in the "Annals" of Tacitus* (Cambridge 2000).

Ohm, T. *Die Gebetsgebärden der Völker und das Christentum* (Leiden 1948).

Onians, R. B. *The Origins of European Thought about the Body, the Mind, the Soul, the World, Time, and Fate* (Cambridge 1954) 2d ed.

Otto, A. *Die Sprichwörter und sprichwörtlichen Redensarten der Römer* (Leipzig 1890).

Page, D. *Euripides: Medea* (Oxford 1967).

Parker, H. "The Teratogenic Grid," in Hallett and Skinner eds., 47–65.

Parrish, D. "The Date of the Mosaics from Zliten," *Antiquités africaines* 21 (1985) 137–58.

Pease, A. S. *Virgil "Aeneid" 4* (Cambridge, Mass. 1935).

———. *Marci Tulli Ciceronis De Natura Deorum* (Cambridge, Mass. 1955) 2 vols.

Pei, M. *The Story of Language* (New York and Toronto 1965).

Pelet, A. "Essai sur un bas-relief découvert en 1845, dans le territoire de Cavillargues," *Mémoires de l'Academie du Gard* (1851) 35–41.

Perelli, L. *Il movimento popolare nell' ultimo secolo della repubblica* (Torino 1982).

Perrin, M. *L'homme antique et chrétien: L'anthropologie de Lactance 250–325* (Paris 1981).

Peterfalvi, J.-M. *Recherches expérimentales sur le symbolisme phonétique* (Paris 1970).

Pilarczyk, D. *"Hominum vultus"* in *Tacitus* (Ph.D. diss. Cincinnati 1969).

Picard, C. "Le geste de la prière funéraire en Grèce at en Étrurie," *Revue de l'histoire des religions* 114 (1936) 137–57.

Pina Polo, F. *"Contra Arma Verbis": Der Redner vor dem Volk in der späten römischen Republik*, trans. E. Liess (Stuttgart 1996). Heidelberger althistorische Beiträge und epigraphische Studien 22.

Pinker, S. *The Language Instinct* (New York 1994).

Polacco, L. *Il volto di Tiberio. Saggio di critica iconografica* (Rome 1955).

Pöschl, V. "Zur Einbeziehung anwesender Personen und sichtbarer Objekte in Ciceros Reden," in A. Michel and R. Verdière eds., *Ciceroniana. Hommages à K. Kumaniecki* (Leiden 1975) 206–26. Roma Aeterna 9.

Post, E. "Pollice verso," *American Journal of Philology* 13 (1892) 213–25.

Prescendi, F. "Il lutto dei padri nella cultura romana," in Hinard ed., 1995.147–54.

Puhvel, J. "Greek ἔχφαρ and Latin *instar*," *Glotta* 37 (1958) 288–92.

Ramage, E. "Cicero on Extra-Roman Speech," *Transactions and Proceedings of the American Philological Association* 92 (1961) 481–94.

Rawson, E. *Intellectual Life in the Late Roman Republic* (Baltimore 1985).

Reekmans, L. "La *dextrarum iunctio* dans l'iconographie romaine et paléochrétienne," *Bulletin de l'Institut Historique Belge de Rome* 31 (1958) 23–95, plus fifteen plates.

Reinach, A. "Signa militaria," in Daremberg and Saglio eds., 4.1307–25.

Reiner, E. *Die rituelle Totenklage der Griechen* (Stuttgart and Berlin 1938). Tübinger Beiträge zur Altertumswissenschaft 30.

Rhodes, P. J. *A Commentary on the Aristotelian "Athenaion Politeia"* (Oxford 1981).

Richardson, E. *The Etruscans* (Chicago 1976).

Richlin, A. *The Garden of Priapus* (New Haven 1983; repr. Oxford 1992).

———. "Not Before Homosexuality," *Journal of the History of Sexuality* 3 (1993) 523–73.

———. "Gender and Rhetoric: Producing Manhood in the Schools," in W. Dominik ed., *Roman Eloquence. Rhetoric in Society and Literature* (New York and London 1997) 90–110.

Ricottilli, L. " '*Tum breviter Dido voltum demissa profatur*' (*Aen.* 1.561): individuazione di un 'cogitantis gestus' e delle sue funzioni e modalità di rappresentazione nell' *Eneide*," *Materiali e discussioni per l'analisi dei testi classici* 28 (1992) 179–227.

———. *Gesto e parola nell'Eneide* (Bologna 2000). Testi e manuali per l'insegnamento universitario del latino 63.

Riese, A. *Anthologia Latina* (Leipzig 1894). 1.1: Libri Salmasiani aliorumque carmina.

Riggsby, A. "The Rhetoric of Character in the Roman Courts," in J. Powell and J. Paterson, eds. *Cicero the Advocate* (Oxford, forthcoming).

Rimé, B., and L. Schiaratura. "Gesture and Speech," in R. Feldman and B. Rimé, eds., *Fundamentals of Nonverbal Behavior* (Cambridge 1991) 239–81.

Robert, L. "Monuments de gladiateurs dans l'orient Grec," in *Hellenica, recueil d'épigraphie, de numismatique et d'antiquités grecques* (Paris 1948) 5.84–86.

Rocchetti, L. "Il mosaico con scene d'arena al Museo Borghese," *Rivista dell'Istituto Nazionale d'Archeologia e Storia dell'arte* n. s. 10 (1961) 79–115.

Rohde, E. *Psyche. The Cult of Souls and Belief in Immortality among the Greeks*, trans. W. Hillis (London 1925) 8th ed.

Röhrich, L. *Gebärde—Metapher—Parodie* (Düsseldorf 1967).

———. *Das grosse Lexikon der sprichwörtlichen Redensarten* (Freiburg 1991).

Roscher, W., ed. *Ausführliches Lexikon der griechischen und römischen Mythologie* (Leipzig 1884–1937).

Rose, H. J. "Celestial and Terrestrial Orientation of the Dead," *Journal of the Royal Anthropological Institute of Great Britain and Ireland* 52 (1922) 127–40.

———. "The Inauguration of Numa," *Journal of Roman Studies* 13 (1923) 82–90.

———. *The "Roman Questions" of Plutarch* (Oxford 1924).

———. "The Folklore of the Geoponica," *Folklore* 44 (1933) 57–90.

Rose, V., ed. *Sorani Gynaeciorum vetus translatio latina* (Leipzig 1882).

Rosenberger, V. *Gezähmte Götter. Das Prodigienwesen der römischen Republik* (Stuttgart 1998). Heidelberger althistorische Beiträge und Epigraphische Studien 27.

Rosetti, L. "Il *De opificio Dei* di Lattanzio e le sue fonti," *Didaskaleion* 6 (1928) 115–200.

Rouquette, J.-M., and C. Sintès. *Arles antique. Monuments et sites* (Paris 1989).

Rudd, N. *Horace: Epistles Book II and Epistle to the Pisones (Ars Poetica)* (Cambridge 1989).

Rudich, V. *Political Dissidence under Nero. The Price of Dissimulation* (London and New York 1993).

Saglio, E. "Adoratio," in Daremberg and Saglio eds., 1.1: 80–82.

Saitz, R., and E. Cervenka. *Handbook of Gestures: Colombia and the United States* (The Hague and Paris 1972). Approaches to Semiotics 31.

Samter, E. *Familienfeste der Griechen und Römer* (Berlin 1901).

———. "Zu römischen Bestattungsbräuchen," *Festschrift zu Otto Hirschfelds sechzigsten Geburtstag* (Berlin 1903) 249–56.

———. *Geburt, Hochzeit und Tod. Beiträge zur vergleichenden Volkskunde* (Leipzig and Berlin 1911).

Saverkina, I. *Römische Sarkophage in der Ermitage* (Berlin 1979).

Saxe, A. *Social Dimensions of Mortuary Practice* (Ph.D. diss. Michigan 1970).

Schauenburg, K. "Die *lupa Romana* als sepulkrales Motiv," *Jahrbuch des Deutschen Archäologischen Instituts* 81 (1966) 261–309.

Scheid, J. "*Contraria facere*: renversements et déplacements dans les rites funéraires," *Annali dell'istituto universitario orientale; sezione di archeologia e storia antica* 6 (1984) 117–39.

———. "The Religious Roles of Roman Women," trans. A. Goldhammer, in P. Schmitt Pantel ed., *A History of Women: From Ancient Goddesses to Christian Saints* (Cambridge, Mass. 1992) 1.377–408.

Schmidt, L. "Die volkstümlichen Grundlagen der Gebärdensprache," *Beiträge zur sprachlichen Volksüberlieferung* (Berlin 1953) 233–49. Deutsche Akademie der Wissenschaften zu Berlin, Veröffentlichungen des Instituts für Deutsche Volkskunde 2.

Schmitt, J.-C. "*Gestus-Gesticulatio*. Contribution a l'étude du vocabulaire Latin médiéval des gestes," in Y. Lefèvre ed., *La lexicographie du latin médiéval et ses rapports avec les recherches actuelles sur la civilisation du Moyen Age* (Paris 1981) 377–90. Colloques internationaux du Centre National de la Recherche Scientifique 589.

———. "The Ethics of Gesture," trans. I. Patterson, in *Fragments for a History of the Human Body*, part 2 (New York 1989) 128–47.

Schofield, M. "Cicero for and against Divination," *Journal of Roman Studies* 76 (1986) 47–65.

Schrader, H. "Einem den Daumen halten, drücken," *Zeitschrift für deutsche Sprache* 8 (1894–1895) 223–26.

Scullard, H. *Festivals and Ceremonies of the Roman Republic* (Ithaca 1981).

Seager, R. "Cicero and the Word *popularis*," *Classical Quarterly* 66 (1972) 328–38.

Seligmann, S. "Auge," in Bächtold-Stäubli ed., 1.679–701.

Settis, S. "Images of Meditation, Uncertainty and Repentance in Ancient Art," trans. P. Spring, in J.-C. Schmitt ed., *Gestures*. Special issue of *History and Anthropology* 1: 1 (1984) 193–237. Originally published as "Immagini della meditazione, dell'incertezza e del pentimento nell'arte antica," *Prospettiva* 1 (1975) 4–18.

Severus, E. von. "Gebet I," *Reallexikon für Antike und Christentum* 8 (Stuttgart 1972) 1134–1258.

Shackleton Bailey, D. R. *Anthologia Latina* (Stuttgart 1982). 1.1: Libri Salmasiani aliorumque carmina.

Shapiro, A. "The Iconography of Mourning in Athenian Art," *American Journal of Archaeology* 95 (1991) 629–56.

Sichtermann, H., and G. Koch eds. *Griechische Mythen auf römischen Sarkophagen* (Tübingen 1975). Bilderhefte des Deutschen Archäologischen Instituts Rom 5/6.

Sinclair, P. "Political Declensions in Latin Grammar and Oratory 55 BCE–CE 39," *Ramus* 23 (1994) 92–109.

Sittl, C. *Die Gebärden der Griechen und Römer* (Leipzig 1890).

Sjöqvist, E. "Pnyx and Comitium," in G. Mylonas ed., *Studies Presented to David M. Robinson* (St. Louis 1951) 1.400–11.

Slater, N. *Plautus in Performance: The Theatre of the Mind* (Amsterdam 2000) 2d ed.

Smith, M. "On the Lack of a History of Greco-Roman Magic," in H. Heinen ed., *Althistorische Studien. Hermann Bengtson* (Wiesbaden 1983) 251–57. Historia Einzelschriften 40.

Smith, W. et al. eds., *A Dictionary of Greek and Roman Antiquities* (London 1914) 3d ed.

Sordi, M. "La tradizione storiografica su Tiberio Sempronio Gracco e la propaganda contemporanea," in *Miscellanea greca e romana* 6 (1978) 299–330. Studi pubblicati dall' Istituto Italiano per la Storica Antica 27.

Stählin, G. "Κοπετός," in G. Kittel ed., *Theological Dictionary of the New Testament* (Grand Rapids, Mich. 1965) trans. G. Bromiley, 3.830–52.

Stannard, J. "Medicinal Plants and Folk Remedies in Pliny, *Historia naturalis*," *History and Philosophy of the Life Sciences* 4 (1982) 3–23.

———. "Herbal Medicine and Herbal Magic in Pliny's Time," in *Pline l'Ancien. Temoin de son Temps* (Salamanca and Nantes 1987) 95–106.

Stears, K. "Death Becomes Her. Gender and Athenian Death Ritual," in S. Blundell and M. Williamson eds., *The Sacred and the Feminine in Ancient Greece* (New York and London 1998) 113–27.

Stemplinger, E. "Der Heilmagnetismus bei Plinius," *Zeitschrift für die deutschösterreichische Gymnasien* 69 (1919) 1–20.

———. "Daumen," in Bächtold-Stäubli ed., 2.174–78.

Stevenson, T. *Miniature Decoration in the Vatican Virgil: A Study in Late Antique Iconography* (Tübingen 1983).

Strzelecki, W. C. *Atei Capitonis fragmenta* (Leipzig 1967).

Stuart Jones, H. *A Catalogue of the Ancient Sculptures Preserved in the Municipal Collections of Rome. The Sculptures of the Palazzo dei Conservatori* (Oxford 1926) 2 vols.

Swedenberg, H. T., Jr., et al., eds. *The Works of John Dryden* (Berkeley 1956–2000) 20 vols.

Talbert, R. *The Senate of Imperial Rome* (Princeton 1984).

Tarrant, R. *Seneca: Agamemnon* (Cambridge 1976).

Täubler, E. *Imperium Romanum. Studien zur Entwicklungsgeschichte des römischen Reichs. I: Die Staatsverträge und Vertragsverhältnisse* (Leipzig and Berlin 1913).

Taylor, A. *The Shanghai Gesture* (Helsinki 1956). Folklore Fellows Communications 166.

Taylor, L. R. *Party Politics in the Age of Caesar* (Berkeley and Los Angeles 1949).

———. *Roman Voting Assemblies* (Ann Arbor 1966).

Taylor, R. "Two Pathic Subcultures in Ancient Rome," *Journal of the History of Sexuality* 7 (1997) 319–71.

Tels-de Jong, L. *Sur quelques divinités romaines de la naissance et de la prophétie* (Delft 1959).

Temkin, O. ed. and trans. *Soranus' Gynecology* (Baltimore 1991).

Thomas, K. "Introduction," in Bremmer and Roodenburg eds., 1–14.

Thommen, L. "Les lieux de la plèbe et de ses tribuns dans la Rome républicaine," *Klio* 77 (1995) 358–70.

Tobin, R. "The Pose of the Doryphoros," in W. Moon ed., *Polykleitos, the Doryphoros, and Tradition* (Madison 1995) 52–64.

Todorov, T. *The Conquest of America: The Question of the Other*, trans. R. Howard (New York 1984).

Torelli, M. *Typology and Structure of Roman Historical Reliefs* (Ann Arbor 1992). Jerome Lectures 14.

Toynbee, J.M.C. *Death and Burial in the Roman World* (London 1971).

Ucelli, G. *Le navi di Nemi* (Rome 1940).

Vasaly, A. *Representations. Images of the World in Ciceronian Oratory* (Berkeley and Los Angeles 1993).

Ville, G. *La Gladiature en Occident des origines à la mort de Domitien* (Rome 1981).

Volkmann, H. "Ein verkannter Strafbrauch der Spartaner," *Archiv für Religionswissenschaft* 32 (1935) 188–91.

Vorwahl, H. "Die Gebärdensprache der Religion," *Zeitschrift für Religionspsychologie* 5 (1932) 121–28.

Wagenvoort, H. *Roman Dynamism. Studies in ancient Roman thought, language and custom* (Oxford 1947).

———. " 'Rebirth' in Antique Profane Literature," in *Studies in Roman Literature, Culture and Religion* (Leiden 1956) 132–49.

Walker, B. *The Annals of Tacitus: A Study in the Writing of History* (Manchester 1952).

Walsh, P. G. trans. *Apuleius: The Golden Ass* (Oxford 1994).

Wanner, H. et al., " 'Dam,' 'dem,' 'dim,' 'dom,' 'dum,' bzw. 'damm' usw.," in F. Staub, L. Tobler, et al. eds., *Schweizerisches Idiotikon. Wörterbuch der schweizerdeutschen Sprache* (Frauenfeld 1881–). Handwörterbücher zur Deutschen Volkskunde 1.

Wardman, A. *Religion and Statecraft among the Romans* (Baltimore 1982).

Warmington, E. H. *Remains of Old Latin* (Cambridge, Mass. and London 1979) 4 vols.

Watson, J., trans., *Quintilian's Institutes of Oratory* (London 1905). 2 vols.

Watson, J. "The Structure of Chinese Funerary Rites: Elementary Forms, Ritual Sequence, and the Primacy of Performance," in Watson and Rawski eds., 3–19.

Watson, J., and E. Rawski eds. *Death Ritual in Late Imperial and Modern China* (Berkeley 1988).

Weickert, C. "Gladiatoren-Relief der Münchner Glyptothek," *Münchner Jahrbuch der Bildenden Kunst* n.s. 2 (1925) 1–39.

Weinreich, O. *Antike Heilungswunder. Untersuchungen zum Wunderglauben der Griechen und Römer* (Gießen 1909). Religionsgeschichtliche Versuche und Vorarbeiten 8: 1.

Wenger, L. *Die Quellen des römischen Rechts* (Vienna 1953). Österreichische Akademie der Wissenschaften, Denkschriften der Gesamtakademie 2.

Weston, K. "The Illustrated Terence Manuscripts," *Harvard Studies in Classical Philology* 14 (1903) 37–54.

Whitbread, L. *Fulgentius the Mythographer* (Columbus 1971).

Wiedemann, T. *Emperors & Gladiators* (New York 1992).

Wille, G. *Musica Romana* (Amsterdam 1967).

Williams, C. *Roman Homosexuality: Ideologies of Masculinity in Classical Antiquity* (New York and Oxford 1999).

Williams, R. D. *The Aeneid of Vergil, Books 1–6* (London 1972).

Wills, G. "John Wayne's Body," *New Yorker*, 19 August 1996, 38–49.

Wilpert, P., and S. Zenker, "Auge," *Reallexikon für Antike und Christentum* 1 (Stuttgart 1950) 957–69.

Wilson, R. Rev. of Holloway, *Journal of Hellenic Studies* 114 (1994) 217–18.

Winkes, R. "Physiognomonia: Probleme der Charakterinterpretation römischer Porträts," *Aufstieg und Niedergang der römischen Welt* I, 4 (1973) 899–926.

Winkler, J. *Auctor & Actor. A Narratological Reading of Apuleius's "The Golden Ass"* (Berkeley 1985).

Winterbottom, M. M. *Fabii Quintiliani Institutionis oratoriae libri duodecim* (Oxford 1970a) 2 vols.

———. *Problems in Quintilian* (London 1970b). Bulletin of the Institute of Classical Studies, supplememt 25.

Wissowa, G. *Religion und Kultus der Römer* (Munich 1912) 2d ed. Handbuch der klassischen Altertumswissenschaft 5: 4.

Wölfflin, E. "Instar, ad instar," *Archiv für lateinische Lexicographie und Grammatik* 2 (1885) 581–97.

———. "Instar," *Archiv für lateinische Lexicographie und Grammatik* 4 (1887) 357.

Wolters, X.F.M.G. *Notes on Antique Folklore on the Basis of Pliny's "Natural History" (28.22–9)* (Amsterdam 1935).

Woodman, A. J. *Velleius Paterculus: The Tiberian Narrative (2.94–131)* (Cambridge 1977).

———. "Tacitus' Obituary of Tiberius," *Classical Quarterly* 39 (1989) 197–205.

———. *Tacitus Reviewed* (Oxford 1998).

Wright, D. *Codicological Notes on the Vergilius Romanus (Vat. lat. 3867)* (Vatican City 1992).

———. *The Vatican Vergil. A Masterpiece of Late Antique Art* (Berkeley 1993).

Wuilleumier, P., and A. Audin. *Les médaillons d'applique gallo-romains de la vallée du Rhône* (Paris 1952).

Wülfing, P. "Antike und moderne Redegestik. Quintilians Theorie der Körpersprache," *Der altsprachliche Unterricht* 36 (1994) 45–63.

Wyse, W. *The Speeches of Isaeus* (Cambridge 1904).

Wyß, K. *Die Milch im Kultus der Griechen und Römer* (Gießen 1914). Religionsgeschichtliche Versuche und Vorarbeiten 15: 2.

Zanker, P. *The Power of Images in the Age of Augustus*, trans. A. Shapiro (Ann Arbor 1988a).

———. " 'Bilderzwang': Augustan Political Symbolism in the Private Sphere," in J. Huskinson, M. Beard, and J. Reynolds eds., *Image and Mystery in the Roman World. Papers given in memory of Jocelyn Toynbee* (Gloucester 1988b) 1–21.

Zschietzschmann, W. "Die Darstellungen der Prothesis in der griechischen Kunst," *Mitteilungen des Deutschen Archäologischen Instituts, Athenische Abteilung* 53 (1928) 17–47.

INDEX LOCORUM

This INDEX includes all passages from Greek and Roman authors cited in the text or notes. Latin authors and works are cited according to the *Index* of the *Thesaurus linguae Latinae* (Leipzig 1990), Greek according to the *Oxford Classical Dictionary* (Oxford 1996) 3d ed.

GENERAL INDEX

ROMAN names are listed according to the form commonly used in English. For a listing of Greek and Latin passages cited, see the *Index locorum*.

Lightning Source UK Ltd.
Milton Keynes UK
UKOW02n1146080317
296091UK00002B/44/P